Dirty Words

THE RHETORIC OF
PUBLIC SEX EDUCATION,
1870–1924

Robin E. Jensen

University of Illinois Press

Urbana, Chicago, and Springfield

Manufactured in the United States of America

1 2 3 4 5 C P 5 4 3 2 1

∞ This book is printed on acid-free paper.

Library of Congress Cataloging-in-Publication Data
Jensen, Robin E.
Dirty words : the rhetoric of public sex education, 1870–1924 /
by Robin E. Jensen.
p.   cm.
Includes bibliographical references and index.
ISBN 978-0-252-03573-9 (alk. paper) —
ISBN 978-0-252-07766-1 (pbk. : alk. paper)
1. Sex instruction—United States—History. I. Title.
HQ57.5.A3J46   2010
613.9'51071273—dc22   2010009557

Dirty Words

For Jake

Contents

Acknowledgments

I have learned so much about research, rhetoric, sex education, and, most importantly, the generosity of others throughout the process of writing this book. I am glad to have this opportunity to think back on and thank those who have played a role in bringing this project to fruition. I am thankful for the editorial assistance of Karen Ross, the editor of *Communication, Culture, and Critique*, who published an earlier version of part of chapter 1 (1.4 [2008]), and Susanna Hornig Priest, the editor of *Science Communication*, who published an earlier version of part of chapter 2 (29.2 [2007]).

This book's claims are grounded in sources housed in several excellent archival repositories. I am indebted to the staff of the Social Welfare History Archives at the University of Minnesota, especially head archivist David Klaassen, for helping me to access such amazing primary sources. My thanks also go to the dedicated individuals overseeing the Special Collections Library at the University of Illinois at Chicago and the University of Illinois Archives in Urbana-Champaign.

Funding for this project came from an Illinois Project for Research in the Humanities (IPRH) fellowship at the University of Illinois at Urbana-Champaign, a Clarke Chambers Travel Fellowship from the Social Welfare History Archives at the University of Minnesota, and a Marianne A. Ferber Scholarship from the Gender and Women's Studies Program at the University of Illinois at Urbana-Champaign. The support and encouragement I garnered from individuals representing these organizations, especially Matti Bunzl and Christine Catanzarite at the IPRH, helped me to find my scholarly voice.

Cara Finnegan repeatedly offered me excellent feedback and encouragement, and I am honored to call her both my mentor and my friend. For as long as I have known her, Cara has modeled for me what it means to be a wonderful mentor, a dedicated member of the scholarly community, and an altogether mighty and awesome woman. These are lessons I will always hold close. Thank you, Cara. I also extend my warmest thanks to Dale Brashers, Stephen Hartnett, and Leslie Reagan for helping me to shape this project when it was in its earliest stages.

I initially envisioned this project while I was at the University of Illinois in the Department of Speech Communication (now the Department of Communication). During this time, friends and colleagues enlightened me, entertained me, and did not seem to mind my inherent corniness—perhaps because we were, after all, in the land of corn. My new friends and colleagues at Purdue University in the Department of Communication have fostered an ideal environment for me to hone in on the questions at the heart of this book (and also to laugh and enjoy myself some along the way).

I feel very blessed to have the support of a wonderful family, and my scholarship has benefited exponentially from that support. In fact, this book would probably not have been completed if my mom had not supplied me with an endless stream of Grand Bagels, if Nana had never taught me to read "da books" many years ago, if Rosemary Jan had not been such an accommodating first student, and if Diana and Bob Jensen had not expressed interest in its content from start to finish.

I owe a great debt to Kendra Boileau, the senior acquisitions editor at the University of Illinois Press, as well as to Susan Zaeske, both of whom went to great lengths to make this book far better than it ever would have been otherwise. And I am also grateful to two anonymous reviewers who provided me with excellent feedback on earlier versions of this manuscript.

Most importantly, I am thankful to and for Jakob Jensen, who was there all along, listening, brainstorming, asking questions, thinking of titles, searching for images, and sustaining me with his dimples and his love. In the words of the novelist George R. R. Martin, "I dreamed of you."

Introduction

On August 22, 1996, the 104th U.S. Congress and President William J. Clinton, a Democrat, passed the Personal Responsibility and Work Opportunity Reconciliation Act. Better known as the 1996 Welfare Reform Bill, this act drastically altered how and to whom welfare benefits are granted in the United States. What many people do not know is that the Welfare Reform Bill also censored public education about sexual health. The bill included the controversial provision that abstinence-education programs be the only federally funded sex-education curricula in U.S. schools. The act defined abstinence education (known today as "abstinence-only" or "abstinence-only-until-marriage" education) as any program that "has as its exclusive purpose, teaching the social, psychological, and health gains to be realized by abstaining from sexual activity." More than a decade later, the government still provides federal support exclusively to schools that offer students abstinence-only education.[1] School districts that want to provide students with information about topics such as contraception, abortion, or homosexuality must go without federal funding. Consequently, many young people confront issues like HIV/AIDS and unintended pregnancy without adequate information about prevention or health care. This problem is particularly difficult to ignore when adolescents in the United States suffer from comparatively higher rates of sexually transmitted infections (STIs), abortions, and unwanted pregnancies than do adolescents in most other developed countries.[2]

Questions about how to approach public sex education seem fixed at the center of U.S. politics. Advocates of comprehensive sexuality education cite studies highlighting the failure of abstinence-only programs to reduce STIs, teenage pregnancies, and abortions.[3] Abstinence-only advocates argue that teaching young people about STIs and pregnancy prevention (i.e., teaching them about "safe sex") also teaches them that sex outside of marriage is permissible. Congressional hearings regularly focus on the content of public sex-education instruction without resolution. School-board meetings become shouting matches over the distribution of condoms in secondary schools. And political candidates avoid discussing sex education on the campaign trail to prevent alienating constituencies. The country's current sociopolitical condition begs a number of critical questions: When did this debate about public sex education begin? How and why did Americans initially introduce the concept of sex education into the public imaginary? What were the major sources of support for and resistance to this movement? And, most importantly, why has the United States made so little progress in keeping residents free of disease and informed about sex?

This book answers these questions by examining rhetorical appeals for and against public sex education in late-nineteenth- and early-twentieth-century U.S. history, as well as public sex-education campaigns and materials. This book offers a story of the emergence of public sex education in the United States that has yet to be told because much of the featured discourse has been erroneously framed as marginal. It is the story of an inner-city educator convincing decision makers and laypeople to include "social purity" courses in public schools, and the story of a Russian immigrant persuading those in power that populations of women, immigrants, minorities, and the poor constituted important members of the public in need of sex education. It is the story of public health advocates creating lecture series, traveling poster campaigns, and medical education about venereal diseases and human reproduction. It is the story of the historical and discursive forces that have framed this work. It is the story of determined women with a vision of truly public sex education and the ethical compromises they made for the sake of that vision. And it is the story of the historically appropriate rhetorical tools public health advocates have used to garner support for increasingly inclusive public sex-education initiatives.

This story transpires amid a discursive setting of ambiguous language because much sex-education discourse in U.S. history has been clouded by ambiguity. Communication is ambiguous when its meaning is difficult to pin down, when the signifier's signified, as the linguist Ferdinand de Saussure would put it, may be a number of different concepts, and the receiver of the message could read its meaning in a variety of conflicting ways.[4] All language is potentially ambiguous because an inescapable lacuna exists between what one says and what one means or thinks.[5] But some language is decidedly more ambiguous than other language, and speakers sometimes employ ambiguity strategically to appeal to several different factions at once. The problem with strategic ambiguity in the case of sex-education discourse is that, although it may allow for a wider berth of acceptance for controversial education programs, such programs often fail to provide students with enough accessible information about sex to foster public health and individual wellness. Ambiguous language such as "abstinence-only" sex education may seem like the only discursive option for pleasing divergent constituencies and getting sex education to American people. But, more often than not, discursive ambiguity leads to misunderstanding, lack of access for underserved populations, and increases in individuals' physical, economic, and social hardships.

This book argues that the Progressive Era (1890–1917) serves as an example of rhetors' dependence on ambiguous language in debates about sex education *and* as the host of notable exceptions. While many of the ideologies driving sex-education agendas at that time were communicated through a veil of ambiguous language, discourse by Margaret Sanger, Ella Flagg Young, and Rachelle Slobodinsky Yarros drew from a variety of rhetorical strategies to make a case for inclusive, accessible, and relatively straightforward public sex-education programs. In this light, the country's current sexual-health problems may be rooted in the distant past, but, surprisingly, so may be the solutions. During and directly after the Progressive Era, Young and Yarros in particular managed to negotiate around norms of imprecision using rhetorical strategies such as infiltrating existing and accepted argumentative spheres, positioning leaders in diverse subject positions, and creating campaigns that conflated ideas of difference and similarity. Their efforts were certainly not without error, but such efforts must be recognized for constituting the emergence of truly public sex education in the United States (i.e., sex education that targets both sexes and a diversity of races, classes, and ethnicities). Their stories and discourses offer contemporary readers distinct examples of sex-education initiatives that fostered clear and practical talk about sex.

My argument is especially pertinent today, as contemporary scholars cite the growth of and support for abstinence-only education as evidence of a contemporary revival of Progressive Era sexual politics.[6] Indeed, questions about public sex education gained a foothold in American politics during the Progressive Era. Unfortunately, the ambiguous rhetoric that some Progressive Era leaders used to talk about sex and sex education have since resurfaced to become fixtures in U.S. discourse, thereby shaping what sorts of information was (and is) available to individuals. By demonstrating that drawing from ambiguous language was not the only way Progressive Era leaders discussed sex education, I hope to revive attempts to talk about sex education in ways that support access, learning, and public health. I offer the historical analyses that follow in the belief that protecting the health of individuals and moving beyond the sex-education gridlock of the present day will necessarily involve understanding where the country has been, what rhetorical strategies were successful in different situations, and how historical figures worked to provide health-care information to diverse members of the population. Scholars, educators, governmental leaders, and concerned citizens who familiarize themselves with the earliest attempts to integrate sex education into the broader public sphere will be better prepared to shape health policy in the years to come.

For the purposes of this book, I use "public sex education" as an umbrella term denoting any experience in which a person acquires information about sex and/or topics related to sexual activity through a program aimed at public audiences. These topics include, but are not limited to, abortion, abstinence, conception, contraception, family planning, masturbation, pregnancy, puberty, reproductive biology, sexual abuse, sexual activities involving one or more person, sexual orientation, sexual pleasure, sexually transmitted infections (sexually transmitted diseases or venereal diseases), and sexual morality. I provide a chronicle of the discursive negotiation that transpired before, during, and directly after the emergence of early public sex-education initiatives in the United States, as well as the public sex-education initiatives and materials that became available during that time. In the broadest sense, I outline how discourse about and artifacts of public sex education shaped and were shaped by a historical context of great social change. The following chapters move chronologically from the mid-to-late nineteenth century to the Progressive Era and World War I to the 1920s, finally tying into the present day. These time periods loosely correspond with the era before public sex education in the United States, the emergence of public sex education, and the integration of sex education into the larger culture. Americans living during these eras saw the beginning of sex-education programs in U.S. public schools, a growing tolerance toward birth control, and an increase in acceptance of female sexual activity outside of procreation.[7] At the same time, Americans experienced these cultural changes in the midst of intense protest from supporters of Anthony Comstock and other conservative vice reformers. Comstock argued that talk about sex should be limited to sermons on the evils of sexual desire and expression outside the act of procreation. In the words of the philosopher Michel Foucault, he took "great pains to relate in detail" the topics that were not to be said.[8] Such opposition made advocating for public sex education not only controversial but also, in some cases, illegal.

Dirty Words: The Rhetoric of Public Sex Education, 1870–1924, offers historical, conceptual, and critical contributions to existing accounts of U.S. sex-education and public health campaigns. This book reconstructs a narrative history of sex-education advocacy during the Progressive Era by recovering voices of women who were central to that process. Despite the fact that the vast majority of scholarship attributes the growth of public sex education to male leaders, this book demonstrates that women were leaders and innovators in early U.S. sex-education movements. I analyze the discourse of Drs. Ella Flagg Young and Rachelle Slobodinsky Yarros, as well as the better-known Margaret Sanger, who promoted the concept of public sex education during and directly after the Progressive Era. Moreover, I contextualize their messages within the major arguments and ideological positions about sex that individuals were endorsing in the late nineteenth and early twentieth centuries. I demonstrate how they used argumentative strategies to rise above and, at times, contribute to the sexist, racist, and classist commentaries circulating during this time. The latter section of this narrative connects these figures' appeals to government-sponsored, postwar sex-education initiatives that targeted underserved health populations, including white women and African American men. In this sense, this historical narrative not only recovers the voices of influential women but also considers how their messages were connected to what public health scholars now call health-disparity work.

This book adds to the conceptual landscape of research on health and sex education by investigating the rhetorical practices surrounding the emergence of public sex education in the United States. While there are several excellent historical and sociological analyses of U.S. public sex education, scholars have yet to analyze discourse surrounding sex education in history, particularly at its inception in the early twentieth century. I illustrate that women in particular struggled for a platform to create and circulate arguments concerning this controversial issue. Although the Progressive Era saw women enter the public sphere to find employment in factories, join social-reform movements, and work as professionals in a variety of fields, many people still believed that women's proper place was in the home.[9] Women such as Sanger, Young, and Yarros were discounted because, for one, they were women, and some people thought it was inappropriate for women to speak in public; and, for another, many people argued that talking about sex in and of itself violated social norms and laws.[10] As these sex-education advocates navigated societal values and obscenity laws, they drew from and created discourses that helped them accomplish their goals in the midst of the many obstacles they faced. The subsequent chapters identify the specific rhetorical patterns and strategies they used and interpret what those patterns and strategies meant for specific groups of individuals.

Taken as a whole, this book also serves as a foundation for analyses of sex-education debates over time and at different moments in history. My goal in exploring the rhetoric surrounding early U.S. public sex education is to establish a basis for the study of sexual-health discourses in other eras and places, thereby highlighting connections between the past and the present. For instance, this book provides some evidence that the argumentative black hole facing sex-education advocates and critics in the twenty-first century is connected to the origins of the debate. I mined archives containing nineteenth- and early-twentieth-century primary sources related to sex education to create an increasingly comprehensive picture of rhetoric about sex education during that time, which helped me identify patterns of discourse that speakers used and surmise if and how those patterns might have survived into the present era. Thus, not only does this book offer critical insights into the rhetorical practices surrounding early sex-education initiatives in the United States, it also creates opportunities for comparison and critique of discourse about sex education in other contexts.

Scholarship from a range of disciplines informs this book, but I repeatedly build from suppositions emerging from public health scholarship and rhetorical studies of the Progressive Era. I employ the work of public health scholars to highlight the interconnected relationship between health science and sexuality. I situate historical sex-education campaigns within the broader context of public health communication in the United States. More specifically, I draw from the history of U.S. public health campaigns to explicate how and why the country's leaders have dealt with venereal diseases, contraception, and public sex education in particular ways. According to the historian Nancy Tomes, the development of germ theory in the 1870s, as well as previous efforts to control the spread of diseases such as tuberculosis and smallpox, played a major role in how officials approached sex education in the twentieth century.[11] What becomes clear in this scholarship is that the relationship between health science and sexuality is a central theme, and frequent point of contention, in U.S. debates about public sex education.

Drawing from my scholarly home in communication and rhetorical studies, this book also works from the supposition that Progressive Era reformers repeatedly put forth progressive messages only in spite of themselves. Although there was never a single progressive movement, and so-called progressive activists were driven by a range of diverse ideological positions, the communication scholar J. Michael Hogan argues that progressive rhetoric is distinct from rhetoric originating at other times in the twentieth century because of its appeal to and faith in public deliberation.[12] I join with scholars of Progressive Era discourse in exploring the deliberative reformation that occurred at this moment in U.S. history, but I also identify the irony inherent in much Progressive Era communication that included sexist, racist, classist, and xenophobic appeals. Often reformers' rhetorical appeals did garner support for much-needed social programs. However, their words in support of, for example, immigration restriction and eugenics were thick with discriminatory language that reiterated social hierarchies. In the present analysis, I have tried to resist the urge to idealize Progressive Era discourse and, in the process, have worked to create a more complete picture of rhetoric's role in Progressive Era social politics. In this way, *Dirty Words* confronts the messy, ironic, and, at times, celebratory nature of early-twentieth-century discursive practice.

My exploration is guided by analytical methods of rhetorical history and criticism, visual studies, and feminist accounts of intersectional identities, focusing specifically on the discursive negotiation of power and agency within particular historical moments.[13] The communication scholar Karlyn Kohrs Campbell defines rhetoric as "the study of the means by which symbols can be used to appeal to others, to persuade."[14] I build from Campbell's definition to explore the discursive strategies individuals used to create support for public sex education in U.S. history. I use public discourses about sex education as a starting point for understanding broader issues such as citizenship, societal power structures, and health-care delivery.

The rhetorical-studies orientation grounding this book emerges from an organic examination of discourse in that the conceptual tools I use as a guide emerge from my interpretation of the discourse at hand. At times, this process led me to engage in a close reading of single texts such as self-contained speeches, essays, or books. In these cases, I focus largely on what the communication scholar Michael C. Leff calls the "rhetorical texture" of the text and Leff's disciplinary colleague Stephen E. Lucas terms the text's "internal dynamics."[15] I analyze the strategies, argument patterns, and style of messages to draw conclusions about how it functioned in context, while still accounting for the discourse's intertextuality with other rhetoric circulating concurrently. At other times, this process led me to analyze communication using a broader lens and approach discourse as fragmented. In these cases, I recognize that text and context are often intertwined to the point where it is impossible to disentangle them. Thus, I follow the advice of the communication scholar Raymie E. McKerrow and take an active role as critic "to construct addresses out of the fabric of mediated experience."[16] I embrace the inherently fragmented nature of communication and bring together distinct but interrelated discursive fragments as "text" and "context" to answer questions about the dynamics of power at play when those fragments interact. In each of these cases, the rhetoric itself and the questions I generated from that discourse, rather than a freestanding theory, was the starting point for analysis. While some might argue that integrating methods of close reading and broader critical-cultural interpretation is paradoxical, I argue that different discourses, communication formations, and research questions demand that critics use diverse lenses for analysis.

Along with this organic approach to criticism, I also focus explicitly on pragmatic aspects of communication, such as discursive tactics and arguments. I seek to answer questions about how, specifically, rhetors worked to convince early-twentieth-century audiences to support public sex-education initiatives. In this way, the narrative in this book offers readers cautionary tales of rhetoric gone awry, a variety of discursive tools that may be helpful in gaining support from audiences, and discussions of argumentative fallacies that tend to emerge in public conversations about sex education. Yet, although I tend to focus on applied aspects of rhetoric, I also strive to avoid the pitfalls of reducing rhetoric to mere strategy by demonstrating how discourse emerges from and reacts to specific cultural values, ethics, and aesthetic norms. No discussion of rhetoric is meaningful without an account of the historical, political, and sociological variables from which it emerges. This book accounts for those variables while emphasizing the practical role rhetoric can play in societal negotiations.

Methods of visual studies and visual rhetoric guide the subsequent analyses and contextualization of featured images. Although, as the communication scholar Cara A. Finnegan points out, a dichotomy of visual and textual rhetoric is a false one,[17] the methods one must utilize to interpret visual forms often differ in some key ways from the methods one uses to interpret textually based communication. Accounting for the visual culture into which an image emerged is central to that process, as is identifying visual "arguments" therein, be those arguments propositional or not. And, as the communication scholar Thomas Benson notes, an analysis of visual rhetoric must address the ways rhetors drew from the realm of the visual to target potential audiences and thereby invited them to participate in the creation of meaning.[18] The cartoons, pamphlet illustrations, and posters that are featured in these chapters provide telling clues about how individuals visualized sexuality, sexual health, and sex education in the early twentieth century.

Feminist scholarship on intersectional identities also grounds the following analyses of women's rhetoric about public sex education, as well as discussions about the representations of women, immigrants, minorities, and the impoverished targeted (or not targeted) by sex-education initiatives. Such work recognizes that women often experience oppression in response to their sex *and* in response to other characteristics such as race, class, sexuality, nationality, and religion. These resulting intersections of subordination function to shape women's sense of self and constrain their discourse and behaviors.[19] In Yarros's case, for example, her difference as a woman *and* an immigrant *and* a person coming from a working-class economic situation upon first entering the United States compounded the power imbalance she experienced while working as a sex-education advocate. But I argue that, in some ways, her intersectionality also helped her to understand, speak on behalf of, and better serve others with intersectional identities who were in need of access to health information. The same could be said for Sanger, who, early in her career, frequently drew from her memories of an impoverished childhood and a constantly pregnant Irish-Catholic mother to appeal for sex education targeting working-class women. As the feminist theorist Kathy Davis maintains, feminist theories of intersectionality "initiate a process of discovery" that attempts to account for the complicated and often contradictory elements of women's discursive and material realities.[20]

To address the questions at the heart of this book, I engaged in an intensive critical-historical study of the Victorian, Progressive, World War I, and postwar eras and traveled to multiple archival repositories to obtain primary documents from those time periods. The major figures featured herein have received little attention over the last century, despite their important roles in the fight for public sex education in the United States. Dr. Ella Flagg Young was the first female superintendent of the Chicago Public Schools, the first female president of the National Education Association, a prolific writer and speaker on topics of education and pedagogical theory, and, most importantly for my purposes, the founder of the first sex-education program in U.S. public schools. I located Young's primary sources in the Special Collections Library at the University of Illinois at Chicago, the

University of Illinois Archives at Urbana-Champaign, and the Social Welfare History Archives at the University of Minnesota. The documents reveal a woman who presented herself as professional, intelligent, and extremely hard-working. Her contemporaries described her as someone who expertly brought together diverse interests in support of a variety of causes. Many of them also perceived her as conservative and even prudish. Regardless of, or perhaps *because of*, her ethos among early-twentieth-century leaders, today we can look back at Young as a champion of and martyr for sexual health.

Like Young, Dr. Rachelle Slobodinsky Yarros played a central role in her community and in the fight to provide women and children with sex education. Yarros moved to the United States from Russia as an adolescent. After learning English and working in a factory for several years, she became the first woman admitted to the Boston College of Physicians and Surgeons. Earning her medical degree granted her the professional credibility to help found the American Social Hygiene Association in 1914 and gain appointment to a special professorship of social hygiene at the University of Illinois Medical School in 1926.[21] I located Yarros's primary sources in the Special Collections Library at the University of Illinois at Chicago and the Social Welfare History Archives at the University of Minnesota. Despite the high number of publicly available primary sources by Yarros, this book is the first large-scale work to analyze her rhetoric about sex education and women's and minorities' right to sexual information.[22] Her writings and speeches draw from her unique position at the intersection of social work, medicine, and education, offering audiences a previously unexplored perspective on early-twentieth-century U.S. social politics.

The Social Welfare History Archives at the University of Minnesota provided the majority of the images featured in this book.[23] While combing the archives in March 2006, I made a discovery that guided my efforts to connect U.S. sex-education history to contemporary health-disparity work: I unearthed a dozen unfiled posters from a social-hygiene campaign targeted at African American men entitled "Keeping Fit: For Negro Boys and Young Men." Unlike the other social-hygiene campaigns I was examining for this book—"Keeping Fit," aimed at white boys and young men, and "Youth and Life," aimed at white girls and young women—"Keeping Fit: For Negro Boys and Young Men" had not been closely examined in existing scholarship on historical sex-education efforts. During this visit, I also found one reference to a campaign aimed at African American women entitled "Youth and Life Exhibit for Negros." Unfortunately, I found no further evidence of such a campaign. Nonetheless, this is the first study to position these additional poster campaigns as early attempts at alleviating health disparities in sex education among minority populations, a primary focus of contemporary public health research.[24] On the whole, the visually and textually based archival sources consulted here offer a representative picture of the debates surrounding public sex education in the United States at the turn of the century, as they encompass a range of media and were created by and targeted at diverse individuals, populations, and ideologies. At the same time, it should be noted that very little evidence exists about how these campaigns and proposals were received by minority and impoverished populations. And although Sanger, Young, and Yarros worked closely with members of these populations or, in some cases, were members themselves, by the time they argued for public sex education they spoke from positions of privileged womanhood. In this sense, as much as they worked to speak for and educate members of overlooked populations, their rhetoric does not adequately represent discourse from within those communities.

The individual chapters follow several different but corresponding aspects of early public sex education in the United States. The chapters trace public debates surrounding public sex education in the late nineteenth and early twentieth centuries; and they analyze sex-education programs and materials that were made available to publics during and directly after the Progressive Era. In analyzing arguments about and artifacts of sex education, this book demonstrates that truly public sex education in the United States was built from the clarion words of important Progressive Era women and frames their discourse as potential models for sex-education advocacy today. Chapter 1 contextualizes the early-twentieth-century discourse featured throughout the book by tying a broader history of the United States in the nineteenth and early twentieth centuries to issues central to sexual politics. This time period saw four major ideological strains of discourse about sex and sex education promoted by Comstockian vice reformers, social purists, free lovers, and social hygienists. The underlying structure of these conversations was predicated on language with multiple, often conflicting, meanings—language with which Sanger, Young, and Yarros largely refused to comply.

A section of this chapter is devoted to exploring the career of the notorious vice reformer Anthony Comstock and the Comstock laws that made it difficult for dissenters to enact public sex-education initiatives. The chapter also examines Margaret Sanger's renowned attempts to dodge Comstock's laws in the early twentieth century, as well as the persuasive appeals in her book *What Every Girl Should Know* and her pamphlet *Family Limitation*.[25] Because figures like Margaret Sanger and representatives of the free-love movement did not use strategically ambiguous language (i.e., language that can be read in several ways to appeal to distinct audiences) to discuss their agendas, they faced substantial censure. Despite this censure, however, they produced some of the clearest, most functional sex-education literature of the day.

In chapter 2, I analyze Dr. Ella Flagg Young's rhetoric in support of the first sex-education program in U.S. public schools and her skillful negotiation of ambiguous public talk about sex. I draw from Young's appeals to the Chicago Board of Education in favor of sexual-hygiene programs, outlines of her sex-education curriculum, editorials and articles about her program, and proceedings of the American Social Hygiene Association. My analysis of these artifacts supports the following contention: by infiltrating existing and accepted argumentative spheres, Young built support for a new, inclusive model of public sex education targeting the largely low-income, immigrant populations that made up the majority of students attending Chicago's public schools. Several years after becoming the first female superintendent of the Chicago Public Schools, Young proposed that the schools integrate scientifically based sexual-hygiene lessons into the curriculum.[26] She argued that these lessons would help keep students safe from venereal diseases and sexual promiscuity. Although Young's program only lasted for one year (the 1913–14 school year), her Chicago Experiment helped to catalyze the emergence of similarly inclusive programs in the years that directly followed.

Chapter 3 takes up several years after the debut of Young's Chicago Experiment to examine the straightforward language evident in wartime social-hygiene propaganda targeted at soldiers. I discuss how social-hygiene advocates used the war as a justification for providing soldiers with information about sex, noting that this was one of the few periods in U.S. history in which there was popular support for sex-education initiatives. During the war, leaders and laypeople alike were convinced that sex-education programs would protect the troops and keep them "fit to fight." Unfortunately, this support generally did not include sex-education initiatives designed for other populations such as women and African American soldiers. So although new sex-education efforts targeted at white soldiers utilized increasingly straightforward appeals, those targeting other populations were largely either shrouded in imprecision, focused on protecting the well-being of soldiers (rather than the well-being of targeted readers), or nonexistent.

Chapter 4 focuses on Dr. Rachelle Slobodinsky Yarros's discursive attempts to build support for sex education targeting women at the end of World War I. Yarros's intersectionality as a Russian immigrant, doctor, reformer, and settlement-house resident convinced her that women from a variety of races and classes need access to public sex education. Her experiences also convinced her that providing men alone with such access would not be enough to slow the spread of venereal diseases, prostitution, and unwanted pregnancies. My analysis of her discourse provides evidence for the chapter's major contention, that Yarros worked to expand the general sense of who should be targeted by sex-education initiatives and modeled rhetorical strategies that garnered support for programs targeting previously overlooked populations.

In chapter 5, I follow up on a project that Yarros helped to spearhead after the war and link my findings about sex-education discourse in the Progressive Era to the emergence of government-sponsored public sex-education programs in the 1920s. More specifically, I analyze the U.S. Public Health Service poster campaigns "Keeping Fit," targeted at young men; "Youth and Life," targeted at young women; and "Keeping Fit: For Negro Boys and Young Men." These campaigns serve as early examples of health-disparity work in the United States. The rhetoric of difference that Public Health Service officials used to publicize these initiatives and separate them from each other functioned, first, to conceal the similarities in the campaigns' information about sex, and, second, to protect the campaigns from criticism. Although each campaign featured distinct images, text, and cultural appeals, they all offered audiences very similar information about sex. In general, they provided audiences of white men, white women, and African American men with equivalent sex educations, and they instantiated a "separate but equal" ideology that became legal in 1896 with the Supreme Court ruling in *Plessy v. Ferguson*.[27] Ultimately, these groundbreaking postwar campaigns targeted at relatively overlooked health populations (women and African American men) were made possible, in part, by the skillful rhetorical efforts of women including Sanger, Young, and Yarros.

In conclusion, I demonstrate how knowledge of the discourses identified in the subsequent chapters can inform contemporary attempts to analyze and create rhetoric about public sex education. Many of the late-nineteenth- and early-twentieth-century ideologies and discursive norms surrounding sex education are still widespread today. Ambiguous language continues to serve as the foundation for many conversations about sexual health and education, but there are few attempts to disrupt this foundation that resemble the work of Sanger, Young, and Yarros. Although ambiguous language may function by appeasing (and often confusing) diverse interests, it does not necessarily contribute to the educational goals that many sex-education advocates hope to achieve: decreasing rates of STIs, unwanted pregnancies, and sexual abuse.

Dirty Words: The Rhetoric of Public Sex Education, 1870–1924, investigates rhetoric about and examples of public sex education in U.S. history, arguing that dedicated women championed inclusive, accessible models of sex education during and directly after the Progressive Era by using contextually appropriate rhetorical strategies. Their legacy is worth revisiting today as Americans search for a sex-education agenda that serves the needs of all and is accessible to all. Analyzing discourse about sex education in years past is a necessary step in crafting contemporary public-policy agendas that foster public sexual health and ensure individual sexual agency.

Dirty Words

ONE

Engaging Ambiguous Discourse

When Dr. Prince A. Morrow founded the "social-hygiene" movement in the early 1900s, his aim was to teach U.S. citizens how to stop the seemingly exponential spread of venereal diseases. In his book *Social Diseases and Marriage*, Morrow claimed that disseminating information about the dangers of venereal diseases would be the best remedy.[1] He wanted citizens, specifically male citizens, to know about reproductive biology, germ theory, and human physiology so they would avoid infecting themselves and others. In the nineteenth and early twentieth centuries, "social" was a common euphemism for sex; "hygiene" was analogous to what "health" is for U.S. citizens today—a moniker with the potential to include topics such as nutrition, medication, sexual activity, and cleanliness. Although many Progressive Era audiences probably suspected that Morrow's "social-hygiene" instruction included at least some discussion about sex, his terminology was ambiguous enough to suggest that sex might not be the primary focus. Morrow's language encouraged audiences to read the movement in one of several ways. His use of phrases such as "social hygiene" was a strategy designed to cushion his potentially offensive endorsement of educating the male public about sex.

Morrow was neither the first nor the last person to use ambiguous language to discuss sex and its instruction, but his ideas helped ring in a new era of modern public sex education in which sex was increasingly framed as neutral or scientific and therefore appropriate for public discussion. As more Americans moved to cities and allegedly fell prey to "urban vices" such as prostitution, erotic literature, and sexual activity outside of marriage, multiple forces set to work warning good citizens away from vice and protecting them from consequences such as venereal-disease infection and familial disintegration. Some of these efforts, including those put forth by Morrow and the social-hygiene movement, involved what amounted to varying forms of public sex education. This controversial concept stirred a range of competing voices, desperate to maintain or affect existing societal power structures and clamoring to promote specific definitions of sex and sex education.

Given the relatively new and potentially alarming idea of teaching the public about sex, many of the individuals who discussed the topic tried to protect themselves from criticism, avoid legal condemnation, and appeal to diverse audiences by strategically using ambiguous language to refer to sexual instruction. In the process, terms such as "sex," "danger," "death," "dirt," "disease," "evil," "health," "love," "pleasure," "reproduction," and "science" were equivocated in ways that made it difficult to differentiate between, understand, challenge, and/or become offended by the positions endorsed. In this context, those who employed straightforward language to talk about sex education were the most vulnerable to attack and were the least likely to get their messages to publics. Thus, in early-twentieth-century debates about whether to educate the public about sex, how to do so, and what, exactly, to teach, strategic ambiguity kept individuals—especially those who had the fewest health resources, such as women, immigrants, racial minorities, and the poor—from garnering the information about sex that they needed.

Ambiguous language also functioned to cloak the extent to which such discourse was raced, gendered, and classed. Many of those conversing about sex education assumed that members of different races, sexes, and classes should receive different types and amounts of sexual information according to their social status. Such differentiation fits into the scholarly assessment of Progressive Era politics in general. Some scholars of the Progressive Era note that race relations generally did not improve during this time.[2] Instead, the early twentieth century is exceptional for its lack of racial progress. Many progressives marginalized African Americans and other minorities by introducing Jim Crow laws in the South and claiming that immigrants and minorities are innately inferior to whites.[3] In discussions about sex, racist views tended to reveal themselves in programs such as the White Cross Campaign (a Women's Christian Temperance Union campaign encouraging young men and women to create a "white life for two" by abstaining from sexual activity until marriage), phrases such as "white slavery," and appeals to improving the "race," an ambiguous term that could refer to either the human race or the white race.[4] Given the racist, sexist, and xenophobic attitudes that grounded even the most tolerant of Progressive Era discourses about sex, it should come as no surprise that women, immigrants, racial minorities, and members of the working classes received little, if any, formal sex education. Although there is evidence that groups of African American women, for example, sometimes were able to create grassroots educational initiatives about sex and birth control for other African American women, these initiatives were rare.[5] So if public sex education at this time was difficult to access and ambiguous in general, it was especially so for members of marginalized groups with few health resources. And health reformers such as the nurse Margaret Sanger dedicated themselves to reversing this situation by making medically accurate information about sex accessible to those who needed it.

Anthony Comstock, Social Purity, Free Love, and Social Hygiene

Four of the major positions on sex and sex education in the mid-to-late nineteenth and early twentieth centuries in the United States were represented by Anthony Comstock's vice reformers, who framed sex as an immoral temptation and worked to silence most public talk about sex; social-purity advocates, who framed sex as equivalent to danger, death, and disease and worked to provide some individuals with fear-based sex education; free lovers, who framed sex between consenting, connected adults as a potential expression of love, pleasure, and health and worked to provide individuals with a program of public sex education; and social hygienists, who framed sex as a scientific category separate from issues of morality and worked to provide individuals with a censored public sex-education program.

Each discursive strain was driven by a set of rhetorical norms and strategies. Comstock utilized strategically ambiguous language to obscure his tendency to apply words such as "obscenity" inconsistently. Social purists employed strategically ambiguous language to speak to and satisfy distinct audiences at the same time. Free lovers used comparatively straightforward language to represent their philosophy, but people from outside the movement introduced ambiguity into the discourses of free love by reading them in ways resistive to what the authors intended. Social hygienists utilized strategically ambiguous language to conceal their value-laden ideology within a scientific agenda and, ultimately, to appeal to both moralists and scientists.[6] Each of these ideological conversations was implicated in patterns of language with multiple meanings. Those who tried to reject that rhetorical foundation often lost the platform to speak, either through legal or popular censure.

Obscenity and Comstock's Double Standard

Beginning in the mid-nineteenth century, the United States experienced an increase in economic mobility, an influx of immigrants, and a rise in urban development. To escape their families' close watch and find employment, many young people moved to cities where men and women fraternized freely, single women became pregnant and sought abortions, and instances of venereal diseases rose dramatically.[7] A rapid increase in prostitution, or "white slavery," allowed men to take advantage of the era's sexual double standards.[8] Although women were expected to remain virginal and "pure" until marriage, men were generally unhindered in their attempts to visit brothels and release their sexual energy prior to marriage. These cultural changes, particularly the increases in prostitution and venereal diseases, taxed the Victorian tradition of dealing with sex by not discussing it at all. Despite the active trade in pornography, contraceptives, and erotica during much of the nineteenth century, mainstream U.S. society generally refused to acknowledge sexual issues in the public sphere.[9] Citizens' sexual silence was often grounded in the belief that children, especially girls and young women, were naturally innocent and modest.[10] The young were generally viewed as blank slates who became interested in sex only when exposed to outside influences. In this light, keeping young people uninformed about sex was also to keep them safe from "self-harms" such as masturbation and sexual experimentation.

Anthony Comstock, the infamous dry-goods sales clerk turned vice reformer, was perhaps the most outspoken proponent of the idea that children were naturally innocent. He argued that giving children information about sex corrupted them and led them toward a life of sin. After serving in the Union army during the Civil War, Comstock married, moved to New York, and began informing New York police officers about the practices, products, and locations of obscenity dealers.[11] In his book *Traps for the Young*, published in 1883, Comstock revealed his dedication to censoring public discourse about sex: "I unhesitatingly declare, there is at present no more active agent employed by Satan in civilized communities to ruin the human family and subject the nations to himself than EVIL READING."[12] Comstock repeatedly referred to himself as "Satan's enemy," and his followers called him an "angel" and the "Roundsman of the Lord" because of his obsession with ridding the public of depravity. Charles Trumbull, the editor of the respected Christian journal the *Sunday School Times* and Comstock's contemporary, went so far as to frame Comstock as a Christ figure who had "risen up veritably in the strength of the Lord to let the Father's will be done through him, at any cost to him."[13] According to Comstock, any public discourse about sex corrupted the nation's young people, and he favored governmental action to prevent discourse about sex from reaching potential converts.

In *Traps for the Young*, Comstock made the following analogy to demonstrate the harms of communication about sex to young people:

> Fill a clean, clear glass with distilled water and hold it to the light, and you cannot perceive a single discoloration. It will sparkle like a gem, seeming to rejoice in its purity, and dance in the sunlight, because of its freedom from pollution. So with a child. Its [*sic*] innocence bubbles all over with glee. What is more sweet, fascinating, and beautiful than a pure, innocent child? But put a drop of ink into the glass of water, and at once it is discolored. Its purity cannot be restored. So drop into the fountain of moral purity in our youth the poison of much of the literature of the day, and you place in their lives an all-pervading power for evil.[14]

On one level, Comstock's language provides evidence that he approached the world from an all-or-nothing, good-versus-evil perspective. He divided people into two distinct groups. On the side of all things good were those people who resembled sparkling, pure gems, untouched by temptation, preserving the innocence of their childhood into adulthood. On the side of all things evil were those people who resembled poison or pollution, those who had been tainted by immorality and squandered their original innocence.

On another level, one that becomes apparent only in light of the discriminatory comments sprinkled throughout his writings and his history of race and class bias,[15] Comstock was building support for vice reformation by appealing to existing understandings of racial hierarchies. He communicated that to be "pure" was to be "light" and uncontaminated by the darkness of sin. "Evil literature"—literature about sex—forever marked what was pure and "discolored" it so that it was never the same. One drop of poison was enough to erase the sparkle from an innocent gem, just as one drop of non-white blood was believed by many eugenicists to ruin a person's moral and physical make-up. The ink that authors use to write about sex contaminated children (and society) in the way that tainted blood contaminated the body. Comstock's strategically ambiguous language allowed him to make such appeals somewhat covertly.

This second reading of Comstock's words is further supported by the scholarship of the historian Nicola Beisel, who argues that Comstock's career as a vice reformer was driven by his desire to preserve the societal institutions that kept upper-class whites in power.[16] He gained the support of elite audiences with discourse framing sex as something that, when placed in the hands of young people, would make them lazy, greedy, lustful, and therefore unable to strive toward excellence and power. He argued that obscene materials could encourage children to masturbate themselves into a state of lunacy or even death. Comstock spoke repeatedly about the important role that traditional, nuclear families and Protestantism played in protecting the young from obscenity and potential ruin. Throughout his career, he campaigned against the burgeoning women's-rights movement by arguing that mothers must continuously monitor their children if their progenies' morality is to remain intact. He claimed, "As soon as the babe is born the duty of the mother is changed. A human soul is placed in her hands to care for, instruct, and bring up for the Master."[17] In this light, any woman who gives birth must dedicate much of her life to guarding the child's innocence in the name of God and her husband. It is for this reason, as well as Comstock's scorn for contraception and family-limitation information, that historians such as Janet Brodie and Carroll Smith-Rosenberg frame his anti-vice crusade as an attempt to limit women's opportunities outside the home and rouse them to have as many children as possible.[18]

In 1873, the Young Men's Christian Association (YMCA) of New York, whose members were also supportive of traditional families and Christian organizations, agreed to fund Comstock's attempts to censor sexual information from the public and form the New York Society for the Suppression of Vice. The following year, Comstock convinced Congress to pass what came to be known as the federal Comstock Law.[19] Formally entitled the Act for the Suppression of Trade in, and Circulation of, Obscene Literature and Articles for Immoral Use, it made illegal the sending of "obscene" materials such as pornography, contraceptives, and abortifacients through the U.S. mail and gave the government the power to search and seize those suspected of doing so. Twenty-four states soon passed "mini-Comstock laws," which deemed the mere possession of obscene materials a crime. Together with the federal law, these state laws made it very difficult for individuals, particularly those who were economically disadvantaged, to acquire information about sex. The possession of books, pamphlets, drawings, articles, dime novels, and even medical tracts discussing sex were regarded as direct action against the state. Violators could face large fines and upwards of six months in prison doing manual labor. As a result, physiological literature at the end of the nineteenth century tended to be vague and less instructive than was literature available earlier in the century. By the time the sexual educator Margaret Sanger went looking for information on contraception in American libraries in 1913, she found virtually nothing because federal and state Comstock laws had banned the distribution of so many books about human sexual physiology.[20]

At this time, obscenity was defined by a British court precedent as anything with the tendency to "deprave and corrupt those whose minds are open to immoral influences, and into whose hands a publication of this sort may fall."[21] This definition was elusive enough to allow Comstock to apply the law sparingly in the cases of his elite supporters. Although Comstock's laws led to the arrest of more than 3,800 people, so-called regular doctors were rarely arrested for providing their middle-to-upper-class patients with abortions, contraceptives, and sex-education materials and/or sending those materials through the mail. In an interview with *Harper's Weekly* in 1915, Comstock explained that "'no reputable physician has ever been prosecuted under these laws.'"[22] Arrest records from this time indicate that "reputable" physicians, for Comstock, must have been synonymous with members of the American Medical Association: they were largely male, white, upper-class, and born in the United States. In this case, strategically ambiguous language allowed Comstock to utilize a double standard so that he could protect influential citizens who sought or provided others with information about sex. At the same time, such language also allowed him to arrest so-called quack doctors and midwives, most of whom were immigrants. This discursive situation left women of the working classes who could not afford to visit a "regular" doctor with little information about sex and sparse access to contraceptives or abortifacients.[23]

Over time, however, Comstock's double standard did not go entirely unnoticed, as support for public sex education grew. During the last few decades of his life, editorials, articles, and political cartoons published in mostly progressive media highlighted the gap between Comstock's words and his actions. For instance, in one political cartoon by Robert Minor, featured in an issue of the New York–based socialist magazine *The Masses*, Comstock stood atop a naked woman, smashing her breast and preparing to cut it off with a sword (see figure 1).[24]

The woman, depicted as twice the size of Comstock, lay provocatively beneath him. Her naked body and dark, loose hair suggested, perhaps, that she was an immigrant or a prostitute. The caption read, "O Wicked Flesh." Although there are numerous elements of this cartoon that deserve attention, I refer to it here as an illustration of the backlash that Comstock experienced

Figure 1. "O Wicked Flesh," by Robert Minor, *The Masses* (1915).

late in his career as a result of societal changes that corresponded with the efforts of Sanger, Ella Flagg Young, and Rachelle Slobodinsky Yarros. Although Comstock claimed to be protecting society by censoring and arresting numerous individuals, political cartoons like this one demonstrated that he wielded his sword of righteousness unevenly. His attempts to remove discussions of sexuality from the public sphere had led him to act foolishly and inhumanely toward those in the working classes, whom he believed to be excessively sexual and immoral. But despite this realization among some individuals, Comstock's sword continued to generate power long after his demise. Until the Comstock laws were finally overturned in 1936, working-class citizens were repeatedly forced to balance their need to communicate and learn about topics such as venereal diseases, contraception, and sexuality with their more pressing need to avoid legal prosecution.

Social Purity: Bridging Comstock and Sex Education

Social-purity advocates worked to shelter children from corruption and preserve the traditional American family in the midst of increasing turn-of-the-century urban vice. Social purists, the overwhelming majority of whom were middle-to-upper-class, white, Protestant women, touted many of the same values as did Comstock by taking a decidedly Christian approach to vice reform and upholding motherhood as women's most important and sacred contribution to society. Yet while Comstock believed that censoring all information about sex from the public was the only way to attend to these issues, social purists believed that some degree of public sex education was necessary to accomplish their goals. Essentially, Comstock and the social purists agreed on what was wrong with society, but they disagreed about how to go about correcting those wrongs. Therefore, much of social purists' discourse was designed to satisfy Comstock's sensibilities and, at the same time, provide white, middle-to-upper-class publics with limited education about sex.

In an effort to successfully navigate this delicate rhetorical situation, social purists frequently utilized strategically ambiguous discourse. Evidence of social purists' attempt to satisfy diverse audiences with the same language emerges directly out of their movement's title. Indeed, pairing "social," a euphemism for sex, with "purity," a word commonly associated with innocence, morality, and a lack of sexual experience, allowed audiences to conceive of the movement in several different ways.[25] Those in favor of public sex education could read the movement as supportive of their goals, and those against public sex education could read the movement as supportive of protecting individuals' sexual innocence. In the end, because audiences could interpret social-purity messages in several diverse ways, social purists gained increased support and managed to endorse a new and controversial topic, public sex education, without censure. At the same time, however, strategic ambiguity obscured the social-purity movement's educational goals (and biases).

For the most part, social purists agreed on several key goals for the movement: eliminating the sexual double standard, abolishing prostitution, and providing "purity education" to the public.[26] Purity education was designed to teach women about their bodies, reproduction, and voluntary motherhood, information that Comstock deemed publicly inappropriate and obscene. But although social purists were willing to discuss sex, they usually did so exclusively by equating it with danger, disease, and death, a choice with which Comstock was more comfortable. The historian Linda Gordon notes that the social-purity movement did not endorse sexual pleasure. Advocates framed sex as an activity that even married couples should regulate and limit so they could conserve their energy for more useful endeavors.[27] In 1890, Frances Willard, a leader in the social-purity, temperance, and woman-suffrage movements, delivered a speech to the National Education Association in which she argued that "vital forces conserved build up the whole being, and especially the brain. The fire in the furnace should drive the ship over the waves, not burn it to the water's edge."[28] Sexual desire, for Willard, was a life force that, if conserved, reinforced and improved a person's physical and intellectual abilities. But if those desires squandered on sexual exploits, a person would have no energy for the waves of everyday existence and be forever anchored to the shores of base craving without the paddle of ambition. Comstock shared the view that sexual activity robbed a person of energy, ambition, and drive and made "real life a drudge and burden."[29] He also joined social purists as they praised women for their ability to tap into their inherent morality and set a positive example for men. Purity educators, like Comstock and most of the general public, assumed that males were driven by their sexual urges. But social purists were distinct in their views that men's sexual urges were socially constructed and could be subdued with the proper sex-education training.

In 1885, the Women's Christian Temperance Union (WCTU) sponsored a social-purity program called the White Cross Campaign, which was designed to teach men how to resist extra- and premarital sexual temptation. The White Cross Campaign originated in the Church of England and encouraged young people to pledge that they would uphold a single sexual standard and create a "white life for two," a pledge that scholars such as the historian Louise M. Newman identify as ambiguously racist in light of WCTU politics.[30] Purity, in this sense, was implicitly equated with Protestantism, as opposed to religious or racial diversity. According to Willard, "the common talk of street and play-ground" could wrench sheltered, innocent children "away from the white line of purity and truth."[31] In a speech before the National Education Association, she wondered why "we send missionaries to the Fijis, but we leave the play-ground of our common schools practically in the hands of a pagan influence," essentially dooming "little children out of sheltered homes to the malaria of associations as harmful to them spiritually and physically as the small-pox would be."[32] Willard veiled her critique of working-class immigrants by referring to them indirectly as "common," "diseased," and "pagan" (likely an insult targeting Catholics). She attempted to frighten parents by reminding them that sin spreads through "association" with the impure, just as disease spreads through contact with the ailing. Children could "catch" depravity at school and therefore must learn "broad, generous and noble ideas concerning the relations of men and women" so they would be immunized against the diversity of ideas they encountered in the world.[33] Although social purists disagreed with Comstock about providing children with sex education, they tended to correlate sexual indulgence with immigrants and members of the working classes. In this sense, they highlighted their similarities with Comstock and his tendency to associate obscenity with those same groups. Likewise, they accented their agreement with Comstock in their willingness to inform the upper classes about sex before informing anyone else. For instance, the American Purity Alliance joined with Moral Education Societies at the end of the nineteenth century to provide purity education to professional and elite members of local communities. These organizations hoped to engage upper-class, white men in their campaign to control the vices of the working classes.

Meanwhile, social-purity advocates were also busy fighting attempts to legalize and regulate prostitution, an effort that was driven largely by sex, race, and class biases. Social purists were determined to abolish prostitution by "rescuing" prostitutes from "white slavery." The United States experienced a widespread panic over the existence of white slavery, lasting from approximately 1908 to 1914. A huge social-purity propaganda campaign fed the panic with pamphlets, books, and journal articles informing women about the dangers of sporting culture and urban night life.[34] In the early twentieth century, the American Purity Association journal *Vigilance* publicized the cadet system in which young men were hired to steal unsuspecting young women from theaters and dance halls and force them into white slavery.[35] "Unsuspecting young women" was code for sheltered, white women who found themselves in the public realm, where nonwhites and members of the working classes could prey upon their innocence and exploit them. According to this report, white, native-born women who worked as prostitutes were usually forced to join the profession and needed to be saved from their unfortunate circumstances. Those women who refused reformers' attempts to rescue them were generally fined and sent to workhouses to be rehabilitated and, ideally, married into middle-class respectability.

Despite what many social purists would have had people believe, however, the number of native, white Christian victims of the slave trade was comparatively small. Many women forced into prostitution in the United States at this time were southern black women sold into northern states, Asian women sold into western states, or Jewish women sold into northeastern states, none of whom were generally the focus of white, Christian, middle-to-upper-class societal concern.[36] The white-slavery hysteria peaked in 1910 with the passage of the Mann Act, which forbid the "transportation of women across state lines for immoral purposes."[37] Women, according to the wording of this act, were simply an illegal commodity without any say in where or with whom they traveled.

At the end of the nineteenth century, the American Purity Association sponsored "mothers' meetings" where women would gather to learn about child-rearing techniques and human physiology.[38] With the "Mothers' Crusade" program, the predecessor to the National Parent Teacher Association, social purists hoped to teach mothers how to raise their children in ways that helped them to retain their innocence (i.e., their whiteness) as long as possible and to avoid temptation from the evils of society as young adults. Willard believed that mothers could help "to push forward the white car of social purity."[39] She reported that many mothers had helped a son to discount "the common school-boy talk upon subjects he had learned to regard as sacred by reason of confidences exchanged between himself and her who bore him."[40] That is, Willard argued that young boys could resist the temptations of "common" talk and degradation that they encountered at school if they had wholesome mothers who conferred with them about retaining their purity. She believed that such discussions would protect elite children from the obscenity that immigrants and working-class children introduced to them. Although the Mother's Crusade program included limited discussions about sex, the social-purity movement saved itself from Comstock's censure by focusing on the central role that morally pure, selfless mothers played in those discussions and the role the program itself played in protecting privileged children from immorality. In the end, social purists used strategically ambiguous language about topics such as purity, innocence, whiteness, and motherhood to have public discussions about sex without overtly upsetting those who did not approve of publicly acknowledging, or teaching about, sex. Unfortunately, the social-purity movement's brand of sex education was hardly all-encompassing in its subject matter and did not serve immigrants, racial minorities, or non-Christians.

A Resistive Reading of Free Love

While social-purity advocates' goal was to maintain existing societal structures and protect marriage and nuclear families, free-love advocates' goal was quite different, as was their justification for supporting public sex education. The free-love movement originated in the early to mid-nineteenth century and remained active throughout much of the Progressive Era. Its adherents aimed to upset existing hierarchies of power and eliminate state-sponsored marriage entirely. In the first American free-love polemic, *Love vs. Marriage*, published in 1852, Marx Edgeworth Lazarus argued that marriage kept people from establishing harmonic equilibrium with those they truly loved because it forced them to deny their attraction to all but their spouse.[41] Ezra Heywood agreed with Lazarus, and in his 1879 free-love tract *Cupid's Yokes*, a work Comstock found "too foul for description," he contended that the state should have no role in the creation and maintenance of individual relationships. Free-love advocates of the nineteenth century held that meaningful sexual relationships only occurred when both partners were truly in love with each other's soul, not when partners felt bound by marriage to have sex. Heywood argued that marriage, in this sense, damned citizens by giving them the "legal license and power to invade, pollute, and destroy each other."[42] Heywood was not arguing that sex was inherently immoral, just that having sex without total commitment to and love for a partner was a form of self-pollution. In fact, free lovers tended to maintain that a lack of sex could harm a person's health. In Ezra Heywood and Angela Heywood's free-love journal *The Word*, they argued that celibacy was harmful to anyone's health and that, to be fulfilled, women, like men, needed the agency to make their own sexual choices.[43] In an effort to provide citizens with the information they needed to make sexual decisions inside and outside of marriage, free-love advocates endorsed public sex-education initiatives. Unlike their social-purity counterparts, free lovers seemed to worry little about appeasing Comstock and the general public when they talked about sex education. According to Heywood, sex "is mystified by ignorance and superstition," and therefore he believed that social problems such as prostitution and venereal diseases would markedly decrease if all members of the public had access to frank information about sex.[44]

The free-love advocate Victoria Woodhull also supported public sex-education initiatives, arguing, "I deem it a false and perverse modesty that shuts off discussion, and consequently knowledge, upon these subjects."[45] Woodhull upped the stakes of the free-love argument even further than did the Heywoods by claiming that marriage was a form of slavery for women. She offered readers a new terminology for discussing relationships: love was marriage regardless of what the state decreed; sex without love was adultery; and sex with hatred was prostitution.[46] In her speeches and writings, Woodhull connected love and emotional commitment to sexual experience and defined sex according to those variables. She explained, "I can see no moral difference between a woman who marries and lives with a man because he can provide for her wants and the woman who is not married but is provided for at the same price."[47] According to this logic, any person who engaged in sex without genuine love was acting immorally. Sex, in this sense, was not inherently moral or immoral, healthy or unhealthy. Rather, sex was to be evaluated by its accompanying level of emotional commitment. Woodhull held that sex had the potential to be the expression of almost any characteristic, depending on the role that love played in its procurement.

Despite Woodhull's relative clarity in outlining her understanding of the movement's position on sex, neither she nor her fellow free lovers could convince the general public that free love was incompatible with promiscuity. Articles in the *New York Times* expressed the opinion of free-love opponents who deemed free love an "ulcerous abomination of unrestrained lust" and a system "where passion and personal inclination shall be the sole bond, and the sole restriction, of union between the sexes."[48] Similarly, the renowned pastor Thomas S. Munnell argued in the *Christian Quarterly* that free lovers emerged from "those sewers in the system of moral reform."[49] The popular framing of the free-love community as licentious constituted an instance in historical debates about sex education in which those outside a pro-sex-education movement developed a resistive reading of the movement's stated goals. In this case, free-love advocates themselves worked to foster a relatively unambiguous reading of their philosophy, but outsider interpretations of free-love discourse rarely corresponded with the intended message.

In an 1871 speech on the principles of social freedom and the free-love movement, Woodhull overtly rejected the tenets of strategic ambiguity by arguing, "To speak thus plainly and pointedly is a duty I owe to myself."[50] She and other free lovers wanted people to understand their position that love, like speech, should be "free" of interference from the church and the state, and "that the very highest sexual unions are those that are monogamic"[51] rather than desultory and promiscuous. Therefore, they strove to present their arguments in a clear, logical manner. In the same speech, Woodhull argued, "I have an inalienable, constitutional and natural right to love whom I may, to love as long or as short a period as I can; to change that lover every day if I please, and with that right neither you nor any law you can frame have any right to interfere. . . . I trust that I am fully understood, for I mean just that and nothing less."[52] Woodhull was explicitly trying to demarcate her rights as an American citizen. What is apparent about this passage in the context of the speech as a whole is that she was not laying out the tenets of free love so much as emphasizing what she and her fellow free-love advocates had the right to do without interference. She was extending the logic of her argument to its extreme to demonstrate that free lovers were well within their rights to critique marriage as a harmful institution. Yet many audience members, including her sister, Mrs. Utie Brooker,[53] took this statement and others like it to mean that the free-love philosophy supported "unrestricted" sex with random and/or multiple partners without emotional or spiritual connection. This interpretation is "grounded in the text itself," even though the author did not intend for her words to be interpreted in that way.[54]

Audiences' resistive readings of Woodhull's words led them to believe that free-love advocates had sex whenever the opportunity presented itself, an assumption that Comstock repeatedly exploited to discredit them as "free lusters." In Comstock's *Traps for the Young*, he argued that for free lovers, "Marriage is bondage; love is lust; celibacy is suicide; while fidelity to marriage vows is a relic of barbarism. All restraints . . . which prevent our homes from being turned into voluntary brothels are not to be tolerated by them."[55] Although Comstock may not have believed that this was the meaning behind free lovers' doctrines, he used their own words against them. By doing so, he encouraged others to read free lovers' messages resistively. Heywood described the situation in *Cupid's Yokes:* "In the distorted popular view, free love tends to unrestrained licentiousness, to open the flood-gates of passion and remove all barriers in its desolating course; but it means just the opposite; it means the expulsion of animalism and the entrance of reason, knowledge, and continence."[56] Indeed, regardless of the "distorted popular view," many free-love advocates maintained long-term monogamous relationships and argued that sexual intercourse should take place in only the most ideal circumstances. Woodhull explained, "To more specifically define free love I would say that I prefer to use the word love with lust as its antithesis, love representing the spiritual and lust the animal."[57] "Love," in this sense, referred to emotional connection and commitment more than to sexual activity, a stance that, if they had understood it, members of the mainstream public may have supported.

And despite what Woodhull's interpretation of free love might lead audiences to believe, the majority of free-love supporters were not convinced that women could or should be equal to men. Gordon claims that the free-love movement was dominated by men. Many of those men were sympathetic to the theories of the British sexologist Havelock Ellis, who argued that women's primary function was to bear children and to subordinate their intellectual and professional pursuits accordingly.[58] In this way, free-love advocates were not as radical or egalitarian as most people understood them to be. But regardless of free lovers' efforts to be forthcoming about the movement's philosophy and goals, resistive readings of free-love discourses worked to widen the gap between what free lovers were saying and what audiences thought they were saying. And this lack of popular support kept free-love-endorsed sex-education initiatives from reaching their target audiences and made it easier for Comstock to jail the movement's devotees.

While social-purity crusaders avoided Comstock's wrath, free-love advocates did not, as they seemed to lack control over how their rhetoric was interpreted by the mainstream public.[59] Framed as moral relativists and sexual hedonists, free-love advocates absorbed the brunt of the fallout from Comstock's laws. Before the federal Comstock Law even went into effect, Comstock managed to arrest Woodhull and her sister, Tennessee Claflin, for using their journal to publicize an affair between a highly regarded preacher, Henry Ward Beecher, and a married woman in his congregation, Elizabeth Tilton. After refusing to post bail, both women spent four weeks in jail before their trial; the charges were eventually dismissed. Their fate was far better than was that of Ida Craddock, however, the spiritualist and free-love author who, after enduring her second Comstock-led indictment and trial, committed suicide to escape her predicament. She left a departure note that explained, "I am taking my life because a judge at the instigation of Anthony Comstock, has declared me guilty of a crime which I did not commit—the circulation of obscene literature."[60] Craddock saw Comstock as the instigator of her legal troubles and, therefore, as an accomplice in her death. On multiple occasions Comstock also arrested Ezra Heywood for writing and distributing works in which he and others argued that the desire for obscene materials was the result of sexual ignorance. Heywood repeatedly claimed that if citizens were to become educated about sex and sexuality, their longing for such materials would disappear, and Comstock openly disagreed with his assertion.[61] Heywood's basic argument was eventually taken up more successfully by members of the social-hygiene movement, who used science to validate their claims and deflect Comstockian critique.

In the last years of his life, Comstock arrested and prosecuted the free-love supporter Margaret Sanger, as well as her husband William Sanger, for distributing information on contraception and sex. Sanger became an especially vocal opponent of "Comstockery," and the debate between Comstock and Sanger is a topic I take up more specifically later in this chapter. Although Sanger was hardly the only person to speak publicly against Comstock and the Comstock laws (members of the National Defense League and the New York Committee of Seven also framed themselves as Comstock's adversaries),[62] she was one of the only individuals to focus almost exclusively on the Comstock laws' impact on women, particularly women from the working classes. She utilized accessible, clear language when talking about sex and providing sex education. And she, like Craddock, Heywood, and Woodhull, confronted significantly more criticism for her support of sex education than did those representing groups such as the social purists and social hygienists, who utilized strategically ambiguous language to endorse sex-education initiatives.

Social Hygiene's Scientific Shield

As the United States entered the Progressive Era, an emerging societal preoccupation with modernization, scientific discovery, and the maintenance of human health shaped discourse about sex education. Comstock's vice reformers, social purists, and free lovers integrated aspects of this scientific turn into their discourses about sex education by referencing topics such as genetic superiority, methods for halting the spread of venereal diseases, and the limitations of biological control over the sex drive. But it was members of the social-hygiene movement, an organization made up of individuals dedicated to principles of modern research methods and scientific findings about sexual health, who integrated the scientific turn into their discourses with the most zeal. Social hygienists developed support for their public sex-education work by using strategic ambiguity to appeal to scientists and moralists at the same time. They also framed sex education as scientific and therefore beyond reproach. Their focus on seemingly unbiased research methods allowed social hygienists to equate talk about sex with scientific pursuits. This focus, in turn, helped them to legitimize their work, protect themselves from Comstock and other opponents of sex education, and create additional support for public sex-education programs. In addition, it allowed them to conceal value judgments within their discourse.

The social-hygiene movement emerged in conjunction with several important scientific discoveries that changed the way Americans were thinking and talking about sex. In 1905, German scientists isolated the spirochete for syphilis, providing them with information about the extreme dangers the venereal disease posed to individuals and public health in general.[63] One year later, scientists developed the Wassermann syphilis blood test, allowing them to easily test individuals for the infection. By 1910, Paul Ehrlich was using chemical therapeutics as a "magic bullet" to treat syphilis.[64] Advances in the manufacturing of rubber made it possible for the military to distribute condoms to soldiers, and in 1904 the army and navy began providing troops with chemical prophylaxis treatments (K-packets).[65] After many years of believing that venereal diseases were a just punishment for immoral behavior, some health and military officials began to encourage treatment of the infected to limit population-level contamination.

Beyond advances in preventing and treating venereal diseases, turn-of-the-century scientists focused increasingly on the study of heredity and its connection to sex and education, a practice that was also central to the social-hygiene movement. In 1883, the British scientist Francis Galton coined the term "eugenics" to "denote the 'science' of improving human stock by giving 'the more suitable races or strains of blood a better chance of prevailing speedily over the less suitable.'"[66] Eugenicists generally believed that characteristics such as intelligence, physical ability, morality, and personality were hereditary traits. In turn, they also came to believe that it would be possible to create a race of people with exceptional abilities by "breeding" only the most gifted and moral citizens.[67] "Hardline eugenicists" argued that the whole of a person's potential existed in his or her germplasm.[68] In this light, the most extreme eugenicists equated sex with reproduction and the future health of the nation, and nearly all turn-of-the-century discussions about sex education ended up alluding to or building from eugenic logic as a framing device.

The hardline eugenicist goal was to encourage those deemed genetically superior to have large families, and eugenicists' ideas about how to accomplish this objective circulated widely throughout mainstream media outlets in the early twentieth century. Much newspaper coverage was devoted to President Theodore Roosevelt's concerns about the "New Woman" who married late, had few children, and worked outside the home. Roosevelt claimed that white, northern-European American women were committing "race suicide" by ignoring their duties as wife and mother. First used by the sociologist E. A. Ross, the term "race suicide" referred to "fears of national decline because the superior white races were not reproducing and the less fit races were."[69] Roosevelt argued that families consisting of virile men, submissive women, and many genetically fit offspring would build a superior nation. In a 1905 speech entitled "On American Motherhood," he argued before the National Congress of Mothers that the country would not prosper unless the "average woman" was "able and willing to bear, and to bring up as they should be brought up, healthy children, sound in body, mind, and character, and numerous enough so that the race shall increase and not decrease."[70] Using the "science" of eugenics to back up his claims, Roosevelt created a message with several different layers of meaning. Although his speech could be interpreted as a statement in support of the human race in general, Roosevelt's dedication to improving the Anglo-Saxon race underlies much of what he said. By referring to ideal children as "healthy" and "sound in body, mind, and character" and then discussing genetic purity, Roosevelt equated those terms with the eugenic vision of hereditary fitness. That is, "healthy," "sound" babies were distinguished not only by their physical health but also by their white skin and their middle-to-upper-class parents. The "average," "good" woman was also distinguished by her white skin and, just as importantly, by her total dedication to raising a large, healthy family.

Several years after he delivered his speech to the National Congress of Mothers, Roosevelt claimed that women's selfishness was behind their decisions to remain unmarried and childless. Such decisions, as he explains in his book *The Foes of Our Own Household*, were the result of their "coldness, love of ease, striving after social position, fear of pain, dislike of hard work, and sheer inability to get life values in their proper perspective."[71] According to Roosevelt, white, native-born women who did not spend their lives raising future citizens were morally inadequate and unpatriotic. Roosevelt implied but never stated explicitly, however, that minority and immigrant women who had no offspring were protecting the country from being overrun by inferior races. For Roosevelt and many other eugenicists, what a woman was expected to know about sex and how she was expected to approach family life depended on her race and class—not all individuals should know (or have access to) the same information. In an effort to prevent race suicide and uphold Roosevelt's vision, the American Eugenics Society tried to pass laws restricting immigration and mandating sterilization of criminals, the insane, and the "feeble-minded." Although the society was not entirely successful, by the second decade of the twentieth century numerous states were passing marriage-restriction and sterilization laws. These mandates limited many individuals' reproductive agency. The American public, constantly confronted by the many available articles, books, pamphlets, and speeches on eugenics and the breeding of a new superior race, was familiar and sometimes in agreement with eugenic reasoning.[72]

Members of the social-hygiene movement repeatedly utilized Roosevelt's eugenic logic to win support for their causes and advocate for public sex education. For example, Dr. Prince A. Morrow, the founder of the social-hygiene movement, framed public sex education as an effort to further the eugenic vision of genetic superiority rather than as an attempt to alter the moral commitments of the country. In the 1890s, Morrow attended an international medical conference in Europe and discovered that venereal diseases were more dangerous and contagious than American physicians had previously realized. He eventually concluded, "The vitality of the *race*, the health of the family, and its productive energy are involved in the conservation of the integrity of functions which these diseases damage or destroy."[73] Morrow justified his discourse about and research in sexual matters, as well as the public sex-education initiatives he was endorsing, by asserting that his work contributed to the well-being of the race.

Morrow came back to the United States determined to protect "the race" by eradicating prostitution and venereal disease, and he founded the American Society for Sanitary and Moral Prophylaxis (ASSMP) to help him power this effort.[74] ASSMP members communicated the movement's emphasis on science and health rather than morality and values by labeling the movement social "hygiene" rather than social "purity." "Hygiene," as I noted in this chapter's introduction, denoted a general concern with human health and those activities believed to promote health. Yet social-hygiene leaders also implicitly supported values such as premarital chastity, monogamy within marriage, and racial and gender inequality, values that complemented the work of social purists. These values were buried within the language of hygiene and the idea that sex was an activity that people were capable of dealing with rationally by resisting temporary pleasures in light of long-term consequences. In this sense, because sex seemed to have less to do with morality than with factual information and logic, those who used a scientific framework to talk about sex during the Progressive Era generally operated outside charges of obscenity and immorality. By convincing some that the social-hygiene movement was purely value-neutral, while at the same time implying to others that the movement supported their values, social hygienists used language "to manipulate conflicting groups into harmonious adjustment."[75]

Social hygienists used their scientific exemption from vice reformers' censorship to push sex education, and the values they endorsed, into the public sphere. They argued that because sex was intimately connected to health, a scientific and therefore value-neutral topic, members of the public should be given a factually based introduction to issues such as reproduction, venereal disease, and puberty. Morrow claimed that the Victorian "conspiracy of silence" had made citizens ignorant about the potential harms of pre- and extramarital sexual relationships. According to social hygienists, sexual promiscuity and immorality were primarily results of sexual misinformation that young people obtained from their peers, quack doctors, and consumer culture. Morrow argued that if young men were educated about topics such as "sexual hygiene, the significance and dangers of venereal diseases, their mode of contagion, and the serious consequences they may entail in married life," such knowledge would be of inestimable service in protecting the "sanctuary of marriage from their invasion."[76] That is, by using science to demystify sex and publicize its potential harms, social hygienists believed that they could appeal to their audiences' rationality and encourage them to remain chaste outside of the marriage "sanctuary." Therefore, they designed classes and materials to provide students with the "right" information about sex and ultimately keep them from having sex until they entered into marriage. Social hygienists disproved rumors about the necessity of sexual activity to male health and the innate moral inferiority of males as compared to females, and they hoped that upon hearing this information people would change their promiscuous ways.[77]

Morrow and the ASSMP introduced a New Purity Plan to the public.[78] This plan sought to improve upon the "old purity plan" of the social-purity movement, in which sex education was aimed primarily at white professionals and elites. Morrow's new plan enlisted social workers, teachers, and physicians to educate the working classes about sex. Morrow instructed these professionals to focus on specific topics (e.g., the dangers of extramarital sex and the ways venereal diseases were transmitted) while educating the working classes and to omit other topics (e.g., the pleasures of sex and unorthodox topics such as homosexuality). In this sense, social-hygiene educators served as censors of information about sex and sexuality as much as they served as instructors about those topics.

Shortly after Morrow died in 1913, John D. Rockefeller Jr. encouraged social-hygiene and social-purity advocates to merge under an umbrella organization, the American Social Hygiene Association (ASHA).[79] The ASHA endorsed mandatory blood testing before marriage, compulsory reporting of venereal diseases by physicians, and a comprehensive program of social-hygiene courses and exhibits in schools, churches, civic organizations, and other cooperative institutions.[80] Members of this organization argued that most parents and church officials were unqualified to provide adolescents with the scientific information about sex that they needed to protect themselves from harm in the cities. The group created a public sex-education campaign that featured lectures in local YMCA buildings and union halls. ASHA lecturers showed audiences shocking slides of people suffering from venereal diseases in an effort to scare them into a continent lifestyle.[81] Although social hygienists worried about frightening girls away from men and marriage entirely, they nevertheless used fear appeals to frame most of their presentations and lessons on sex. Charles W. Eliot, president emeritus of Harvard College and the ASHA's first president, expressed the views of many of his fellow social hygienists by claiming that sex education should describe and illustrate "the contagions of syphilis and gonorrhea, from which proceed some of the most horrible evils which afflict modern society."[82] He wanted students of sex education to be especially well versed in the negative consequences of pre- and extramarital sexual activity so their terror would override their desire to have sex outside of marriage.

Midway through the Progressive Era, social hygienists decided that adults were unlikely to alter their ingrained sexual behaviors after hearing several lectures on sex education. A better use of resources, they reasoned, would be to teach the young about chastity before they formed bad habits. In this vein, social hygienists began to advocate for the implementation of social-hygiene courses in public schools. By the early 1900s, public-school attendance was increasing, and the curriculum was shifting from a classical model of education to a pragmatic model that included lessons about hygiene, temperance, and general health.[83] American cities were heavily populated with immigrants and rural farmers looking for work in factories. Those new to the city often sent their children to public schools during the day, where young people could learn how to function within an urban, capitalist society by following a curriculum for "complete living."[84] Much of the curriculum was devoted to the Americanization of immigrants, and students were just as likely to learn about table manners as they were to read Plato's *Republic*. Because attendance was high following the passage of child-labor laws, public-school teachers were positioned to disseminate social-hygiene messages efficiently. Social-hygiene lessons in public schools (which began to proliferate after Dr. Ella Flagg Young's Chicago Experiment paved the way in 1913) were ultimately designed to squelch children's curiosity about sex while providing them with the scientific "facts" they would need to protect themselves from urban harms. Sex, according to such lessons, was not immoral, because reproduction was a necessary part of life.[85] But sex without reproductive goals, they instructed, would stunt young people's evolution into civilized society and give them venereal diseases that put society as a whole in danger. So, although social hygienists claimed to provide citizens with value-neutral information about sex, they actually provided them with only the information that would create a generally negative and forbidding view of sexual activity. The information they provided concerning sex was, although better than nothing, limited and largely unconnected to issues such as desire and pleasure, values that fell primarily within the realm of free-love advocates. Social hygienists' success in building support for sex education was due, in large part, to their use of strategic ambiguity to appeal to scientists and moralists at the same time, as well as their framing of sex education and research as scientific and therefore beyond reproach.

Margaret Sanger and Educating Working-Class Women about Sex

Some individuals from this time period could not easily be classified into one of these four ideological positions. Margaret Sanger, for example, defined herself as a free-love supporter and sought support from free-love-oriented groups. But Sanger's discourse about public sex education tended to differ from that of other free-love advocates (and even from the members of Heterodoxy, a feminist organization with free-love sympathies based in Manhattan's Greenwich Village) because she focused her attention primarily on providing working-class women with sex education.[86] Toward the beginning of her long career as a nurse and women's health activist, she dedicated herself to providing women with straightforward, accessible information about sex, no matter if she had to break laws to accomplish this goal. In her 1915 article "Comstockery in America," she explained that she had resolved herself to "giving [sexual] information to women who applied for it. I resolved to defy the law, not behind a barricade of law books and technicalities, but by giving the information to the workers directly in factory and workshop."[87]

Unlike most sexual educators of the day, Sanger agreed with the anarchist Emma Goldman, who claimed that women, like men, should be able to experience sexual pleasure without worry that their activities might result in an unwanted pregnancy. Education about "birth control" or "family limitation practices" emerged from the idea that women should have control over the size of their families and the number of times they gave birth, regardless of how often they engaged in sexual activity. In this way, birth-control and family-limitation education encouraged women to separate sexual pleasure from reproduction and contemplate sex apart from its potentially negative consequences. Sanger adopted many of Goldman's political stances, most of which emerged from a distrust of the legal system.[88] In Sanger's work with the Industrial Workers of the World, she discovered that radical socialist groups, like mainstream political organizations (including free-love groups), often ignored the needs of women and children. Therefore, she, like Goldman, concluded that direct action was the only way to bring issues of gender equality and social justice into the public spotlight.[89] In 1916, after returning from a world tour promoting birth control, Sanger set up the first birth-control clinic in the United States, which provided women with sex education and fitted them for contraceptive devices.[90] She went to jail for failing to staff a registered doctor at the clinic (no doctors were willing to volunteer their services). It was not until five years later that Dr. Rachelle Slobodinsky Yarros managed to establish the next birth-control clinic in the United States.

Today, Sanger is best known as the founder of the modern birth-control movement, but, especially at the beginning of her career, she was also a key player in the fight to get coherent sex education to publics of working-class women. Her passion for this cause emerged largely from her early personal and professional experiences with working-class women and families. Sanger was the sixth of eleven children, and her Catholic mother suffered physically, emotionally, and economically to give her offspring life.[91] Sanger attributed her mother's early death at the age of forty-nine to her many years of child bearing. In the conclusion of her book *What Every Girl Should Know*, Sanger's grief and anger over her mother's death is evident. She argues that women have allowed themselves to become child-bearing machines, "bowing to the yoke of motherhood from puberty to the grave. No other thought has entered the mind except to be a good mother—which has usually meant a slave-mother."[92] As an adult, Sanger would be reminded of the trials of the working-class "slave mother" as she trained as a nurse and worked as a social advocate for the poor. Her own intersectional identity as a woman and a former member of the working class helped her to realize that many women like her mother did not know basic information about sex or have access to contraceptives. She set out to give them the information they needed with a determination and directness that some believe eventually sent Anthony Comstock to his grave.[93]

Communicating *What Every Girl Should Know*

In 1911, Sanger began giving sex-education lectures in her home to children and their mothers. Her talks focused on issues such as sexuality, pregnancy, venereal diseases, and reproductive biology.[94] She justified her teaching and encouraged others to head similar educational efforts by speaking to socialist women's groups about the harmful effects of "public prudery" on working-class women and children. Her work eventually led her to publish a regular column in *The Call*, a New York socialist newspaper, on women's sexual health. But on June 12, 1913, *The Call* left a conspicuous blank space in its pages. At the top of the space was the title of the column that had been scheduled to appear, "What Every Girl Should Know," along with an addendum: "By Order of the Post Office—NOTHING."[95] The federal Comstock Law had censored Sanger's article on venereal diseases.[96] But Sanger's resolve to educate working-class women about sexual health remained intact. Two weeks after her article was censored, the ruling of a U.S. district court lifted the ban on her work, enabling Sanger to publish her article as she had originally intended.[97]

In 1914, Sanger published a compilation of her columns, including the specific column that so incensed Comstock, under the title *What Every Girl Should Know*. The book sold well from the beginning and was reprinted numerous times over the next sixty-five years.[98] Even the U.S. government eventually recognized the merits of Sanger's work and, without giving credit to its author, distributed the section on venereal diseases to troops during World War I.[99] In 1927, Sanger published a revised version and changed the title to *What Every Boy and Girl Should Know*. The retitled book, unlike its predecessor, included information about male anatomy and discussed the "spiritual communion" of sexual activity. Although *What Every Boy and Girl Should Know* was also republished and reprinted many times, it is Sanger's first book that contemporary scholars identify as the precursor to the canonical *Our Bodies, Ourselves*.[100]

What Every Girl Should Know stands out among other Progressive Era discourse on sex and sex education because it offered clear, coherent information about sex to working-class women and their children, a group that few sexual educators at this time viewed as worth their educational efforts. Unlike social purists and social hygienists, Sanger generally avoided sexual euphemisms and spoke directly about the "sex subject and the importance of sex education for boys and girls,"[101] a choice that made her extremely vulnerable to Comstock's censorship. She was straightforward about targeting her book at working-class women and girls and encouraging them to band together as females to upset societal inequalities. Although some of her statements were intended to thwart her critics or shame the middle and upper classes for their role in upholding "Comstockery," Sanger repeatedly spoke directly to working-class "girls," providing them with advice, information, and the occasional admonishment. At times she confronted them openly, exclaiming, for example, "How long will you endure this, working women?"[102] and dedicating her book "to the working girls of the world."[103] At several points, Sanger used traditionally masculine analogies so her female readers would realize the strength they had when they joined together as, for instance, an "army."[104] She also highlighted and celebrated traditional bonds between women, such as those between mothers and daughters. She explained, "Too much importance cannot be attached to the necessity of an early confidence between the girl and her mother."[105] Mothers, according to Sanger, usually provided their daughters with great support, understanding, and love as they experienced biological changes that male family members could not fully appreciate. When a young girl had a close and honest relationship with her mother, she would "be prepared for the changes taking place within herself, and consequently be practically immune from the influence of a bad environment, which otherwise might affect her in a way detrimental to her health and happiness."[106] Here, Sanger's language reflected her experience as a socialist worker and mirrored that of social-purity advocates who supported "mothers' meetings" and believed that mothers could help to shelter their daughters from evil and harm.

But Sanger described the steadfast connections between mothers and daughters to accomplish a goal very different from that of social-purity advocates. She wanted to demonstrate that women's relationships with each other were vital to the fabric of society and therefore capable of drastically changing that society. She claimed that, just as the daughter needs her mother to guide her into womanhood, women in general need each other so they can give voice to their unique experiences and needs. Sanger did not mention the high degree of intolerance members of different cultures, races, and religions tended to demonstrate toward each other in the early-twentieth-century United States, and in this respect she utilized a form of rhetorical evasion rather than strategic ambiguity. By highlighting the intersectional bonds of gender and class, she worked to call attention away from what made her readers different from each other so they could focus on their similarities. According to Sanger, societal problems such as venereal diseases, prostitution, and sexual abuse would "exist until women rise in one big sisterhood to fight this capitalist society which compels a woman to serve as a sex implement for man's use."[107] In this sense, *What Every Girl Should Know* was distinct from other Progressive Era sex-education literature not only because it addressed working-class women but also because it clearly pointed to men as the cause of women's ignorance about sex and encouraged women to act together to change the system.

What Every Girl Should Know was also unique because it dealt with topics that were especially pertinent to women and generally not addressed in other sex-education literature. The book consisted of seven short chapters and was largely organized according to a woman's life cycle from girlhood to menopause, thus emphasizing the book's target audience in its form and its content. Sanger introduced her book by maintaining that "every girl should first understand herself; she should know her anatomy, including sex anatomy; she should know the epochs of a normal woman's life, and the unfoldment [*sic*] which each epoch brings."[108] She carefully explained processes that other works by social purists, free-love advocates, and social hygienists did not address because they did not pertain directly to men. For instance, not only did Sanger discuss why and how menstruation and pregnancy occurred, she also posed and answered questions about those processes that women might be too embarrassed to ask their male doctors. Sanger wrote that "one of the common questions asked by young women in early married life is how to tell if they are pregnant."[109] She answered this query in detail, explaining that pregnant women usually experience an enlarging of the breasts, changes in the nipples and areolas, and nausea. Sanger also noted that many women know nothing about menopause when they enter into it. To alleviate this problem, she mapped out what they should expect. Sanger's candid discussion about the lived experience of pregnancy and menopause allowed women to understand changes in their bodies and what those changes might mean. This woman-centered health information would have helped readers to better care for their bodies and control, to some extent, their reproductive destinies.

Later in the book, Sanger disproved sexual-health myths that often worked to subordinate women. She assured her readers that the absence of the hymen, "a thin membrane or film" covering the vagina, is not necessarily a sign of sexual experience. In fact, she claimed that some babies were born without hymens, and some prostitutes' hymens remained intact for all of their lives.[110] Young women, according to Sanger, should feel no shame for entering the marriage bed without a hymen, and their husbands should not assume that the lack of a hymen means their new wives have been unfaithful. She attempted to dispel the myth that menstruating woman are unclean, and she bemoaned the fact that some women will "bear the most intense pain rather than allow the men working with [them] to suspect that she is menstruating."[111] Sanger argued that women, specifically working women, must not be ashamed or feel embarrassed or unclean during menstruation. Instead, they should be straightforward about their needs as women and demand a day off from work each month so they can better care for themselves. Sanger implied that women should be proud of their "powers of motherhood" and the process of menstruation that signals those powers.

But what really separated Sanger's views on motherhood from the views of others was her contention that women who decided not to become mothers could proudly "enter into public life unhampered by the details of kitchen and babies."[112] She directly challenged the traditional role of women as, first and foremost, mothers by claiming that all women, no matter what their reproductive abilities, choices, or actions, could be valuable to society. Sanger explained, "More and more is [woman] realizing that motherhood is only one of her capabilities; that there are certain individuals more fitted for motherhood than others, just as individuals are better fitted for nursing, teaching, etc."[113] Sanger was one of the few Progressive Era individuals willing to publicly state that some women are better suited for roles other than motherhood. Her position directly contrasted with the views of vice reformers, social purists, social hygienists, and even most free-love advocates.

In addition, *What Every Girl Should Know* stood out from most other Progressive Era literature providing information about sex because Sanger went beyond the identification of basic physiological information to acknowledge and discuss women's "sexual impulses" and desires. To bring "every girl" her due education, Sanger identified the scientific names for the reproductive body parts and functions using relatively "plain sexual talk." She focused most particularly on the female processes of menstruation, conception, pregnancy, and menopause.[114] Her appeal to the purity of science resembled the language of the social-hygiene movement and appealed to a modern faith in all things scientific. Sanger's acknowledgment of the male sex drive was not unusual for sex-education literature of the time. Yet, in the spirit of feminist and free-love philosophies, Sanger also acknowledged that females, like males, experience sexual desires that they must learn to manage and control, a claim with which many early-twentieth-century Americans were either unfamiliar or in disagreement. Sanger claimed that both boys and girls acquire two impulses when they reach puberty: "the desire to touch or caress," and the desire to engage in sexual activity with members of the opposite sex.[115] She argued that girls are more likely to experience the former, and boys are more likely to experience the latter, but nonetheless, members of both sexes feel both impulses. Similarly, she noted that girls, like boys, can and do masturbate, although she warned against it for everyone. She contended that it would be simple for her, as a nurse, "to fill page upon page of heartrending confessions made by young girls whose lives were blighted by this pernicious habit."[116] In this light, Sanger implied that women and girls had to know about sex not only because of their reproductive capabilities but also because of their sexual desire and the dangers associated with such desires.

Suppressing Sanger's Ideas about Sex

The same year that *What Every Girl Should Know* was first released, Sanger began writing for, editing, and publishing a newspaper, the *Woman Rebel.* Her discourse, at this point, lacked the strategic ambiguity that was generally used by social purists and social hygienists. Her straightforward style, especially when it was targeted at working-class women, had Comstock convinced that she was supplying vulnerable individuals with obscene ideas that would lead to their downfall. He became obsessed with censoring her work. Of the nine issues of the *Woman Rebel* that Sanger released, Comstock managed to suppress seven of them under the Comstock laws.[117] Unlike *What Every Girl Should Know*, which focused on sex education and did not mention contraception, the *Woman Rebel* was aimed primarily at building support for birth control. The newspaper also dealt with a range of other topics, such as the evils of various churches, capitalism, and the prevalence of abortion in the United States (Sanger did not support abortion).

The publication of the *Woman Rebel* signaled the beginning of a shift in Sanger's focus. For the remainder of her career as a social reformer, she would devote herself almost exclusively to the birth-control movement. In an effort to gain favorable publicity and funding, she allied herself with middle-to-upper-class, eugenically inclined interests and began disassociating herself from free-love and socialist groups.[118] With the *Women Rebel*, however, Sanger had only just begun this transformation and was still amenable to the language of protest, revolt, and sex education on a broad scale. Yet, because of Comstock's efforts, few early-twentieth-century individuals would ever read the newspaper that aimed "to stimulate working women to think for themselves and to build up a conscious fighting character."[119] For a short while, Comstock must have felt both celebratory and relieved when he managed to keep Sanger's discourse out of the limelight.

But his celebration was to be short-lived. In the July 1915 issue of the *International Socialist Review*, Sanger fired back at her censorious contemporary with "Comstockery in America."[120] "Comstockery" was a term originally coined by the playwright George Bernard Shaw in 1905 to mean excessive public prudery. Comstock tried to redefine the term in his favor to denote "applying of the noblest principles of law . . . in the interest of Public Morals, especially those of the young,"[121] but he did so with little success. By this time, not only was Sanger incensed about Comstock's censorship of the *Woman Rebel;* she was also angry that he had arrested her husband, William Sanger, for distributing her birth-control pamphlet *Family Limitation.*[122] This charge landed William in jail for a month. Sanger wrote "Comstockery in America" in Europe after traveling there to escape a criminal trial for sending the *Woman Rebel* through the U.S. mail.

Sanger was no less straightforward in this article than in her previous work, and she blamed Comstock repeatedly for infringing on Americans' personal liberty and setting up innocent people to be arrested under his laws. She began by making Comstock out to be a dimwit in the eyes of the international community: "There is nothing which causes so much laughter or calls forth so many joking comments by people in Europe as Comstockery in America."[123] She then provided some background on Comstock, summarized several of his "persecutions" as a special agent for the postal service, and exposed the double standard under which he seemed to operate, so that middle-to-upper-class women could obtain sexual instruction and contraception from their doctors, while working-class women were forced to go without. As a nurse, Sanger claimed that she saw well-to-do women obtain sexual information fairly easily. At the same time, she saw economically disadvantaged women, uninformed about matters of sex, birthing more children than they could care for, and sometimes left with no choice but to seek illegal abortions. Therefore, Sanger exclaimed, "COMSTOCKERY MUST DIE! EDUCATION ON THE MEANS TO PREVENT CONCEPTION AND PUBLICITY OF COMSTOCK'S ACTIONS IS THE SUREST WEAPON TO STRIKE THE BLOW. WHEN PEOPLE HAVE THE KNOWLEDGE TO PREVENT CONCEPTIONS THEN THE LAW BECOMES USELESS AND FALLS AWAY LIKE THE DEAD SKIN OF A SNAKE."[124] Sanger framed Comstock as a devil who, by making it impossible for working women to obtain information about sex, robbed them of the health and happiness they deserved.

Sanger began her self-imposed exile in Europe by striking one final blow at Comstock before he died at the end of 1915. She ordered her American supporters to publish and distribute her pamphlet *Family Limitation*, a work that the historian Joan Jensen calls "the best contraceptive advice of the day."[125] Sanger's supporters eluded Comstock well enough to distribute approximately 160,000 copies of *Family Limitation* from 1914 to 1917. The pamphlet was as accessible and candid as anything Sanger ever wrote. For example, in the introduction she told women, "The inevitable fact is that unless you prevent the male sperm from entering the womb, you are going to become pregnant," and no amount of praying, denying, or avoiding could change that fact.[126] Then she used the rest of the pamphlet to supply readers with specific directions about how to prevent conception. She included recipes for douches and vaginal suppositories, encouraged women "to know their own bodies" by observing their bodily patterns and cycles, and described how to use contraceptives such as sponges, condoms, and pessaries. In other editions of *Family Limitation*, Sanger included several drawings of the female reproductive system. In one illustration, a pessary covered "the mouth of the womb," and in another, a human finger was inserted into the vagina, pointing to the location a woman should place a pessary in her body.[127]

Comstock and the courts deemed these images extraordinarily obscene, and Comstock spoke against Sanger's arguments that women desired sex beyond what was required for reproduction and were healthiest when they were able to satisfy sexual desires. He demonstrated his disgust for such ideas when a *Chicago Tribune* reporter asked him about Sanger and the birth-control movement. He responded with questions of his own: "Are we to have homes or brothels?" and, "Can't everybody, whether rich or poor, learn to control themselves?"[128] In *Family Limitation*, Sanger, like Comstock, worried that U.S. homes were becoming brothels, but her anxieties were rooted in different concerns. For Comstock, women's demands for contraception signaled their lack of self-control and therefore their potential for prostitution. Sanger, however, channeled Victoria Woodhull's vocabulary to claim that when women were forced to have sex without the desire to do so it was "an act of prostitution and is degrading to the woman's finer sensibility, all the marriage certificates on earth to the contrary notwithstanding."[129] In the end, Sanger's earliest writings on sex education and contraception offered working-class women information about sex that was clear enough for them to understand and use. In the process of putting Sanger's ideas to work, however, her readers would also have been challenging the societal power structures that Comstock and his elite supporters wanted to protect. Without the strategic ambiguity used by social purists and social hygienists to broach the topic of public sex education, Sanger was an easy target for those who resisted changes to the sexual hegemony. Yet, for those women who managed to gain access to them, *What Every Girl Should Know* and *Family Limitation* provided them with what others were generally unwilling to discuss—especially without ambiguity, vague euphemisms, and censorship.

Early U.S. Discourse about Sex Education

Margaret Sanger's rhetoric, by providing working-class women with accessible, easy-to-follow information about sex, was exceptional in that most talk about sex at the time was strategically ambiguous and exclusionary. Several other, less well-known women also worked to provide publics with accessible sex education during and directly after the Progressive Era. Along with Sanger, these women initiated sex-education movements that were truly public, targeting women, immigrants, minorities, and the working classes. The present chapter illustrates some of the cultural hurdles they had to negotiate along the way. Of the four major ideological positions on sex education at the time, represented by Comstock supporters, social purists, free lovers, and social hygienists, none consistently framed women as autonomous individuals in need of sex education for their own well-being; and discussions about sex education for nonwhite, non-Christian groups were largely nonexistent. Arguments about public sex education in general were becoming increasingly common during this time, but arguments about sex education for women, immigrants, minorities, and the poor were rare.

Ambiguous language helped communicators talk about sensitive topics and suffer a minimum of public criticism, but such language also allowed them to implicitly communicate exclusionary biases about race, class, and gender. Comstock and the anti-vice crusaders of the late nineteenth century equated sex with evil and immorality. Comstock interpreted the definition of "obscenity" ambiguously, which allowed for the inconsistent enforcement of federal and state Comstock laws. He worked to maintain elite control over discussions about sex by exempting "regular" doctors and their well-to-do clients from legal censure, punishing instead members of the working classes, immigrants, and free-love advocates. Toward the end of his career, Comstock suffered some backlash for his contradictory readings of obscenity, but his laws remained valid nonetheless.

Social purists touted many of the same values as did Comstock and his vice reformers, but they did not argue that all talk about sex should be stricken from the public sphere. They used strategically ambiguous language to promote an early form of sex education and to appease Comstock by touting his value system. By focusing on "purity," social purists promoted several distinct interpretations of their movement's philosophy. "Social purity" could denote a program designed to bring messages about the social (that is, sex) to audiences. Yet "purity" could also stand for a lack of sex and therefore innocence and/or "whiteness" and being native to the United States. In this sense, to have sex outside of marriage was to be Other, and, vice versa, to be racially or ethnically Other was to be impure regardless of individual actions. White women who became prostitutes were known as "white slaves" because their heritage granted them a reputation for inherent purity and a lack of sexual agency. This reputation allowed them a chance at reform and rehabilitation into mainstream society. They were labeled "slaves" because many people could not believe that such women would or could consciously choose to trade sex for economic gain. "Other" prostitutes, however, were generally believed to be lacking in inherent purity and therefore incapable of reform. Purity, in this sense, was something a woman was either born with the capacity for or not.

For the most part, free-love advocates set themselves apart from other voices in the sex-education debates by using comparatively straightforward language and by communicating ideas about love and sexual relationships that differed markedly from those of most others (although often their ideas were still predicated on discriminatory ideas about gender, race, and class). Those outside their sex-education movement read the movement's messages in ways that group members had not intended. Free-love advocates ultimately could not escape resistive readings of their messages. Thus, they developed an unshakable reputation for supporting random sexual coupling, a reputation that discredited their calls for public sex education. Lacking the leeway that strategic ambiguity would have afforded them, many from their ranks suffered stigmatization, legal action, and social ostracism at the hands of Comstock and his supporters.

Social hygienists, much like social purists, were generally more successful than free-love advocates at protecting themselves from critique and legal censure. Yet they differed from social purists because they framed their work as scientific and therefore factual and argued that providing citizens with value-neutral information would stifle their curiosity about sex rather than excite their passions. In this sense, the words "science" and "scientific" functioned as shields that kept members of the public from confronting the level of value-dependency at work in the social-hygiene movement's philosophy. Members of the social-hygiene movement were invested in controlling the types and amount of citizens' sexual activities for numerous reasons, some of them decidedly moral. They utilized strategically ambiguous language to tailor their messages to several groups. In the process, they earned a Comstockian exemption from obscenity laws. This exemption allowed them to push social-hygiene education into public arenas and limit the type and amount of sexual information that individuals received.

Margaret Sanger joined the conversation about sex and sex education as a free-love sympathizer. What set her discourse apart from that of others was that she offered women-centered information about sex and reproductive biology to audiences of working-class women. Unlike many of her contemporaries, Sanger was more concerned with providing women with the information they needed than she was with eluding Comstock's laws or cultivating an uncontroversial public image. She traded strategic ambiguity for discourse that amounted to direct action against the state and, as a result, suffered more criticism and legal censure than did others. Sanger's *What Every Girl Should Know* stands out among discourse about sex from this era because it was clearly targeted at working-class women and girls, dealt with topics that were especially pertinent to women and were, for the most part, not addressed in other literature available to the public, and went beyond basic physiological information to acknowledge and discuss women's sexual impulses and desires.

In sum, this chapter has situated discourse about sex education in the late-nineteenth and early-twentieth centuries as emerging from a network of ambiguous language and biases that kept sex education from reaching many members of the population. And it is from this complex arena that Drs. Ella Flagg Young and Rachelle Slobodinsky Yarros, as well as Margaret Sanger, worked to transform discursive ambiguity into rhetorical access.

TWO

Championing the Chicago Experiment

In the fall of 1913, over twenty thousand Chicago high school students completed the first public sex-education program in U.S. schools. The program consisted of three lessons designed to inform students about "personal sexual hygiene," "problems of sex instincts," and "a few of the hygienic and social facts regarding venereal disease," respectively.[1] The previous year, the founder of the program and superintendent of Chicago Public Schools, Dr. Ella Flagg Young, had proposed to the Chicago Board of Education "that specialists in sex hygiene who lecture in simple, yet scientifically correct language," provide such a course in all twenty-one high schools.[2] Young insisted that the courses be accessible and easy to understand. She also resolved that they be separated by sex to respect norms of modesty and that their content be grounded in recognized scientific facts. Yet members of the board still resisted instituting a program their constituents were sure to reject, especially in an era when Comstock laws remained influential. The *Chicago Tribune* reported that Young "had been told she had better not advocate the adoption of instruction of sex hygiene in the schools because in so doing she would arouse the opposition, then dormant, of certain members of the school board."[3] Yet advocate she did. By the end of the summer, after Young agreed to change the name of the "sex-hygiene" talks to "personal-purity" lessons, she had not only convinced the Board of Education to vote in favor of her Chicago Experiment, she had garnered enough community support to institute the initiative that fall.

In the spring of 1913, a sample of female graduates of Young's program was asked to critique the personal-purity lessons. Their statements provide insight into how desperately many young women needed information about sex at this time, as well as how difficult it was for them to talk about sex at all. One high school freshman wrote of her lack of knowledge concerning anything related to sex before her attendance at the social-purity lessons, explaining that her "instincts and imagination told me some things and then I overheard a conversation between mother and a lady visitor, so guessed at part of it, but I did not have any definite information until the [personal-purity lessons]."[4]

Older students also used vague language to report their lack of parental guidance and high degree of confusion about sex. Many of them cited similarly uninformed peers as their primary source for information about puberty, reproduction, and sex. A high school junior explained, "Got my first information from my girl friends. Was very glad to hear lectures and want to hear more, for while my mother knows a lot, she won't tell me a thing." Likewise, a high school senior lamented, "Mother told me about menstrual periods after they arrived," and, "I was told a great many things by girl friends at ten years of age which I did not understand very well." After completing the Chicago Experiment's courses, she concluded "that I should have been told earlier by an older person and not by girls who had a wrong view."[5] This young woman waited seven or eight years before escaping the "dark view" of sex-related issues she developed after receiving information about sex from children. Prior to attending the lessons, all three of these young women were so uninformed about "things" that they were unprepared for the changes in their bodies, as well as for the physical and emotional transformations accompanying such changes. Their comments demonstrate that they were extremely grateful and quite relieved to attend the school's social-purity lessons.

That girls, most of whom were working-class immigrants, would have access to such lessons was unprecedented. Young's inclusive approach to sex education, targeting girls and boys, immigrants and the poor, young and old, introduced U.S. citizens to a brand of sex education that was truly public. Young's ideas, and the strategically fragmented argumentation style she used to present them, were an important departure from the rhetorical patterns of ambiguous language underlying most discussions about sex education.

While sex education initiated by social hygienists, social purists, and free-love advocates often targeted men, native-born Americans, and the middle to upper classes, the Chicago Experiment targeted all young people attending Chicago public schools. At this time, the majority of Chicago Public School students were members of low-income, immigrant populations. Although the program Young championed ultimately lasted for only one year, the ways she talked about education, health, and citizenship functioned as a model and a catalyst for talk about sex education and traditionally marginalized populations in the years that followed.

My analysis of discourse surrounding the Chicago Experiment diverges from the work of the historian Jeffrey P. Moran, who positions Young's initiative as an example of sex education emerging from the broader social-hygiene movement.[6] I argue that, while Young drew from some ideas that were compatible with the tenets of the social-hygiene movement, she made unique persuasive appeals that differed in important ways from other sex-education advocates at the time and that ultimately helped her to garner much-needed support for public sex education in general. In the process of reconstructing Young's appeals in favor of the Chicago Experiment, I focus on analyzing how she persuaded the Chicago Board of Education to allow her to establish these lessons in the midst of Comstockian vice reform. As a well-known educator and administrator, Young had a vested interest in seeing that the Chicago Public Schools succeed in helping the city's children grow into self-sufficient adults. Over the course of her career, she served in almost every capacity an educator in the Chicago Public School system could serve, from teaching in the elementary schools, high schools, and normal schools to holding numerous administrative positions. She became the first female superintendent of the Chicago Public Schools in 1909. In 1910, she was elected president of the Illinois State Teachers' Association and president of the National Education Association. These positions offered Young numerous opportunities to reach a broad public, and she used them to speak and write about educational theory, ethics, and the connections between schools and society.

Despite Young's designation as the first person to institute sex education in a U.S. public school system, sex education was one topic she did *not* speak about very often or for any extended period of time. She never made sex education the sole topic of her speeches or writings, which may explain the lack of scholarship on her sex-education advocacy. Instead, she campaigned for public sex education in general and the Chicago Experiment in particular by broaching the topic in the midst of other conversations. Specifically, Young created support for sex-education programs in the public schools by inserting pro-sex-education arguments into seemingly unrelated conversations. Her persuasive appeals seemed to garner force (i.e., by helping to convince the Chicago Board of Education and others to support the Chicago Experiment despite pressure to do otherwise) because she used the taken-for-granted assumptions from those conversations to justify her plan. In this way, she traded ambiguous talk about sex education for strategically fragmented (but also logical and accessible) rhetoric in favor of public sex education. There were three specific Progressive Era conversations into which Young incorporated arguments for public sex education. These conversations focused on a philosophy of education that connected learning to future citizenship, the credibility of modern research methods and scientific facts, and the importance of physical fitness and its relationship to intellectual growth. By interweaving ideas about public sex education into these conversations and using their assumptions to justify the Chicago Experiment, Young helped decision makers to accept sex education as something that was logical to provide all individuals regardless of race, class, or sex.

Because Young communicated in a strategically fragmented way about sex education, inserting the topic briefly into addresses before the Chicago Board of Education or stating her opinions to *Chicago Tribune* reporters, who then abbreviated her claims into quotations for their articles, the discourse that serves as the artifact for this chapter's analysis comes from a variety of different sources, such as Progressive Era newspaper interviews and reports, educational journals, books and articles that quote Young and discuss her work, and conference proceedings. All of these sources feature either Young building an argument for public sex education or leaders and community members responding to her arguments. After collecting these materials from the Social Welfare History Archives at the University of Minnesota, the Special Collections Library at the University of Illinois at Chicago, the archives at the University of Illinois at Urbana-Champaign, and numerous other sources, I selected the texts quoted here because they provide insight into the discursive process concerning sex and education that encompassed Chicago during the Progressive Era. All discourse, whether a seemingly self-contained speech or a series of disparate argumentative appeals, draws from diverse sources to create meaning.[7] The rhetoric analyzed here offers a sense of how Young's arguments interacted with other discourses and helped to catalyze longer-lasting sex-education programs in the years that followed.

Chicago's First Century: Diversity and Growth

Debates about sex education in the Chicago Public Schools reflected the complexion of the city of Chicago as it emerged from a cow town to a teeming metropolis of immigrants and business tycoons with their virtues and vices. Certain aspects of Chicago's history probably played a central role in helping to make the Chicago Experiment a reality, including its large and diverse immigrant populations, atrocious tenement districts, extreme cases of class inequality, widespread health disasters, emerging reform traditions, and growing public school system. As city officials realized that inattention to any segment of society eventually affected the entire city negatively, inclusive attempts to educate the public about achieving and maintaining health seemed increasingly appealing.

By 1870, Chicago was growing faster than anyone could have anticipated. New railroads, as well as its location near river, canal, and lake, helped Chicago grow to three hundred thousand citizens. Immigrants poured into the city from Germany, Ireland, Poland, Sweden, and other European and far-eastern nations looking for work and a better life in the western "new world." In 1890, not quite 80 percent of Chicago residents were either immigrants or children of immigrants, and Chicago became one of the largest cities in the United States, second only to New York. The city's population was doubling every twenty years, reaching almost 1,700,000 in 1900.[8] It was, in the words of the historian Donald L. Miller, "the fastest-growing city in the world."[9]

Incoming residents brought with them a range of diverse religious ideologies (such as Roman Catholicism, Judaism, Protestantism, and Gnosticism), cultural practices, and political ties that needed to be accounted for by legislators, educators, and city planners. Newcomers joined existing Chicago residents, largely middle-to-upper-class Protestants, who controlled much of the city's economy.[10] Chicago immigrants tended to live in wards distinguished largely by their inhabitants' country of origin. In this way, they were able to preserve many cultural practices and largely keep their distance from those with different ethnic, religious, and geographic heritages. Numerous organizations, such as the German Mutual Benefit Society, the Irish National League of America, and the Norwegian Relief Association, formed in the late nineteenth century to promote solidarity among immigrants from specific countries. Some ethnic groups created and patronized their own schools, saloons, churches, and stores.[11]

After the Great Fire of 1871, which killed approximately three hundred people and left ninety thousand without homes, workers flocked to Chicago to help with the rebuilding effort. But by 1872 the number of workers far exceeded the number of jobs.[12] Some new residents found employment in the Union Stock Yards, and much like Jurgis Rudkus, Upton Sinclair's protagonist in *The Jungle*, they experienced long hours, low pay, unsanitary conditions, hazardous working environments, and a lack of job security.[13] Other unskilled workers found employment as factory workers, street cleaners, railroad employees, and domestic servants. Native-born Americans were usually the first to obtain jobs, while the newest immigrants and African Americans were forced to fight for the jobs that remained. A number of southern African Americans began migrating north to urban centers like Chicago beginning in the late 1800s. Men, women, and entire families hoped to find work and escape both de facto and de jure racial discrimination. The so-called Great Migration continued into the 1920s and between 1916 and 1919 saw over fifty thousand black southerners move to Chicago.[14]

Regardless of their race or ethnicity, in many cases all but the youngest of Chicago's children had to work to help support the family. Young people living in Chicago's slums grew up quickly as they struggled to survive horrendous living conditions. They labored in factories doing repetitive and sometimes dangerous tasks in dark, stuffy rooms. Some children sold newspapers and cigars on the streets, returning home at night to rundown shacks without heating or plumbing where as many as ten or twelve slept in a single room. A dinner of thin soup did little to quell their stomachs as they lay, exhausted, on hard floors. During the day, those rooms would often transform into work sites where women and children toiled making clothing, crafts, and other items for sale.[15] Constant hunger and inadequate shelter, in combination with very little parental supervision, led some children to steal and engage in other criminal activities. If caught by the Chicago police and deemed guilty by the court, these child delinquents would often be detained in cells with adult criminals or removed from their families to live in orphanages or foster homes.[16] More often than not, their futures offered only more of the same: dangerous work, no rest, and an unending search for food and shelter.

But not all of Chicago was impoverished, and the city's wealthy circles were hardly lacking in material goods or in the educational opportunities Young championed. The richest 20 percent of Chicago residents controlled over 99 percent of the city's wealth. Company owners, stockbrokers, politicians, architects, and other members of Chicago's upper classes built beautiful homes, traveled to Europe for extensive trips, attended exclusive dinner parties with friends and business associates, and received the very best in schooling and medical care.[17] Chicago offered affluent residents and visitors stunning hotels, gourmet restaurants, theatrical productions, musical performances, and art museums. Chicago's royal families became members of exclusive clubs such as the Chicago Club, the Calumet Club, and the Chicago Woman's Club. At least until the barrage of reform activity around the turn of the century, Chicago's well-heeled tended to put as much distance as they could between themselves and those less fortunate.

Yet even Chicago's moneyed citizens could not overlook the city's health crises that often arose from tenement neighborhoods and thus threatened their own well-being. Venereal diseases such as syphilis and gonorrhea were passed from prostitutes to their customers and vice versa, and seemingly upstanding men infected their wives and future children. Chicago's problems with waste disposal and drainage in the nineteenth century made the area a breeding ground for diseases such as cholera, typhoid fever, dysentery, and tuberculosis, diseases that crossed boundaries of race and class. In the summer of 1854, an average of sixty residents a day died of cholera.[18] Even by 1882, after health officials created a sewer and water-purification system and raised many city buildings above the water line, half the children living in Chicago never reached the age of five. A better understanding of germ theory encouraged city officials to give more control to the Chicago Public Health Department, which helped to create over sixty licensed city hospitals, fund public vaccination programs, and oversee building safety inspections.[19]

In preparation for the Chicago Columbian Exposition of 1893, Chicago politicians became more dedicated to preventing the spread of disease and working to achieve a level of public health. They founded several city units, such as the Drainage and Water Supply Commission and the Department of Street and Alley Cleaning in the Department of Public Works, which worked to reduce the amount of mud, garbage, and open sewage ground into city streets, thereby helping to lower the city's mortality rate.[20] At the same time, organizations such as the Chicago YMCA and YWCA and the Chicago Bicycle Club encouraged citizens to increase their level of physical activity by exercising in gymnasiums and riding bicycles throughout the city. By the end of the nineteenth century, Chicago's reputation as a health disaster was improving.

The city's reputation as a moral disaster, however, remained intact. According to the historian Lisa Krissoff Boehm, from the late nineteenth to the mid-twentieth century, Chicago "reigned as the urban troubled spot."[21] The city was known primarily for its red-light districts, political dishonesty, tenement dwellings, and labor unrest. William T. Stead, an English journalist and the author of *If Christ Came to Chicago!* (1894), was one of many critics who argued that Chicago was designed purely for corrupt citizens' financial gain.[22] These commentators noted that Chicago politicians and police officers were often paid by gambling-house owners, red-light-district administrators, and building contractors to overlook illegal activity. In some cases, such as the Iroquois Theater fire of 1903 that killed almost six hundred theatergoers, such payoffs severely compromised residents' safety. By 1910, the city boasted over a thousand brothels and an ever-growing crime rate. The following year, the Chicago Vice Commission published *The Social Evil in Chicago*, a report designed to bring attention to the city's moral decline, and released it to the public in the style of a muckraking exposé. The report argued that as many as one in every two hundred Chicago women had worked as a prostitute.[23]

Chicago's "underworld" existed alongside its tradition of activism and labor reform, a pairing that eventually led to an outpouring of social programs along the lines of the Chicago Experiment. The city was the site of numerous labor strikes in the last decades of the nineteenth century, many of which were initiated by trade unions representing brick makers, masons, and other skilled workers. National organizations such as the American Federation of Labor, founded in 1886, fought for an eight-hour workday and improved working conditions for members. Some of these labor battles, such as the 1886 Haymarket Riot, ended with deaths and casualties on both sides. Other battles, such as the 1894 Pullman Sleeping Car Company strikes, were less violent but largely unsuccessful for the striking laborers.[24]

After Chicago's World Columbian Exposition in 1893, the city became, in the words of Boehm, a "breeding ground for social action."[25] Reformers worked to help the impoverished and to overcome the public image of Chicago as dirty and vice-ridden. Perhaps the most celebrated achievement of Chicago's reform tradition was Jane Addams's settlement house, Hull-House, which opened its doors to the public in 1889. Hull-House housed (mostly) female doctors, lawyers, social workers, artists, and educators who provided their indigent neighbors with bathing facilities, educational opportunities, a community center, child care, and more.[26] Reform-oriented Chicago women also joined the Women's Christian Temperance Union and the Citizen's League to curb alcohol consumption, the Women's Aid Association and the Chicago Exchange to create orphanages, and the Illinois Women's Suffrage Association to earn women the vote.

Many Chicago women and men also worked to improve the lives of residents by renovating the public school system. Prior to 1857, when the city founded the Chicago Public Schools, public education transpired in dilapidated rooms. One teacher often oversaw seventy to one hundred children ranging in age from four to twenty-one.[27] The teachers did not give students grades, spending the majority of their time keeping order in the classroom and encouraging students to memorize passages from textbooks. Students had few incentives to attend school consistently, and few did. These poor conditions encouraged many middle-to-upper-class parents to send their children to private schools, where students were assured, if not an excellent education, at least their own seat and a teacher who greeted them by name.

But as the city grew, so did the number of children attending public schools. In the 1892–93 academic year, enrollment was up almost 300 percent from twenty years before.[28] These higher attendance rates only made the schools' problems more salient. By 1900, the Chicago Public Schools included fifteen high schools, two hundred and thirty-four elementary schools, and one teachers' school. Almost 90 percent of the budget for these institutions came from property taxes, and many businesses found ways to avoid paying what they owed the city. Underfunded, unorganized, and disconnected from the communities they served, the Chicago Public Schools lagged behind the schools of comparable U.S. metropolitan areas.

Fortunately, budget reforms, the creation of the Chicago Teachers Federation in 1897, and the publication of the Harper report in 1898 (detailing the public school system's deficiencies)[29] helped to turn the schools around. During the first decades of the twentieth century, the Chicago Public Schools began offering students industrial and technical training to better prepare them for employment in the city. Institutions of higher learning such as the University of Chicago, Northwestern University, Lake Forest University, and St. Ignatius College established themselves in the community. Their accompanying medical schools and research facilities made Chicago one of the country's leaders in scientific research. Co-educational universities began opening their doors to women, and organizations such as the Women's

Physiological Club and the Moral Education Society—which offered well-to-do women access to information about reproductive biology—flourished. Although the Board of Education and the Chicago Teachers Federation often disagreed about how to lead the schools into the twentieth century, the Chicago public schools, as well as neighboring educational institutions, had improved greatly since their inception fifty years earlier.[30]

Overall, Chicago was conducive to programs (like Young's) that accounted for its many competing needs. Attention to the city's differing interests and populations became important to city officials as large numbers of immigrants, southern migrants, and eastern capitalists moved there in the nineteenth century to build a prosperous life. Once in Chicago, however, many working-class residents had difficulty finding employment and supporting their families. They lived in tenement districts that contrasted drastically with the mansions of Chicago entrepreneurs such as J. P. Morgan and Marshall Field. No one was immune from the many epidemics that swept the great city, nor from the smell of the Union Stock Yards. Thus, over time, city officials granted the Chicago Health Department increased funds to improve the state of public health. Progressive Era Chicago was thick with labor strikes and an infrastructure of reformers determined to improve city social institutions. Chicago's many paradoxes—extreme poverty and excessive wealth, selflessness and greed, vitality and death, magnificence and repugnance—opened up space for risk-taking that seemed to play a role in making the Chicago Experiment and its inclusive model of public sex education a reality.

The Chicago Experiment

Another possible reason why the first sex education program in U.S. public schools originated in Chicago was because Young's ideas about sex education were not wholly new to the city. In the early twentieth century, Chicago developed an infrastructure of support for public sex education. The Chicago Society of Social Hygiene, an outgrowth of Dr. Prince A. Morrow's American Society for Sanitary and Moral Prophylaxis, formed in 1907. The group focused primarily on educating boys and young men about the dangers of premarital sex. In the society's review of its first year's work, the secretary claimed that the organization's aim was to "give the boys a chance" in an environment that incessantly inflamed their burgeoning sexuality.[31] The society depended largely on circulars to educate boys about the consequences of "illicit sexual indulgence," consequences that affected everything from the health of the body to one's success in business transactions.[32] According to this organization's mission statement, prospective brides need not be informed about such dangers if their future husbands knew how to avoid passing venereal diseases on to them. Society members assumed that "good" girls, lacking the overpowering sexual instincts of their male counterparts, would avoid sex outside of marriage. Therefore, they could only contract syphilis or gonorrhea if their husbands passed the diseases on to them. But not all young women were "good," and therefore a society circular entitled "Sexual Hygiene: A Circular of Information for Young Men" warned that "every prostitute, public or private, acquires venereal disease sooner or later; hence all of them are diseased some of the time, and some of them practically all of the time."[33] The society labeled any woman who had sex outside of marriage a prostitute and a person from whom men must protect themselves. Prospective brides, by contrast, were framed as women who were innocent (i.e., sexually ignorant) and therefore in need of male protection from the underworld of red-light districts and venereal diseases. This dichotomous portrayal of women, as well as the contention that women did not need sex education in their own right, was something the social-hygiene movement continued into the First World War.

While Young attended several social-hygiene conferences during her career and integrated some social-hygiene tenets into the Chicago Experiment, she was not an official member of the Chicago Society of Social Hygiene or the American Society of Sanitary and Moral Prophylaxis. Her work as superintendent demonstrated that she disagreed with several of the Chicago Society of Social Hygiene's methods. For one, Young was much more inclusive than were social hygienists about who should have access to information about sex, perhaps because her perspective as a woman in educational administration made her sensitive to the harms of exclusion. Young argued that girls, like boys, must receive information about "personal purity" directly from physicians and other experts. She maintained that they should not be forced to remain ignorant of such matters and depend on their male suitors for protection; and ultimately one of her major contributions to the sex-education movement in Chicago was her insistence on including girls in the social-hygiene agenda. She repeatedly demanded that boys and girls be separated during these lessons not because she wanted the sexes to receive different information but because she wanted them to feel comfortable enough to ask questions and comment on the lessons.[34] Young feared that young people would be less likely to engage in such classes if they were in mixed company. And by arguing that sex-education courses be a mandatory element of the Chicago Public Schools' curriculum, Young also insisted that those who subscribed to religions other than Christianity (the social-hygiene movement often aligned itself with Christian organizations), as well as those representing diverse racial and ethnic backgrounds, receive sex education.

Young also separated herself from social-hygiene advocates in that she disfavored using leaflets to educate young people about sex. Instead, she promoted a public dialogue in which people discussed sexual issues with medical professionals and educators rather than reading about those issues by themselves. In her 1911 annual report as superintendent, she acknowledged that "in some cities, leaflets dealing with the physiological and medical phases of purity and impurity have been prepared for the upper grades and the high schools, and their results have been, so the testimony runs, valuable."[35] But she went on to note, "I believe, however, that modest yet intelligent talks on the obligation to keep body and mind pure should be given to all children by teachers qualified for such delicate yet forceful thought and speech."[36] Accomplished speakers, according to Young, could balance modesty with intelligence, delicacy with force, and they could ensure that discussions veered in moral directions. Unlike leaflets, speakers could also answer questions, vary the content of lessons for different venues, relate to students on a personal level, and, perhaps most importantly, ensure that everyone understood what was being discussed.

Evidence of Young's dedication to the movement for public sex education emerged when she became superintendent of the Chicago Public Schools in 1909. She created a Committee of Sex Hygiene, headed by Walter T. Sumner, a member of the Chicago School Board and dean of the Chicago Cathedral of Sts. Peter and Paul. Sumner and the committee recommended that the city offer instruction on issues related to sex and "that the best way to approach this matter in the interest of the children in the public schools at the present time is through the parents."[37] Young used the committee's recommendation to convince the Board of Education to fund sex-education lessons for adults in 1912. Like the personal-purity courses that came later, local physicians delivered these lessons, and audiences were separated by sex. Courses for women were held during the day, and courses for men transpired in the evenings.[38] In the end, more than two thousand adults representing a range of cultures and ethnicities attended one of the forty lessons held in schools throughout Chicago. At the end of the year, Young suggested that parents "bring their older children with them because the lecture heard by parent and child would form a subject of conversation that might not otherwise be broached by the parent."[39] Not long after she made this call, Young proposed to extend her idea by introducing sex-education courses directly into the public schools' curriculum.

In proposing the Chicago Experiment before the Board of Education, Young recommended that, beyond the three talks for high school students, children in the middle and upper grades of elementary school also attend one lesson on personal purity given by a health professional and "that teachers in the lower grades and nurses be requested to endeavor to guard the young children from practices taught by the unchaste."[40] In this way, the Chicago Experiment was designed to begin educating very young students about physiology (a controversial idea even in contemporary society) and to continue offering them increasingly more information as they advanced through the grades. Teachers worked to supply children with only the information they deemed appropriate for their ages, a practice that would have been more difficult had the courses depended on written texts anyone might find and read. Young held that the youngest students would merely need to be "protected" from the "unchaste," but in later years they would need to learn about the technical aspects of physiology and chastity so they could protect themselves from the evils of society. After years of working with children, Young concluded, "But early, much earlier than we have dared to advise, some knowledge must be imparted because of the vulgarity, obscenity, or enticements which may influence the thought, the acts, the lives of the children."[41] That is, Young believed that the environment in Chicago, with its high rates of venereal diseases, prostitution, and pre- and extramarital sex, demanded that schools begin providing sex education to students as soon as possible. Like others before her, she argued that if the schools provided students with information about sex before they encountered vulgar sources, students would be more likely to resist sexual temptations in the future, protect themselves from venereal diseases, and grow into healthy, self-sufficient citizens.

But Young also framed public sex education in ways that others before her had not. During the 1913–14 academic year, the journal *Vigilance* reported, "Mrs. Ella Flagg Young, Superintendent of Schools in Chicago, has at last triumphed after a long, hard fight, and the subject of sex hygiene is now part of the Chicago high school curriculum."[42] In the ensuing section, I explore the ways Young fit arguments for public sex education into three distinct conversations and why doing so helped her to "triumph," at least temporarily, in the fight for public sex education in the United States.

Young's Appeals for Public Sex Education

Young inserted arguments for public sex education into three specific Progressive Era conversations and then used the assumptions from those conversations to convince audiences of the necessity of sex education in Chicago Public Schools. These conversations focused on a philosophy of education that connected learning to future citizenship, the credibility of facts and scientific research methods, and the importance of physical fitness and its connection to intellectual growth. The arguments that emerged in these separate conversations implicitly came together to help convince Chicago citizens that teaching all members of society about sex was logical on a variety of different levels.

The Chicago School Philosophy of Education

Young helped to found the Chicago School philosophy of education, and on occasion she interjected conversations based on this philosophy to argue for sex-education courses in the Chicago Public Schools. Existing theories of education framed schooling as the passing on of information from teacher to student, as preparation for an occupation, or as an exercise in mental discipline. But the Chicago School connected learning with citizenship and emphasized the idea that schools should be places where young people learn to function within a democracy. The historian Mary Herrick dates the emergence of the Chicago School of educational philosophy in the 1890s and identifies John Dewey as its spokesperson.[43] Dewey worked as a professor of philosophy and pedagogy at the University of Chicago from 1884 to 1904 and is known today for his many writings on pragmatism, psychology, and education. He repeatedly argued that schools must educate the "whole child" by emphasizing lived experience over abstract concepts. In *Moral Principles in Education,* Dewey explained that society should "demand for and from the schools whatever is necessary to enable the child intelligently to recognize all his social relations and take his part in sustaining them."[44]

Dewey held that schools must link lessons to students' experiences outside of school in order to make those lessons salient and useful to them.[45] Teaching children classic literature, for example, was not instructive if that literature did not resonate with their day-to-day lives. In this light, schools that focused primarily on teaching children to follow directions or memorize instructions did both the children and society a disservice because "the society of which the child is to be a member is, in the United States, a democratic and progressive society. The child must be educated for leadership as well as for obedience."[46] According to Dewey, schools must inspire all children, regardless of race, religion, or class, to think and act on their own so they are able to oversee a functional society in the future.

In 1895, at the age of fifty, Young began taking graduate courses under Dewey in the Department of Education at the University of Chicago. After finishing her dissertation in 1900 and publishing it as *Isolation in the School* in 1901,[47] Young worked as the director of Dewey's famed Chicago Laboratory School and as a professor of education at the University of Chicago. Young and Dewey worked together closely over the years, and, according to both parties, the intellectual relationship was beneficial. Dewey claimed that he learned as much from Young's experience as a Chicago educator as she did from his graduate seminars. He admitted, "I was constantly getting ideas from her. . . . More times than I could well say, I didn't see the meaning or force of some favorite conception of my own until Mrs. Young had given it back to me."[48] The two scholars developed a similar philosophy of education, but according to the historian Ellen Condliffe Lagemann, it was Young who tended to apply that philosophy to real-world situations;[49] and it was Young who used the Chicago School's logic to support sex-education programs that would serve the diversity of students attending the Chicago Public Schools.

Young's work with Dewey solidified her conviction that Chicago schools should supply all students with tools for future citizenship. In her 1911 annual report as superintendent of schools, Young claimed that the goal of the Chicago Public Schools was to "invigorate and strengthen the children for their future as citizens in this republic."[50] Yet, as Dewey explained in *Moral Principles in Education*, the Chicago School's conception of citizenship went far beyond voter training. Although the child is to be a "voter and a subject of law," the child must also become a responsible family member, a worker "engaged in some occupation which will be of use to society, and which will maintain his own independence and self-respect," and "a member of some particular neighborhood and community, and must contribute to the values of life, add to the decencies and graces of civilization wherever he is."[51] In this light, schools must "train young people for citizenship" by helping them to develop into multifaceted, self-sufficient individuals, capable of meeting the demands of life in the twentieth-century United States. Young, along with other Chicago School advocates such as Dewey and Jane Addams, viewed the environment in which students lived, and the skills they required to navigate that environment, as the most important variable dictating schools' curricula.

The environment students were entering (Progressive Era Chicago) was decidedly multifaceted. Therefore Young argued that students needed to be taught to deal with diverse ideas and to respect difference. In Young's review of Dewey's book *Democracy and Education*,[52] she argued that Americans needed to "make education the great instrumentality helping children and youths to grow into citizenship in a government intended to be of, by, and for all."[53] By alluding to Abraham Lincoln's "Gettysburg Address," Young communicated her view of education as an institution designed to speak to and unify diverse elements of society. According to Young, students learned how to be responsible members of society, capable of compromise and self-representation, when they became familiar with the range of perspectives and information they might encounter in their everyday lives. She held that schools that followed this model of education aided the country "in awakening the American people to the many aspects of knowledge and training," so as to add "to the grandeur of the future of America."[54] In this sense, the nation's future depended on its schools' ability to inspire self-sufficiency, critical thinking, and intellectual curiosity in each of its young people.

Young used the argument that students' environments, experiences, and goals should dictate their program of study to convince Chicago residents to support sex-education courses in the Chicago Public Schools' curriculum. She argued that students' biological and physical environments demanded that they learn about sex in the schools. In terms of biology, Young took Dewey's call for teaching the "whole child" quite literally. As early as 1868, she was providing teachers-in-training attending the Chicago Normal School with Saturday-morning lectures entitled "The Human Body—Parts and Uses."[55] She maintained that "children should be taught to know something of the wonderful structure and mechanism of the body," including how to care for the body by keeping it "clean" and "pure"; and children "should be made to realize that knowledge of their environment comes by way of the organs of special sense; that the interchange of thought with parents and friends is effected through the action of nerve and muscular structure."[56] Young reasoned that because students' bodies were their connection to their environment, they must learn about all of their bodies' "parts and uses." She did not explicitly mention the reproductive organs or secondary sexual characteristics in this passage. However, by using the words "clean" and "pure" to talk about instruction concerning the body, words that were popular among social-purity advocates, she gestured toward the body's sexual functions and features. By referring to body parts as "wonderful" and "special," she worked to replace the often negative connotations of sexual bodies with positive connotations about how even the body's sexual "parts and uses" play a role in individuals' connections with each other. She reminded her students that bodies need to be "properly" cared for to be useful in adulthood. She also reasoned that because young people do not inherently know how to protect their bodies from dirt, disease, and abuse, someone must teach them.

Young drew from the Chicago School rationale that public schools must teach young people what they need to know to navigate their environments, especially if students are not learning that information at home. This reasoning was evident in Young's 1911 report as superintendent of schools, in which she argued that the schools must teach students about finances because "the economical use of money and material is, to a considerable extent, neglected in our homes."[57] On several different occasions, Young used this same logic to argue that schools should teach students about sex. She explained that sex education was a job that "should be done in the home, but which is done in only a few homes."[58] She claimed that "the parents who have the courage, intelligence, and tact to explain the sex organs and functions to their children are so rare that it needs must fall on the school system to convey this information."[59] Others in favor of public sex education had long argued that parents were not teaching their children about sex. For instance, the president of the Chicago Department of School Patrons, Mrs. William S. Heffernan, told the *Chicago Tribune* in 1913, "There is a whole lot of objection to the teaching of sex hygiene in the schools. It is said that it should be taught in the home, but it is evident that it is not being taught in the home."[60] But Mrs. Heffernan and others like her did not link their argument to the Chicago School's assumptions about citizenship. Young, by contrast, argued that children's bodies were tools for interacting with society as citizens and that schools had a responsibility to society at large to teach all students about the sexual aspects of their bodies when their parents were not providing them with that information.

When Young became superintendent of the Chicago Public Schools, she surveyed the schools under her charge and concluded that the "rigid exclusion of sex knowledge from the schools" might lead one to believe that "children were supposed to know all about these particular organs, their functions and abuses, or else were supposed to learn of them by accident or the good graces of their fellows." As a result of this lacuna in the curriculum, she found that students "usually learn [about these issues] in a grossly perverted way through the bad graces of the evil minded among their companions."[61] In this case, Young argued that students' biology *and* their physical environments demanded that the public schools teach them about sex. Here, the "evil minded among their companions" served as a synecdoche for Chicago's underworld. Young implied that girls and boys *will* encounter "perversion" and "bad graces" while making their way in Chicago—especially those living in low-income areas—and they must be prepared to meet those challenges and resist temptation. Students must face what Young called "the low and brutal"[62] when they are in the "real world," and thus their schooling must address these issues. In an "environment filled with temptation,"[63] students would not be able to realize their potential as self-sufficient citizens if they had not been taught how to deal with temptation. By excluding information about sex from the curriculum, Young maintained that the city of Chicago was setting itself up for inheriting a generation of citizens ignorant about sex, perverted, or "evil minded."

Yet not everyone agreed that Chicago's environment demanded its residents learn about sex at school. Some critics argued that students needed to learn about sex, but at home with their parents. An editorial published in the *New York Times* about the Chicago Experiment argued that learning such information at school would have a "demoralizing effect" that would break down the "barriers of polite reticence" and lead to an outpouring of sexual promiscuity among young people.[64] Still other public voices argued that sex education was unnecessary entirely. For instance, in a letter dated December 11, 1913, the governor of Illinois, Edward F. Dunne, explained his fear that if sex education was provided in the public schools, "it may create, and probably will create, in [students'] young minds a prurient curiosity which will induce, rather than suppress, immorality and unchastity."[65] Dunne assumed that young people would not necessarily come into contact with "prurient" information about sex if they did not encounter it in school. Of course, his view failed to account for children living outside the middle-to-upper-class bubble of parental protection. From this perspective, students' environments did not demand that they attend sex-education courses or otherwise learn about sex and sexual "vices." Similarly, after hearing about Young's Chicago Experiment, one mother warned that any attempt to "instruct" her children about sex would force her to "horsewhip the 'educator,' and thus give him or her a needed lesson in respecting the rights of parents to bring up their little ones in innocence of the terrible evils of life."[66] Like Governor Dunne, this individual argued that if parents protected their children from sexual information, their children could grow up without having to know about or deal with such issues. Therefore, she held that sex education was not a tool students needed to become self-sufficient members of society. If parents simply taught their children to "ignore" the "terrible evils of life," rather than to question or interact with them, those children could remain innocent of such topics indefinitely.

But the ever-increasing rates of venereal diseases, prostitution, and other "promiscuous" activity in Chicago countered this line of reasoning. No matter how innocent the child or vigilant the parent, young people living in Chicago would have to deal with sex in one way or another. If environment should dictate curriculum, as the Chicago School's philosophy of education suggested, then Young's proposal in favor of including sex education in public schools made logical sense to a growing number of individuals. People across the country held up Young's program as a valiant effort to provide children with the information about sex they needed to be self-sufficient citizens. For instance, the editor of the *St. Petersburg (Fla.) Times* argued that "no crusade against vice, however well-intentioned or spectacular, is complete unless it includes tactful tuition of children in their formative years."[67] Although what the editor meant by "tactful" is unclear, this quotation implicitly acknowledges that children would encounter sex in their environment and thus the topic must be included in their lessons.

Ultimately, Young's pairing of the Chicago School's philosophy of education with ideas about the sexual nature of students' biology and physical environment, as well as the claim that parents were not teaching children about sex at home, helped some decision makers consider the importance of providing all Chicago's children with information about sex. By introducing arguments about sex education into conversations concerning education and citizenship, Young eased audiences into thinking about a controversial issue and encouraged them to consider the topic outside of the emotionally charged debates that tended to surround such issues. But the Chicago School's philosophy of education was not the only conversation into which Young inserted arguments in support of public sex education. She also argued for public sex education using popular assumptions concerning scientific facts and modern research methods.

The Morality of Scientific Information

Beyond the Chicago School's philosophy of education, Young incorporated arguments in favor of sex education into conversations about the credibility of scientific facts. But rather than simply appealing to the certainty of scientific reasoning in the fashion of social-hygiene advocates, Young extended the logic in those conversations to argue for the inherent morality of scientific information. In this sense, she proceeded from the assumption that morality and science were not mutually exclusive; Young held that they naturally overlapped, and she framed her appeals accordingly.

The Progressive Era is well known for its infatuation with modernity, science, and technical expertise. During this time, scientific methods became the driving force behind the management of research institutions, factories, public schools, and social organizations. Young, like many of her contemporaries, argued that science focused on getting at the "truth" more than other methods of inquiry. She explained that "impartial, sympathetic investigation called scientific" had brought "the modern world to her feet" by promoting an attitude of "the intelligent seeker after truth," which "cannot be taken by one whose premises are false, or whose conclusions are biased by individual likes and dislikes."[68] According to Young and other Progressive Era modernists, science stripped away everything but unencumbered fact. The scientist used an objective, and therefore trustworthy, stance to find out about the world and relationships between things in the world.

This scientific mode of analysis helped people to justify the study of topics such as sex and sexual health that had long been deemed inappropriate for public discussion. Members of the social-hygiene movement argued that because scientific research demonstrated that the spread of venereal diseases was directly related to sexual activity, social institutions such as schools, churches, and community centers had a responsibility to provide citizens with information about topics such as venereal-disease transmission, prostitution, and chastity. To assure that the information these institutions made available to the public was accurate and "decent," institutions tended to stress the scientific foundations of their sex-education efforts. For instance, when the Chicago Society of Social Hygiene released sex-education pamphlets in the early twentieth century, the group ensured readers that only the "facts well known to all physicians are herewith presented."[69] Another Chicago Society of Social Hygiene pamphlet aimed to give readers "the protection afforded by the plain truth."[70] Similarly, according to Dr. Maurice A. Bigelow, a biology professor and leader in the American Social Hygiene

Association, the social-hygiene movement was founded on the "undisputed facts of sanitary science."[71]

The claim that scientific information was more credible than other types of information positioned the testimony of medical experts as especially convincing. Arguments grounded in medical and scientific authority served as the basis for many Progressive Era movements, including the social-hygiene movement. For instance, Dr. Prince A. Morrow, the founder of the social-hygiene movement, argued that physicians were "the only competent authorities in this matter [venereal-disease infection]."[72] He explained that sex education would be most persuasive "coming from a medical man, whose right to speak authoritatively on questions of hygiene cannot be questioned. . . . Medical tracts are not to be recommended as a rule, as they are too often the resource of quacks."[73] The Chicago Social Hygiene Association also worried about "quacks," and an association pamphlet warned readers against the "dangerous misinformation furnished by 'quack' newspaper advertisements."[74] Association members argued that only those trained in scientific methods could be trusted to convey truthful information about sex.

In contrast to social hygienists, social purists—or "moralists," as they were often called—argued that talking about sex was only legitimate if it encouraged individuals to act morally. Social purists were not fully convinced that scientific information about sex necessarily encouraged morality. Morrow explained the seemingly "irreconcilable conflict between moralists and the hygienists" by noting that moralists "look upon vice as far more disastrous to society and the individual than its resulting physical maladies; that it is a moral evil that should be combated by moral means alone." Social hygienists, however, "look upon the effects of vice, the diseases it engenders, their menace to the public health, their morbid irradiation into the family and social life, and their pernicious effects upon the descendents and the race as the greater evil."[75] Morrow and his fellow social hygienists struggled to convince social purists that hygiene and morality did not have to be mutually exclusive; they could work jointly to better modern society. Social hygienists had some success in bringing the social-hygiene and social-purity movements together (as with the merging of the American Federation for Sex Hygiene and the National Vigilance Committee in 1913 into the American Social Hygiene Association). However, members of social-purity organizations such as the American Purity Alliance remained wary of medical experts who attempted to heal patients of venereal diseases without teaching them that having sex outside of marriage was morally reprehensible.[76]

When Young began campaigning for the Chicago Experiment, she worked to bring these two factions, neither of which had managed to get a sex-education program into the public schools, together. She argued that scientific facts about sex were not only credible, a position that most Progressive Era citizens already upheld, but that they were also inherently moral. While social hygienists were arguing that issues of health and morality *could* work together, Young argued that they *always* worked together because they were one and the same. She extended the assumptions of the social-hygiene movement to demonstrate that the Chicago Experiment would not excite students' dormant sexual curiosity because scientific facts were incapable of inspiring such excitations. Certainly she recognized that "quacks" and other laypersons could misrepresent science and trigger young people's interest in sex. But, to counter this concern, Young assured her constituents that if responsible scientific "experts" bequeathed students with information about sex, then the students could not be corrupted by such lessons.

Given this reasoning, Young worked to prove that the Chicago Experiment would include only scientifically generated information and that certified experts with scientific backgrounds would be in charge of the lectures. On numerous occasions, Young assured her constituents of the "scientific basis of instruction,"[77] and she repeatedly noted that "the instruction will be given by physicians" with "fine training."[78] More specifically, she explained that lecturers would be "specialists in sex hygiene who lecture in simple, yet scientifically correct language."[79] Young guaranteed her constituents that the lessons would discuss only scientifically based information about sex in a manner that was neither confusing nor potentially exciting. In this way, she assured them that students would not have their morality tested in the classroom. If anything, Young argued that students would emerge from the Chicago Experiment more firmly committed to a chaste lifestyle then they had been before enrolling in the courses.

Other sex-education advocates backed up her claims. For instance, in 1912 R. E. Blount, a biology teacher from Chicago, asserted that "the scientific way of looking at sex cannot possibly harm a child."[80] He, like Young, held that if students learned about sex through the findings of medical experts, rather than "quacks" or those uninformed by modern research methods, they would not be tempted to have sex outside of marriage. In a *Vigilance* article, Young explained that many parents of children in the Chicago Public Schools also agreed with this reasoning. She noted that once parents learned the scientific nature of the proposed courses, their opposition all but disappeared: "Parents who first objected are now on our side, and the only opposition that now exists comes from outside sources and from persons who do not really understand what we are teaching."[81] Young argued that once parents realized that the personal-purity lectures were delivered by "medical men" (and medical women for courses targeted at girls), parents no longer opposed them.

Young's reasoning complemented social hygienists' arguments about the necessity of including sex education in the public schools. According to the historian Jeffrey P. Moran, social hygienists argued that "average parents [in the Progressive Era] did not possess scientific information about sexual hygiene and other critical aspects of modern living and suffered from overly traditional and ineffectual attitudes."[82] Thus, so-called average parents (much less parents fraught with economic and social adversity) were not capable of providing their children with scientific lessons about sex. What parents taught their children about sex, if they taught them anything, was probably not grounded in science and therefore was not inherently moral. By contrast, Young argued that students who learned about sex at school from medical experts conversant in scientific facts could be assured both an education in morality and in issues of sex.

Yet some vocal opponents of the Chicago Experiment could not be convinced that scientifically grounded sex-education lessons were interconnected with morality. Dr. Charles Keene argued that "it has never been proven that knowledge compels purity,"[83] shrewdly using the language of scientific method ("proven") to demonstrate that science may not be inherently moral. Similarly, Dr. Richard Cabot delivered a paper before the Congress of the American School Hygiene Association in 1911 in which he admitted, "I have very little confidence in the restraining or inspiring value of information, as such. I have seen too much of its powerlessness in medical men and students."[84] Cabot argued that many "medical men," who were well aware of the scientific facts about sex and other potentially vice-ridden topics, still behaved in ways that many people considered immoral. Scientific degrees did not prevent them from having sex with prostitutes, masturbating, or having pre- and extramarital affairs, behaviors that social purists condemned. And many Catholics in particular not only denounced Young's attempts to equate science with morality but also rejected entirely the "cult" of scientific worship. These critics held that religion, the only true teacher of morality, was being replaced by science to society's detriment. They argued that Young's lessons were examples of "modern fad[d]ism," providing students with degrading and transitory information. These claims were particularly forceful in Progressive Era Chicago, where the Catholic church's influence was extensive, and church leaders were ever wary of Protestant and governmental clashes with their teachings.[85]

Many public advocates of scientific inquiry, however, were convinced by Young's equation of science with morality and concluded that "Mrs. Young's plan for personal purity talks to the elementary pupils is way in advance of anything yet advocated in that line."[86] These supporters hoped to continue Young's Chicago Experiment in order to meet the "almost universal demand for more plain facts."[87] In this case, Young's arguments in favor of sex education seemed to encourage people to support the Chicago Experiment because she grounded her argument in the assumptions of scientific credibility and, more specifically, in the social-hygiene movement's rationale that scientific facts about sex could work in conjunction with a moral agenda. Then she pushed that reasoning one step further to argue that scientific facts about sex were inherently moral and therefore incapable of corrupting or harming students who learned them in school. Beyond Young's arguments concerning the inherent morality of scientific information and her arguments concerning the Chicago School's philosophy of education, Young incorporated pro-public-sex-education arguments into one final conversation: she appealed to popular assumptions about the science of physical health as it related to intellectual growth.

Physical Health and Argument from Classification

A third conversation into which Young incorporated arguments in favor of public sex education involved the importance of students' physical health and the connections between health and intellectual ability. According to the historian Ruth Clifford Engs, Progressive Era citizens tended to be well versed in the various health-reform movements surging at the time. These movements focused on issues such as temperance, anti-tobacco and narcotics, disease prevention, nutrition, and physical exercise. So-called clean-living movements were designed to reform public as well as individual health practices and improve U.S. society.[88]

Young, an advocate of health reform on many levels, worked throughout her career to enhance Chicago students' physical health. This was no easy task in a city where impoverished, uneducated families were prevalent. She repeatedly argued that students who were hungry, dirty, sick, or unable to breathe clearly would not be able to concentrate on learning while at school. In this respect, she shared the opinion of a larger movement, which she recognized during a speech before the National Education Association in 1911, noting that the school patrons who "form a department in the National Education Association are making tremendous efforts toward carrying this idea of the physical well-being of the children into every school in the land, and they will succeed because those women are in earnest."[89] Young and the school patrons of whom she spoke argued that the schools had as much responsibility to care for students' physical health as they did to care for students' intellectual growth. She represented their beliefs, as well as her own, by explaining, "It has long been customary to say that education deals with the physical, the mental, and the moral development," with no one area any more important than the others.[90] Some of these patrons were members of the American School Hygiene Association,[91] which was formed in 1906 to encourage U.S. public schools to make students' physical health a chief curricular goal. They agreed with health enthusiasts such as Dr. Dudley Sargent, who identified a correlation between physical fitness and mental capacity.[92] Sargent, who headed the Harvard Hemenway Gymnasium for eighteen years and established one of the first teachers' colleges for training in physical education, held that fit students tended to be smarter students and vice versa.

Young had national support from Sargent, American School Hygiene Association members, and others when she introduced programs into the Chicago Public Schools designed specifically to ensure that students were physically healthy. As superintendent, she earned a reputation for prioritizing student health by maintaining a penny lunch program, building school bath houses, regularly flushing school buildings with fresh air, and prohibiting teachers from disciplining students with corporal punishment. Young reasoned that teachers who struck students when they misbehave could not then credibly teach them to care for and respect their bodies.

After many years of surveying the students attending the Chicago Public Schools, Young announced in 1912, "The fact is indisputable that a large proportion of our boys and girls are ill developed physically."[93] She explained that students had acquired curved spines from slouching, shriveled muscles from lack of activity, and weak lungs from contaminated school buildings. She noted their "defective eyes" and "the uneven shoulders and hips that begin to be noticeable in many children after they have attended school two or three years" and argued that students' health problems were evidence "of the need for the betterment of conditions surrounding the work with the book and the pen" in her schools.[94] According to Young, these conditions had to be remedied because they limited students' aptitude for learning and their potential as future citizens. Unhealthy students made for unhealthy adults, incapable of contributing to the larger society. In an effort to reverse the damage from which many students had been suffering, Young mandated that the schools provide students with better and longer physical-education classes. Her proposal matched up with the goals of the American Association for the Advancement of Physical Education (AAAPE), which was formed in 1885 to advocate for the inclusion of physical-education courses in the schools. Young, like members of the AAAPE, contended that students needed to move their bodies during the school day to counteract the physical effects of being shoved into desks and hunched over books. She claimed, "More exercise out of doors should be offered not alone to boys but to girls also, who are living under the limitations of city life."[95] She hired female physical-education instructors to ensure that girls' feelings of modesty did not keep them from participating in and enjoying physical exercise. Young pointed out that she was not the only educator dedicated to improving students' health. She told members of the National Education Association that "today all over this country, in the large cities and towns, special effort is made to get at the physical condition of the children and see that they neither injure each other nor are injured by the surroundings of the school."[96] According to Young, many of the nation's schools were already actively playing a role in fostering students' health and public health in general.

In the process of positioning herself as a champion of students' health, Young cleverly included public sex education in her agenda to improve Chicago students' physical well-being. While discussing the connections between students' bodily health and their intellectual development, Young spoke about sex-education courses as just one more effort to realize her broader health agenda. In doing so, she made students' attendance at the personal-purity talks seem as innocuous as their participation in a nutrition course or a physical-fitness program. In various speeches and writings, Young reminded citizens that they largely supported health-reform movements and had already tacitly approved of using the schools as a vehicle for improving the physical health of Chicago's young people. As sex-hygiene instruction offered students information they needed to become physically healthy, Young implied that personal-purity talks were simply an extension of what schools already offered students. By classifying sex-education courses as a subcategory of health education, she worked to convince audiences that including sex-hygiene talks in the curriculum was neither extraordinary nor potentially harmful to students. Young demonstrated that health education had long been accepted in schools, and thus this particular type of health education would be accepted by the public as well.

Young encountered little opposition to programs designed to improve students' physical health, and therefore she also hoped to avoid opposition when she began discussing sex hygiene as a topic that students must learn in the schools. She repeatedly grouped together "gymnastics, physiology, and hygiene"[97] to make her pairing of sex education with other types of health education seem natural. She justified this classification by arguing that a child "is told in school that if he doesn't keep his skin clean, his system will fill up with poison, that if he abuses his stomach, he'll suffer with indigestion, if he gathers the contagion of tuberculosis, he'll die of consumption." However, she emphasized that the school never offered the child "a word of sex organs and the terrible cost of abuses."[98] Underlying her claim was the contention that education about "sex organs and the terrible cost of abuses" is no different from education about health topics such as bathing, digestion, or epidemiology. She worked from the assumption that citizens could generally see the value in teaching children about proper bathing, dietary habits, and disease prevention. Therefore, she implied that their reasoning would be inconsistent if they did not also see the value in teaching children about sex hygiene as well. If anything, the "poisons" that developed from dirty skin or poor diet were less harmful to children than the diseases that resulted from pre- or extramarital sex. Young argued that students needed "simple healthful talks" about sex in the same way they needed talks about other health topics.[99] In this light, she framed the Chicago Experiment not as a program designed to work in isolation from other educational programs but as an extension of a program the schools had already implemented. And by the summer of 1913, even the National Education Association categorized a conference panel on "sex hygiene" as a subset of health education, which demonstrated that Young's classification of public sex education was shared by others across the country.[100]

Young further connected sex hygiene with physical health and activity by arguing that the two could work together to keep children from "abusing" their sex organs. She observed that in schools where students were kept physically and mentally occupied, "Little nervous strains were worked off by the way those children directed their energies and their interests with the things about them."[101] Young reasoned that children who were given lots of opportunities to run around, play, and explore the world would not have energy left to direct toward masturbation or sexual experimentation. By contrast, children rarely let out of their desks, particularly those children who also lived in the close quarters of overcrowded tenements, would be less able to work off their "nervous strains" in wholesome ways. In this light, active school children who learned how to care for and protect their bodies in sex-hygiene courses would have neither the energy nor the desire to, as Young put it, "misuse" their bodies.

In summary, Young classified sex education as a subset of health education and then reminded audiences that they generally approved of having the public schools disseminate information about health. She used the assumptions of Progressive Era health movements, which connected physical health to intellectual growth, to justify her support for public sex-education courses, and she demonstrated that students who had an outlet for their physical energy while in school would be less likely to masturbate or otherwise "misuse" their bodies. Although many audiences, including members of the National Education Association, seemed to be convinced by Young's argument from classification, some, like Dr. Charles H. Keene, remained skeptical. Keene argued that sex education was more complicated than other types of health education and therefore was "not a matter to be left to an athletic or football coach."[102] Keene was against providing sex-education courses in the public schools, but he conceded that health educators who had "been properly trained" in the science of venereal diseases and morality could be trusted to provide "this instruction" to parents. In this sense, Young's attempt to classify sex education as a subset of health education convinced even some critics of public sex education that teaching young people about sex was not as shocking as many had believed. While they may not have accepted Young's inclusive model of public sex education, enough decision makers did accept her model to make the Chicago Experiment a reality.

The Chicago Experiment Discontinued

Dr. Ella Flagg Young infiltrated existing and accepted conversational spheres to help convince Chicago citizens to support the Chicago Experiment. She communicated within the frames of three different philosophical conversations to make a strong case for public sex education. The inclusive model of public sex education she championed—one that served diverse people and provided them with standardized lessons—functioned as an important departure from the ambiguous rhetoric grounding most discussions about and artifacts of sex education in the Progressive Era.

Before leaving the topic of Young's Chicago Experiment, I will address one final aspect of the experiment's application: its short life span. In the earliest days of the Chicago Experiment, several signs indicated that the personal-purity lessons Young designed had the potential to become fixtures within the Chicago Public School system. For instance, only 8 percent of parents removed their children from the first round of lessons, and, according to the social-hygiene advocate Mabel Wright, 90 percent of surveyed graduates found the lessons helpful and worth continuing in the future.[103] Although the reliability of Wright's study may be questionable, and many low-income parents may not have had the time or resources to remove their children from the lessons, at the very least Wright's research demonstrates that the young women quoted at the beginning of this chapter were not alone in their gratitude for the personal-purity talks. Several study participants suggested the lessons be altered in various ways, but very few argued the program should be discontinued.

Despite these successes, by November 1913, the Washington, D.C., Post Office Department deemed transcripts of the personal-purity lessons "unmailable" under the federal Comstock Law after the National League for Medical Freedom attempted to send them to Chicago Public School students' parents so the parents could better understand and support the information their children were learning in schools.[104] Some opponents of the talks jumped on this national ruling as evidence of "the extent of the evil [public sex education] is causing." For example, a writer for the *Lawrence (Kans.) Gazette* observed that "the government has taken a hand in the nasty reform inaugurated by the sex hygiene cranks, and has barred lectures given to public school pupils from the mails," before noting sarcastically, "of course the government will permit these fellows to make their talks just as nasty as they please, or as the school authorities will stand for, but it balks at carrying their stuff through the mails."[105] The *Gazette* writer argued that if the lectures were too obscene to go through the U.S. mail, then they were surely too "nasty" to be included in the public school curriculum. The Chicago Board of Education caved in to this pressure and voted against continuing the personal-purity talks in the 1914–15 school year.

Young, at this point, was caught in the middle of a larger fight for control between the Board of Education and the Chicago Teacher's Federation about teachers' right to participate in union activities, a right that Young supported. Ultimately, the board's backlash against Young and her support for teacher unionization led her to resign as superintendent briefly in 1913 and then permanently in 1915.[106] Thus, in 1913 she had few professional resources left to devote to saving the Chicago Experiment, and she was probably not prepared to withstand further indictment as a "sex-hygiene crank." When the board first called for her resignation in 1913, members held that, among other things, Young's sex-hygiene courses were an "unwarranted interference with the rights and prerogatives of the parents."[107] Board members repeatedly criticized Young's support for progressive educational initiatives such as Montessori training and vocational instruction, and their pleas for her resignation cited Young's support for sex hygiene as her most obvious and grave fault. Tellingly, Young's successor, John D. Shoop, was a vocal opponent of teaching sex hygiene in the Chicago Public Schools.[108]

This chapter's goal is not to point out that Young's program, in the end, did not last. Young introduced a new, inclusive model of public sex education to American citizens—one that catered to both sexes, many ages, and a range of classes, races, and ethnicities. The aim of this chapter has been to decipher how she built support for applying that model in the public schools when no American before her had accomplished such a feat. Nonetheless, students of rhetoric, history, and health may wonder about a connection between the Chicago Experiment's abrupt and untimely ending and the strategically fragmented argumentation strategy Young used to gather support for it. Did the circuitous nature of her argument make it more difficult for her to defend public sex education when she found herself confronted directly about the experiment? Would a direct argument in favor of sex education have provided her with the tools to defend the Chicago Experiment? Perhaps one limitation of utilizing a strategically fragmented argumentation strategy, which involves inserting arguments into other lines of discursive logic, is that it may not withstand direct attack. Young accomplished her short-term goal of getting sex-education courses into the public schools by indirectly suggesting that such a program made sense.[109] But argumentation by suggestion tends to lack the conviction that wins propositional arguments. When Young found herself on the defensive side of the sex-education controversy, she had few choices beyond retreat. Direct confrontation probably would not have served her in the early stages of her fight for the Chicago Experiment because, at the very least, it was not a rhetorical style that suited her approach to bureaucracy or the political context. But by the end of 1913,

Young found herself in a dilemma because her brand of argumentation was not providing her with the infrastructure to uphold the Chicago Experiment for any extended period of time. Strategically fragmented argumentation initially got Young's foot in the door, but it could not take her any further into the schoolhouse.

Once the Chicago Experiment was under way, Young continued to face an audience of people who were, at worst, violently opposed to and, at best, ambivalent about sending the city's children to public schools to learn about sex. But no matter what individuals thought about the Chicago Experiment, as a result of Young's work they had witnessed a program of inclusive public sex education, and they were discussing if and how similar programs might fit into the nation's future. Once rhetors introduce new appeals into public discourse, other rhetors can draw from those arguments more readily as their ideas and logical patterns are already circulating in existing patterns of discourse.[110] Young's program was short-lived, but it publicized an innovative sex-education vocabulary, complete with logical warrants and justifications, that health advocates could use to promote future programs. In this way, the Chicago Experiment served as a catalyst for the proliferation of public discourse about sex education in the pre- and postwar United States. Young may not have been able to champion public sex education over the long term, but other sex-education advocates such as Dr. Rachelle Slobodinsky Yarros adopted an increasingly direct rhetorical style that helped to carry the legacy of the Chicago Experiment into the future. It could be argued, however, that Yarros's goals were not quite as daunting as were Young's, as World War I changed the cultural landscape in ways that buttressed campaigns for public sex education.

THREE

Propagating Wartime Sex Education

When the Chicago School Board decided not to continue Dr. Ella Flagg Young's Chicago Experiment after the 1913–14 school year, many Chicago residents probably believed that the city (and the nation) would revert back to talking about and creating sex education using primarily ambiguous language. But the years during and directly before World War I were hardly a return to routine, as the threat of war altered social norms and public expectations. Social-hygiene advocates wisely used the impending war as a justification for providing soldiers with information about sex—information that they argued would allow soldiers to make the "right" decisions about sexual activity outside of marriage. They held that soldiers who were not informed about sexual issues were more likely to become infected with venereal diseases, which would leave them physically unable to defend the country. Arguing in this way, members of the American Social Hygiene Association (ASHA) and the Committee on Training Camp Activities (CTCA) convinced government leaders to mandate that soldiers in training camps receive multiple compulsory lectures on venereal diseases, chastity, and prostitution. These lectures were part of a huge propaganda campaign that also provided white soldiers with access to sex-education pamphlets, exhibits, and films. As one wartime ASHA pamphlet explained, such materials dealt with "sex hygiene and the venereal diseases in plain outspoken language illustrated with effective drawings, anatomical diagrams, and photographs."[1] Wartime social-hygiene advocates used every means available to them—verbal, visual, textual, mediated—to make information about sex accessible to white soldiers.

For example, many men who enlisted during World War I were treated to a viewing of the motion picture *Fit to Win: Honor, Love, Success*, prepared by the Office of the U.S. Surgeon General. The film followed the stories of four young men who joined the military and promptly received education about sex from their company commander. Their newfound knowledge was tested when they went on leave in a neighboring town. While Billy managed to avoid alcohol and sex entirely, his companions found themselves drunk and in a "bawdy house," where they were tempted by sexually available women. Of the remaining four men, Hank retreated from the house in the midst of his seduction, and Kid and Jack had sex but accepted prophylactic treatment when they returned to camp. Hank, Kid, and Jack all contracted venereal diseases, but because they listened to their company commander and were willing to comply with a harsh round of treatment, they suffered no permanent damage for their transgressions. Chick, however, not only gave in to temptation at the bawdy house but also refused prophylactic treatment. Over the following months, he became crippled and developed gonorrheal rheumatism. Chick was subsequently discharged to the care of his doting (but ignorant) mother and shamed father. By contrast, Billy received a hero's welcome home at war's end (see figure 2). He was happy, healthy, ready to marry his sweetheart, and extremely grateful for the lessons about sex he learned from his company commander a year earlier.[2]

This chapter analyzes social-hygiene materials such as *Fit to Win* that were produced by the U.S. government (via the ASHA and the CTCA) leading up to and during the First World War, focusing specifically on arguments therein about why specific audiences should or should not have access to sexual information and what information that access should include. Such materials offer evidence that the war altered individuals' willingness to support public sex education for soldiers, making it possible for social hygienists to forgo ambiguous language for a more direct discourse about sex education targeting the enlisted—or at least the white, male enlisted. Unfortunately, these materials did not extend to the approximately four hundred thousand African American soldiers who enlisted in the U.S. armed forces during the war. Training camps in the United States at this time were segregated, which meant that African American soldiers generally did not

The Story of a Motion
Picture Drama
Prepared for
The Surgeon General

Figure 2. "Fit to Win:
Honor, Love, Success; the
Story of a Motion Picture
Drama" (1918). Courtesy
Social Welfare History
Archives, University of
Minnesota.

have access to the lectures, films, and social-hygiene entertainment that
their white counterparts enjoyed. In addition, although CTCA members
spoke throughout the war about the importance of providing African American soldiers with social-hygiene materials targeting them specifically, such
materials were never produced. Thus, while white soldiers were granted
better sex education than had been available to almost anyone in the past,
African American soldiers were not granted such education and suffered

from discriminatory governmental policies such as mandatory prophylaxis treatment after a leave.[3]

Similarly, only a comparatively small amount of governmental support for sex education during the war included initiatives designed for civilian populations including women. Most social-hygiene documents targeted at white, female audiences offered very little concrete information about sex and focused on training women to protect men (rather than themselves) from venereal diseases. Correspondingly, a central element of social-hygiene propaganda targeting white soldiers involved training readers to differentiate between safe and unsafe women. Such appeals depicted women as potential obstacles to the war effort and the social-hygiene movement rather than information seekers or decision makers. Although new sex-education efforts targeted at white soldiers utilized increasingly straightforward appeals during the war, most efforts targeting white women offered vague and insufficient information. Wartime propaganda materials implicitly, but repeatedly, justified the differences between these efforts by arguing that white, privileged women did not need sex education in their own right. Even worse, women who were not white or privileged, like men who were not white or enlisted, were not targeted by any wartime CTCA or ASHA social-hygiene efforts. Thus, while the war has been celebrated for advancing public sex-education efforts in the United States, this chapter builds from existing historical accounts of World War I social-hygiene efforts and analyses of unique primary sources to demonstrate that wartime propaganda must also be recognized for its patterns of exclusivity, which left many people without access to the information they needed.

The First World War and Social Hygiene

By the early twentieth century, many Americans harbored stereotypes about the immorality of soldiers and sailors. In years past, army camps had been surrounded by brothels, saloons, and other unsavory establishments. Enlistees, many of whom had never been away from their immediate families, were especially vulnerable to the lure of vice. Moreover, most people believed that soldiers needed to exercise their sexual "muscles" in order to fight with passion on the battlefield, so military and government officials tended to condone or even encourage soldiers' weekend trips to houses of prostitution. They also tolerated the hoards of young women who followed the troops from camp to camp as "hookers," a moniker that emerged during the Civil War for women who trailed General Hooker's regiments.[4] But the United States entered World War I with new information about the harms of venereal diseases. No longer could casual sex be passed off as a harmless activity soldiers needed to indulge to prepare for battle. Venereal diseases such as syphilis and gonorrhea could incapacitate soldiers completely, and thus government officials shifted from ignoring these diseases to considering novel methods for thwarting their spread.

While the United States was mobilizing for its entry into World War I, the ASHA leader Walter Clarke predicted that keeping soldiers healthy would play a large role in procuring a U.S. victory. He argued, "That army and navy which is the least syphilized will, other things being equal, win."[5] Clarke's colleague Arthur Spingarn echoed his logic and concluded, "Venereal disease is the greatest single factor in the non-effective rate of the Army."[6] Clarke, Spingarn, and other advocates of sex education contended that not only would a venereal disease–ridden army create a decrease in soldiers' efficiency and make it all but impossible for the Allied forces to triumph, it would, perhaps even more importantly, symbolize U.S. weakness and moral decay. Using this line of reasoning, they quickly convinced Congress that the country's reputation and victory in Europe depended on the government's willingness to teach soldiers how to avoid contracting venereal diseases. In this respect, the war served as a justification for providing many of the country's young men with increasingly straightforward education about sex. Just five days after the United States officially entered World War I, Congress created the Committee on Training Camp Activities to oversee this educational endeavor.

The CTCA, headed by Secretary of War Newton Baker and working in cooperation with the ASHA, was designed with the single purpose of keeping the troops free of venereal disease and consequently in top fighting form.[7] CTCA and ASHA officials approached venereal diseases as if they were physical manifestations of U.S. wartime enemies and thus not issues to be taken lightly. They introduced multiple lines of defense against venereal diseases that were designed to build from each other and function as a cumulative fortress from infection. On a social level, the organization provided white soldiers with "wholesome" recreational activities to divert their attention from sex, alcohol, and gambling. They sponsored sporting events, craft huts, classes on a variety of different subjects, musical groups, clubs, libraries, theaters, and hostess houses where modest young women could visit soldiers under the watchful eyes of Young Women's Christian

Association (YWCA) staff. Hostess houses in particular offered white soldiers a temporary refuge from the rough environment of camp life, and house "matrons" oversaw formal dinners, dances, social gatherings, and even hostess-house weddings. Hostess houses also functioned as receiving areas for visiting family, friends, and community members.[8]

On the level of law enforcement, Congress and military officials created moral or "pure" zones around the camps in which alcohol, prostitution, and gambling were prohibited. One ASHA pamphlet informed civilians, "The Government has since the beginning of the war waged a vigorous campaign against vice and liquor in the vicinity of the camps and cantonments."[9] The CTCA's law-enforcement plan focused on punishing prostitutes and "charity girls" for their exploits rather than on reprimanding soldiers for having illicit sex. Under what came to be known as the American Plan, any woman found within a pure zone who was suspected of prostitution (i.e., sex outside of marriage) could be arrested, submitted to compulsory physical examinations, and detained indefinitely.[10] The CTCA created a Committee on Protective Work for Girls (later the Section on Women and Girls within the CTCA's Law Enforcement Division) designed to solve the "girl problem," which involved those females "who proved to be a menace to the health and morals of the fighting force of this country."[11] The committee monitored pure zones, bringing "suspicious" women (some as young as eight years old) into protective custody, lecturing them on the evils of promiscuity, and funneling those deemed "feeble-minded" into institutions and those deemed "promiscuous" into detention houses.[12] Detained women, almost all of whom were members of the working classes, would be treated for venereal diseases if they were infected and then assigned in-house tasks ranging from sewing to farming in an effort to keep them away from those in uniform. White soldiers, however, were hardly reprimanded for illicit sexual activity unless they contracted a venereal disease, in which case they were treated and educated against engaging in hazardous behaviors in the future. Under the American Plan, officials worked to protect white soldiers, not necessarily women, from harm.

The CTCA's Social Hygiene Instruction Division created a propaganda campaign to teach white soldiers about sex and the dangers of venereal diseases. Division leaders used a variety of educational materials to reach white soldiers and impress upon them the serious nature of their message. According to an ASHA pamphlet on sex education and the soldier, "The three most forceful public methods of appealing to the soldier [were] the placard exhibits, the stereomotorgraph, and lectures."[13] Sex-education exhibits and accompanying materials such as pamphlets and books were constantly on display at all camps and army posts, domestic and abroad. The CTCA used the exhibits and the stereomotorgraph—essentially an electric light box that presented revolving slides—to feature diagrams, drawings, and photographs illustrating the immediate signs of venereal diseases, the causes of infection, and the long-term consequences of venereal diseases left untreated. CTCA lectures were delivered by civilian physicians who traveled to training camps and discussed sex "chiefly from the medical angle."[14] CTCA officials worried that by emphasizing the moral rather than medical reasons for avoiding sex, they would alienate the fun-loving soldiers they were trying to reach. Thus, many wartime sex-education messages targeting the troops minimized appeals to religion and values and maximized appeals designed to elicit audience fear regarding physical consequences—a point to which I will return shortly.

Beyond exhibits, slides, and lectures, the CTCA also depended heavily on pamphlets to communicate with white soldiers about sex in a relatively clear, straightforward manner. A number of pamphlets went into detailed discussions about nocturnal emissions, erections, masturbation, marriage, and parenthood. For example, a representative pamphlet entitled *Manpower* described "the influence upon the development of the [male] body and personality of the secretions from the sex glands," as well as common problems with the male reproductive organs.[15] Some pamphlets also specified a number of dangerous activities that unmarried men should avoid, such as "spooning" or reading "smutty stories," because they often led to poor judgment and unsanctioned sexual behaviors. Then, of course, they discussed gonorrhea, syphilis, and other venereal diseases. *A Few Facts about Syphilis* and *A Few Facts about Gonorrhea*, for example, were "to be distributed by the treating physician to infected persons."[16] These pamphlets were designed for those who had already contracted venereal diseases, and their aim was to get soldiers into treatment as quickly as possible. They offered thorough descriptions of the disease in question, breaking the signs of infection into different stages and laying out how one could recognize the disease in male and female bodies. Both pamphlets identified ways for readers to avoid passing their infections on to others (e.g., "sleep alone, and practice continence"—which may have also functioned as an implicit warning against homosexual behavior) and encouraged them to follow their physicians' orders. These pamphlets were distributed to soldiers before the soldiers were sent to their camp's chemical prophylaxis center. Providing soldiers with venereal-disease treatment became a controversial part of the CTCA campaign after officials realized that, despite the CTCA message of chastity, many soldiers were continuing to contract venereal diseases during their enlistment period.[17]

One central idea highlighted in CTCA pamphlets targeting white soldiers was that chastity and masculinity could coexist, especially during the war—a point that the historians Allan M. Brandt and Nancy K. Bristow also discuss.[18] Some pamphlets communicated this idea succinctly and without much explanation: "You don't need sexual intercourse to be healthy. If you don't believe this ask any famous athlete."[19] According to the social hygienist Paul Strong Achilles's 1923 review of wartime social-hygiene literature, the pamphlet *Friend or Enemy?* went into more detail on this topic, explaining "the manly ideal for the young man outside of marriage is the ideal of a sexually continent life, wherein the individual masters his impulses and refrains from all forms of sexual indulgence." Similarly, the pamphlet *Health for Men* worked to disprove the myth that male genitals would shrink without frequent sexual use. Such materials assured enlisted men that potential physical complications they may have attributed to lack of sex were, in fact, due to other causes and would only be exacerbated if they engaged in sexual activity. In addition, CTCA materials held that soldiers who had sex outside of marriage demonstrated their lack of mental strength and thus their lack of masculinity—an idea that reversed long-held beliefs about a man's virility and his performance defending the country.[20]

A second message many CTCA pamphlets featured was that failure to follow instructions on matters of social hygiene would result in physical and mental pain. Fear appeals threatening physical pain involved descriptions of individuals who had illicit sex, caught a venereal disease, and then found themselves permanently paralyzed or crippled (much like Chick in *Fit to Win: Honor, Love, Success*).[21] Some such appeals even threatened "rotting flesh and bones" or the development of a variety of specific chronic illnesses such as locomotor ataxia or rheumatism.[22] Such excruciating conditions would, at best, make a functioning soldier into a menace to his comrades and, at worst, make him into a liability to the war effort and the country as a whole.

But even worse than the risk of physical harm was the psychological harm ("softening of the brain") that a number of pamphlets cited as resulting from illicit sex and untreated venereal diseases. In a pamphlet entitled *Colonel Care Says*, readers viewed a certificate granting entrance to the "National Asylum for the Insane." Words covering the certificate asked soldiers, "Will They Ever Have To Make One Out For YOU?" (see figure 3).[23]

The pamphlet also featured a newspaper clipping from the *New York Evening Post* reporting that 15 percent of patients admitted to (already over-crowded) state hospitals for the insane were infected with syphilis. Pamphlet authors argued that "loony," "poor half-wits" forced "behind the gates of one of these nut-farms" eventually wished they had followed their colo-nel's instructions and abstained from sex outside of marriage. Readers were persuaded to conclude that the physical and mental pain that resulted from venereal diseases was far worse than any fleeting pleasure gained during a weekend on the town. And one way CTCA materials encouraged white soldiers to ensure their health and avoid future pain was by training them to differentiate between "temptresses" and "sweethearts." According to social-hygiene documents, soldiers' ability to make this differentiation would guide them in their path toward lifelong wellness. As one CTCA pamphlet ex-plained in characteristically blunt slang, "Only a poor boob pays his money, loses his watch, gets the syph, and brags that he's had a good time."[24]

The Temptress and the Sweetheart

As the historian Nancy K. Bristow argues, the majority of government-sponsored wartime social-hygiene pamphlets framed the women with whom soldiers came into contact in mutually exclusive ways.[25] I argue that this framing implied that women, regardless of their race or class, did not need

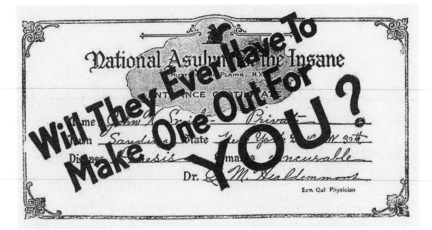

Figure 3. "Colonel Care Says" (1918). Courtesy Social Welfare History Archives, University of Minnesota.

sex education in their own right. Women who were sexually available to soldiers were working against the U.S. war effort by potentially infecting them with venereal diseases and enticing them to break their moral codes. For example, one pamphlet's cover featured a woman with short sleeves and pouty, red lips smiling seductively over her shoulder. She asks, "Hello, Soldier Sport, want to have a Good Time?" (see figure 4).[26]

The pamphlet informed readers that although a woman may look attractive and clean, "It's a 90 to 1 shot that she's poisoned." According to this pamphlet, "A German bullet is a damn sight cleaner than a whore," and whores were defined as "girls who are willing 'to give you a good time,' whether they be plain or fancy, priced or private." In this framework, if a

Figure 4. "Hello, Soldier Sport, Want to Have a Good Time?" (1918). Courtesy Social Welfare History Archives, University of Minnesota.

woman was sexually available outside of marriage (signs of which included a "painted face," revealing clothing, and a pushy personality), she was a temptress and probably also a German sympathizer masquerading as an American sweetheart. Although such a woman's "come-on stares" were "hard to resist sometimes,"[27] CTCA officials positioned them (and the venereal diseases they potentially carried) as physical manifestations of the evils emanating from international enemies. Soldiers were ordered to retreat from temptresses as soon as they identified them.

Visual portrayals of "evil," sexually available women (also referred to as "hardened prostitutes," "Come-on Queens," "she-hookers," "Chippies," "Harpies," and "Molls") existed in contrast to portrayals of the "American Sweetheart," who was also frequently referenced in wartime social-hygiene propaganda. CTCA educational materials implied that such a woman (signs of which included a lack of make-up, conservative clothing, and a submissive personality) would never dream of tempting a soldier with pre- or extramarital seduction; she was, after all, the woman soldiers fantasized about marrying when they returned from duty. During the war, one pamphlet encouraged soldiers to visualize how a sweetheart "may be waiting for you in some farmhouse, or in some cabin on a mountain creek, in a blue print dress and a white sunbonnet."[28] This pamphlet's cover featured a wholesome young woman looking seriously into the camera. She seemed to be posing for a professional photographer, perhaps for a school yearbook picture (see figure 5). Her body was covered by a modest, collared shirt, and her face was positioned as the focus of the image.

The photo's caption read "The Girl You Leave Behind." The pamphlet's inner pages instructed soldiers to keep the picture where they could see it, "so that it may remind you at all times of the girls, like your sisters, who have suffered in the war, and of the girl you left behind, but who is now waiting for you."[29] The picture was issued to soldiers to help them remember that their actions during the war could affect their long-term plans, plans that no doubt included a sweet, innocent wife and healthy offspring. In *Fit to Win: Honor, Love, Success,* Billy modeled this scenario as "the thought of his sweetheart sustains him when later he encounters an even more seductive type" and promptly refused her attentions, thus saving himself from potential disease and immorality.[30]

Like many other similar pamphlets, this CTCA pamphlet pitted the "girl you leave behind" against the sexually available temptress. Readers learned that by accepting the sexual invitations of a woman, they were "shaming and

Figure 5. "The Girl You Leave Behind" (1918). Courtesy
Social Welfare History Archives, University of Minnesota.

insulting the girl you hope to marry some day, and who is waiting for you
here at home, whether you know her yet or not." Soldiers were encouraged
to imagine their homecoming with the girl they left behind: "Suppose when
she ran out down the lane or down the street to meet you, you had to turn
away, to draw back from her . . . because you were afraid you might harm
her."[31] The pamphlet contended that if soldiers came home from war with
venereal diseases they would not be worthy of their sweetheart's love or the
middle-class life they dreamed of building with her. They would not be able
to protect her, or their future children, from the diseases they carried with

them. A temptress might offer soldiers temporary pleasure, but she also forced soldiers to risk their health, victory on the battlefield, self-respect, and happiness after the war's end. An American sweetheart, however, offered enduring love, safety, respectability, and a family that would grow to support the nation in the future.

These pamphlets' dichotomous images characterized women according to their sexual relationships with men. Such depictions did not lead to the conclusion that women, like men, should have access to sex education. While soldiers had to have enough education to choose which women with whom to involve themselves, women were framed as either already overly knowledgeable about sex or, ideally, never needing to know much about sex at all. And the latter could easily transform into the former if she found herself in the wrong company, for, as the *Girl You Leave Behind* pamphlet explained, "every hardened prostitute who offers herself to you was a young girl once, till some man ruined her."[32] These documents ground their argumentative justifications in the assumption that men were active decision makers while women were obedient followers, capable only of hoping they would not be led down the wrong path by a man. The pamphlets implied that it was too late to supply information to the sexual temptress as she was already diseased (at least 90 percent of the time, anyway), sexually active, and no longer a viable marriage partner. In a 1918 ASHA pamphlet, the social-hygiene advocate Katherine Bement Davis voiced this position by noting that a young woman who had "crossed the line" and had become a "temptress" was "dangerous, not only to the young men whom she allures, but, earning money easily, dressing more showily, furnishes a dangerous example to girls of weak will and unsatisfied desires."[33] In this light, most CTCA officials, especially those in the Committee on Protective Work for Girls, thought it more rational to send the temptress to a detention center than to provide her with information about sex and venereal diseases.[34] She was best kept away from society, as she was dangerous not only to herself and the men who desired her but also to the girls who tried to model her way of life.

This was especially the case for African American girls and women, whom the CTCA characterized as inherently immoral and overly sexual. Although postwar, government-sponsored social-hygiene materials would imply that African American women had the potential to be innocent sweethearts, CTCA rhetoric during the war generally grouped all African American women together as active or impending temptresses. Thus, CTCA leaders argued that it would be dangerous for African American women to be near the troops, as they would surely seduce soldiers and infect them with diseases.[35] And while the seduction of African American troops by "colored clandestine prostitutes" was a concern of the CTCA, the organization's major worry was, in the words of the CTCA leader Arthur B. Springarn, that "in many southern cantonment cities, the major part of the sex relations of white troops is with colored women, among whom the incidence of venereal diseases is extremely high."[36] Given that African American women were repeatedly stereotyped as persistent sexual temptresses with no hope for reform, those who were found to be infected with venereal diseases were likely to be detained in jails long after they had been treated for their illness. Social-hygiene education was not something that the CTCA provided for African American women outside, let alone inside, jail—although it should be noted that the historians Susan Smith and Jessie Rodrique find that some African American women gained access to information about birth control through the educational efforts of African American women's clubs.[37]

On the other side of the spectrum, CTCA pamphlets implied that the sweetheart remained pure because she was white, innocent, sheltered, and uninformed about sex. Therefore, the very act of educating her about sex would rob her of what the CTCA celebrated about her. According to social-hygiene materials for the enlisted, the sweetheart needed men to protect her from being corrupted by the evils of premarital intercourse because she was totally unaware of such issues. In the event of her marriage, sex would be only a means to an end—bearing and then mothering children—rather than a meaningful activity in itself. In this respect, a woman's sexual instruction need not begin until her marriage, at which point her white husband (who already knew about sex as a result of his public education while enlisted) would guide her through the process. It was implied that he, and perhaps the girl's mother, would provide the young bride with only procreation-oriented accounts of sex and sexuality. Those women who married men who did not qualify for enlistment were apparently out of luck. Ultimately, wartime social hygienists argued (implicitly and explicitly) that they would prefer to protect respectable women (i.e., white, middle-to-upper-class virgins) from sexual information entirely, which may explain why so few resources were devoted to social-hygiene initiatives targeting women of any race or class during the war. But such reasoning does not also explain why African American soldiers had little access to social-hygiene education while their white counterparts had more access than ever before.

Social Hygiene and the African American Soldier

Although some CTCA officials spoke in favor of providing African American soldiers with social-hygiene materials designed specifically for them, such resources had not materialized by the time the troops began to demobilize in late 1918 and early 1919. On the whole, African American soldiers' health was never framed as a priority in the years before and during the war. According to the historian Vanessa N. Gamble, by 1900 most health professionals agreed that, in general, African Americans were in poorer health than were whites and that their poor health status had the potential to negatively affect the health of whites. Indeed, most discussions about African American health among these (primarily white) early-twentieth-century health professionals focused on, as Dr. C. E. Terry explained in 1915, "its relation to white mortality" and health. Authors reporting in medical journals and the popular press repeatedly justified their attention to the high rates of diseases such as tuberculosis, pneumonia, pellagra, syphilis, and gonorrhea in African American communities by noting that those diseases could spread to whites.[38] For instance, Dr. L. C. Allen spoke before the ASHA in 1914 and alerted its members to the impact that African Americans' diseases could have on their own health: "From dirty homes, in these disease-infested sections, negro people come into intimate contact with white people every day that passes. We meet them in our homes, offices, stores, in street cars, and almost everywhere we go." Although he argued that "the fact is not pleasant to contemplate," Allen contended that there were "colored persons afflicted with gonorrhea, syphilis, and tuberculosis employed as servants in many of the best homes in the South today. In every instance the employer is, of course, unaware of the risk being taken."[39] According to Allen, the fact that African Americans were disproportionately suffering from a range of illnesses did not, in and of itself, constitute a problem that warranted attention. Furthermore, he implied that African Americans were to blame for the "disease-infested sections" in which many of them lived, their dirty habits, rather than economic and political inequalities, having instigated and propagated the squalor. The historian James H. Jones notes that numerous late-nineteenth- and early-twentieth-century health advocates criticized poor African Americans for supposedly neglecting to follow basic tenets of sanitation and fostering the spread of disease in their communities.[40]

Although there was some disagreement about the causes of African American health disparities, some argued that it was rooted in, as Gamble puts it,

African Americans' "proclivity for sexual promiscuity and alcohol and their ignorance of the rules of cleanliness and personal hygiene."[41] The idea that African Americans were less civilized than whites and therefore less able to control their physical desires—making them dirty literally and figuratively—prevailed even among some notable leaders in the fight against racial segregation and inequality. In 1899, W. E. B. Du Bois, the famous African American sociologist and political activist, claimed, "Sexual looseness is to-day the prevailing sin of the mass of the Negro population."[42] Du Bois separated himself from many segregationists and eugenicists by maintaining that such "sexual looseness" derived, in most cases, from discriminatory social policies rather than inherent racial inferiority. However, his willingness to concede that African Americans tended to be more sexually promiscuous than whites demonstrated the strength and pervasiveness of such beliefs at the time. In a 1915 article published in *Social Hygiene*, Dr. Ernst Boas summarized some of the period's popular beliefs about African Americans and venereal diseases, noting that he did not share these opinions because they were not derived from scientific data. According to Boas, many people believed that "negros are an inferior race and therefore more prone to the ravages of syphilis. If a southern physician is asked what percentage of negros in his experience are syphilitic, his offhand estimate will usually be about 75 percent."[43] Both male and female African Americans were often framed as driven by their sexual urges and therefore as natural carriers of venereal diseases, but in many cases the African American male was a special focus of criticism. It was believed that, as Dr. Thomas W. Murrell argued in 1910, "A negro man will not abstain from sexual intercourse if there is the opportunity and no mechanical obstruction."[44] In this way, the African American male was likened to an animal lacking restraint or reasoning and who could thus not learn to behave in ways that subverted his immediate desires.

Despite this framing of the African American male as unteachable, during the war some ASHA and CTCA leaders argued that African American troops needed to learn about sex for many of the same reasons that white troops needed to learn about sex. In an article published in *Social Hygiene*, Arthur B. Spingarn explained that "nearly ten percent of our military forces are to be selected from [African American] ranks and the success or failure of our arms may be determined to no inconsiderable extent by [their] efficiency."[45] As a whole, members of these government-led and affiliated organizations seemed to agree that providing African American soldiers with information about how they could avoid catching venereal diseases would help keep soldiers healthy and defending the country to the best of their ability. Spingarn went so far as to lay out very specific instructions for moving forward with such an initiative, explaining that because there were supposedly higher rates of illiteracy among African American soldiers, "there should be special lectures by colored physicians who are familiar with the race psychology and who can make a special appeal to race pride and desire to excel, and special exhibits and literature particularly adapted to their needs."[46] However, as the CTCA devoted more and more resources to educating white soldiers about social hygiene, they put forth little effort focusing their attention on African American social-hygiene efforts. By the time the war was drawing to a close, the CTCA, along with local chapters of the YMCA and the YWCA, called for the formation of recreation and education programs targeted at African American troops that would be equivalent to those provided white troops. Calls so late in the fighting did not produce very much in the way of educational opportunities and only illustrated the organizations' failure to adequately provide social-hygiene programs and materials for African American soldiers for the better part of the war.[47]

The historian Nancy K. Bristow argues that the lack of social-hygiene resources devoted to African American soldiers during the war was at least partially related to widespread racial strife in the United States going into the war.[48] In the post–Civil War years, southern states were struggling with Jim Crow laws and de facto policies that deprived African Americans of a range of opportunities such as the right to vote and left them vulnerable to horrendous violence and mistreatment. In 1916 alone, more than fifty African Americans were lynched by white mobs throughout the southern states. As southern African Americans migrated north to find employment and leave Jim Crow behind, many white northerners worried about losing jobs and business to the newcomers. Rather than finding the welcoming land of opportunity of which they had dreamed, many African American migrants encountered a hostile reception in northern states. Mounting tension between the races exploded the summer of 1917, when violent race riots in East St. Louis, Illinois, left approximately one hundred people dead and six thousand African Americans homeless. Smaller-scale riots also took place in Chicago and Danville, Illinois; Lexington, Kentucky; New York; Newark; and Waco, Texas.[49] The riots transpired largely in African American districts of the cities, which were notoriously riddled with vice because local officials and reformers zoned saloons, brothels, and similarly insalubrious businesses outside of white neighborhoods.[50] The ASHA member Frank J. Osborne spoke of a typical U.S. city where "the colored district was inhabited by many prostitutes and others living from the proceeds of prostitution, and soldiers who visited the city were securing large quantities of liquor."[51] In this respect, African Americans were often framed as inherently more vice-ridden than whites, even though zoning laws and discrimination, rather than choice or preference, forced them to live in cities' most dangerous, run-down quarters.

In the years before the United States entered the war, some African Americans saw the country's impending involvement as an opportunity to prove themselves as valuable citizens. African American leaders argued that their participation in the war would usher in an era of racial respect, equality, and opportunity. W. E. B. Du Bois wrote in the April 1918 issue of the National Association for the Advancement of Colored People's journal, *Crisis*, that "out of this war will rise, too, an American Negro, with a right to vote and a right to work and a right to live without insult."[52] There was some question among government officials about whether African American men should be drafted, given the hostile, violent interactions among whites and blacks throughout the country, as well as rumors that German agents would persuade African American soldiers to join their cause.[53] But ultimately the need for soldiers was too great, and all male citizens between twenty-one and thirty-one years of age, regardless of race, were required to register under the Draft Act of 1917. To alleviate southern worries that arming the children and grandchildren of slaves would result in violent mob attacks on white soldiers and civilians, African American enlistees were dispersed in relatively small numbers in training camps throughout the country. Most training camps were completely segregated, which CTCA officials argued would further help to keep racial hostilities at bay.[54]

But segregation posed a number of pragmatic problems for the CTCA, not the least of which was that the organization found itself needing to duplicate all facilities and programs for African Americans that were made available to whites. Leaders initially expressed their dedication to duplicating all programs, but they never followed through with their promises. African American women employed by the YWCA were able to erect a model "colored" hostess house in Long Island, and then seventeen others throughout the country's training camps, but these facilities were underfunded and did not even begin to satisfy the needs of all enlistees of color.[55] Thus, African American soldiers found themselves without facilities to receive their guests, play a game of ball, or even, in some cases, buy a stamp. Female African American visitors sometimes had no access to restrooms, and the soldiers themselves were excluded from attending lectures, films, and other forms of visiting entertainment with their white fellow soldiers. This meant, first of all, that African American soldiers did not have frequent access to social-hygiene information, as they were excluded from the "compulsory" social-hygiene lectures put on by the CTCA. Literate African American soldiers may occasionally have been provided with social-hygiene pamphlets, but because the pamphlets were not targeted specifically at African Americans soldiers, they went first and usually only to white soldiers. This was especially true when CTCA workers were instructed "to distribute the pamphlets on the basis of one to five," which probably meant that soldiers were encouraged to share the pamphlets but, in actuality, meant that the pamphlets went to white soldiers initially and then were gone before they made it to African American soldiers.[56]

The lack of facilities and leisure options for African American soldiers in training camps also meant that there was very little to keep them occupied when they were not training. Thus, while CTCA officials hosted a number of in-house events to keep white soldiers from going into towns and encountering vice, they encouraged African American soldiers to take their leaves in neighboring towns. Such counterintuitive policies demonstrated that the health and well-being of African American soldiers was not the CTCA's priority, especially because such excursions into southern towns positioned African American soldiers in segregated communities where they had limited access to entertainment and were repeatedly treated poorly by local law enforcers and civilians.[57] And while the CTCA offered African American soldiers little in the way of social-hygiene education, they tended to institute even stricter social-hygiene penal codes for African Americans than they did for white soldiers. For instance, some camps required that all African American soldiers returning from a leave receive chemical prophylaxis treatment, regardless of whether they claimed to have engaged in sexual activity or not.[58] Thus, African American soldiers during World War I did not get the social-hygiene education that white soldiers received *and* they were punished and treated for venereal diseases, no matter their choices or actions. In comparison, white women fared better than did African American soldiers in terms of access to sex education. But just as African-American-targeted health efforts tended to be driven by concern for other populations (such as white soldiers and civilians), most government-sponsored social-hygiene materials targeted at white women during the war also seemed to be driven by concern for the health of others (white soldiers).

Social-Hygiene Propaganda Targeting Women

On the whole, given the extreme threat venereal diseases posed to soldiers and U.S. security during World War I, CTCA and ASHA officials were willing to trade a bit of young women's supposed innocence for their participation in the war effort to protect the troops against vice. Thus, they created several texts that one could categorize as wartime sex-education messages for women that were distributed to white women who were involved in the war effort. But, as the historians Nancy K. Bristow and Stacie A. Colwell argue, these texts did not teach women very much about their bodies or sex. While social-hygiene pamphlets targeting white soldiers outlined specific problems soldiers might encounter with their genitalia and information about masturbation and seminal emissions, most materials for white women were composed of euphemistic language that discussed sex, reproduction, childbirth, and venereal diseases in only the vaguest sense.[59] In the words of one ASHA pamphlet, sex education targeting white women avoided "accentuating" issues such as venereal disease and sexual activity.[60] The CTCA, in particular, largely avoided any indication that white women had sexual desires of their own, a point the group reiterated by framing reading audiences as innocent sweethearts rather than sexual temptresses. Bristow claims that although the CTCA earmarked sex-education programs for women, the organization's focus always remained on the health and well-being of white soldiers, those whose sexual desires were recognized by government officials.[61] And officials reasoned that no one would be better at persuading men to become their best selves than their future wives.

The CTCA's pamphlets for women of "respectable" ilk worked to ensure, first and foremost, that they did not give in to the "lure of the uniform" and become conduits for venereal diseases among soldiers. While social-hygiene pamphlets targeting white soldiers informed young men that they were solely responsible for leading women down the path of chastity, pamphlets targeting white women positioned readers as agents with the ability to say "no" to misguided suitors. Such pamphlets did not necessarily include detailed information about *why* women might say no or *what* exactly they were refusing, but they did grant white women a small degree of agency and encouraged them to use that agency to benefit the country. In an essay entitled "Social Hygiene and the War: Woman's Part in the Campaign," the ASHA member Katherine Bement Davis explained, "The 'lure of the uniform' is everywhere recognized. Young girls, thrilled with patriotism, sometimes fail to realize that the uniform covers all the kinds of men there are in the world."[62] She went on to argue, "Any soldier or sailor who asks a girl to yield to his desires as a patriotic act is not worthy of his uniform. Patriotism makes no such demands. Real patriotism seeks to protect—not to defile—womanhood."[63] Davis and other social hygienists defined womanhood according to a female's ability to remain chaste until marriage. This particular pamphlet informed white women that, despite what their friends and companions might encourage them to believe, war did not change these expectations. Soldiers might mislead them, and in those cases it was their duty as proud U.S. citizens to defend against sexual advances.

Similarly, in *The End of the Road*, a female-targeted sex-education film that framed white women's purity as their contribution to the war effort, the author explained that "war conditions have disturbed the emotional equilibrium of the people and have tended to multiply the intricacies of sex reactions, particularly among young girls brought into social contact with the soldier." *The End of the Road* was created "to stimulate and strengthen the efforts being made to teach the womanhood and girlhood of our country the vital need of right social adjustments." A pamphlet about the film argued that war could disrupt cultural mores, particularly those having to do with sex, because it tended to heighten people's emotional responses and drowned out their rationality.[64] This claim's force was grounded in the widespread idea that women were inherently more emotional than were men and concluded that women were therefore particularly susceptible to the emotional havoc war wreaks on people's sense of morality and ethics. This being the case, the CTCA was obliged to remind white girls and women that they had to partake in "right social adjustments" for the sake of the country at large.

The CTCA also created social-hygiene pamphlets, posters, and films targeted at white women aiding the war effort. These materials encouraged women to take actions to protect soldiers from themselves. Such messages emerged from the assumption that, while women were more emotional than men, they were also naturally morally superior, a theme that was evident throughout the nineteenth and early twentieth centuries in discourse about abolition, temperance, woman suffrage, education, and social work.[65] The CTCA claimed that it was the young woman's patriotic obligation to guide soldiers toward morality because women could "do more than anyone else to encourage the men of their acquaintance to lead clean lives."[66] Patriotic young women were instructed to dress conservatively because baring their arms, backs, or ankles "may do harm by arousing [men's] emotions [that would be] hard to control."[67] They were also instructed to eschew suggestive language to avoid unnecessarily exciting soldiers' passions. For women, being patriotic meant "helping the boys, who are risking everything for us, to live up to the very best of themselves; it [meant] backing up our government in a tremendous movement for a cleaner, finer race."[68] Under the circumstances of war, white women were granted the agency to help white soldiers make the right sexual choice. Yet white women were not generally given the same detailed information about sex that was provided to enlisted white men, as CTCA officials argued that women risked losing the sanctity of their minds and bodies if they learned as much.

Despite Bristow's claim about the lack of instructive sex-education texts for women during the war, my research in the Social Welfare History Archives at the University of Minnesota demonstrated that some World War I–era sex-education messages aimed at white women involved in the war effort *did* communicate much-needed information about sex. Dr. Mabel Ulrich, for instance, wrote and published several pamphlets targeted at girls and women that included decidedly more details about sex than did other comparable works aimed at women. In *Mothers of America*, Ulrich encouraged those providing young girls with sexual information to proceed "in a simple, direct but perfectly definite fashion."[69] Then she went on to demonstrate what she meant by "simple" and "direct" in her pamphlet *For a New World: The Girl's Part*. She defined the reproductive parts of female and male bodies using technical terms such as "uterus," "vagina," and "testicles." She also laid out the conception process, explaining, "When a baby is about to be created this is what happens: the penis is introduced into the vagina, and the sperm-cells are thrown about the opening of the uterus (womb)."[70] Ulrich's description of conception was remarkable because it included an overview of how the male and female reproductive organs worked together, a biological process that much sex-education literature circumvents even today. Her additional discussions about issues such as sexual attraction, premarital "fondling," and venereal diseases in women were similarly unique, offering just as much (or perhaps even more) information to white women as was available to enlisted white men. In this sense, Ulrich's pamphlets resembled Margaret Sanger's sex-education materials targeting working-class women. Yet the CTCA and the ASHA offered sex-education messages of this nature virtually no support, and by the end of the war the movement for white women's sex education (not to mention African American women's sex education) was in desperate need of organizational assistance, resources, and public backing.

At War's End

Scholars of public health and U.S. history have long celebrated the government's increased support for sex education targeted at enlistees during World War I. Indeed, this chapter has demonstrated that ASHA and CTCA officials provided soldiers with increasingly accessible information about sex, and they crafted a justification for this move by drawing from popular rhetoric concerning the country's need for efficient, healthy troops. Wartime social-hygiene propaganda characterized women as either pure or diseased and encouraged soldiers to differentiate among women along those lines. These characterizations of women fostered the assumption that they did not need access to clear information about sex as they were either oversexed and therefore ruined, or innocent and therefore vulnerable to corruption as they awaited marriage. The CTCA offered African American soldiers little to no social-hygiene education during the war, choosing instead to target their educational efforts at white soldiers and to regulate African American behavior and health with law-enforcement initiatives and discriminatory policies. Correspondingly, social-hygiene materials targeting white women during the war generally did not offer readers the same level of detailed information about sex supplied to white soldiers in comparable texts. African American women were not the target of any government-sponsored sex-education initiatives. Fortunately, as Smith and Rodrique's work demonstrates, in some communities African American women took it upon themselves to educate other African American women about topics related to sexual health such as personal hygiene and birth control.[71] These were not explicit sex-education lessons, but they were excellent examples of grassroots efforts led by U.S. women who attempted to alleviate the gaps in health care perpetuated by government agencies and organizations. While the war was an important moment in U.S. efforts to offer some individuals sex education, the number of individuals excluded from sex-education access left public health advocates with much to accomplish in the postwar years.

When the war ended, the CTCA and all of its programs were absorbed into the Interdepartmental Social Hygiene Board, the Venereal Disease

Division of the U.S. Public Health Service, and the ASHA. Leaders of these organizations hoped to build off of wartime support for public sex education and supply sex-education programs to civilians, thus warding off venereal diseases and other sex-related public health problems. One ASHA pamphlet on continuing the work of the CTCA explained that "the Government has declared a new war on an old enemy, Venereal Disease (gonorrhea and syphilis). The men who were *fit to fight* Germany must be kept *fit to win* honor, love, and success." The War Department wanted to ensure that "the men it has safeguarded against venereal diseases shall return to their citizenship in the new civilization *fit to live* and work for their country's progress under the great peace they have won."[72] Whatever men were doing—fighting, winning, or simply living—this ASHA pamphlet argued that they needed sex education to maintain their fitness as citizens (an appeal reminiscent of Ella Flagg Young's arguments aimed at the Chicago Board of Education).

Unfortunately, in the push to ensure that the sex-education movement would survive after the war, many social-hygiene advocates were continuing their pattern of gearing sex-education programs toward white men rather than African American men, women, and immigrant populations. As I detail in the next chapter, during and directly after the war, Dr. Rachelle Slobodinsky Yarros noted these patterns of exclusion. She then crafted public arguments to generate social-hygiene advocates' support for sex-education programs, targeting women from a range of races, classes, and backgrounds. Her discourse stands today as a compelling example of internal persuasion and a catalyst in the movement toward U.S. public sex education.

FOUR

Speaking for Women at War's End

By the end of World War I, Dr. Rachelle Slobodinsky Yarros had traveled throughout the United States giving hundreds of talks on sex education under the auspices of the U.S. Public Health Service (PHS) and the American Social Hygiene Association. She provided her audiences with straightforward information about the "prevalence and dangers of venereal diseases and prostitution," the value in keeping sexual desires under control, and the details of conception and reproduction.[1] In this respect, Yarros was just one of many advocates of public sex education who argued that it was vital for U.S. soldiers to learn how to protect themselves from venereal diseases and who worked tirelessly during the war to ensure that as many white men as possible were provided with a sex education.

Yet, what made Yarros different from her fellow lecturers was that she gave the majority of her sex-education talks to girls and young women, providing them with information and anecdotes garnered from her work as an obstetrician and gynecologist in Chicago's poorest communities. Despite wartime framing of women as unnecessary targets of sex education, Yarros maintained that it was just as important to deliver sexual information to them as it was to distribute the information to white soldiers. Thus, during the war Yarros spoke about sex to audiences composed of women from a variety of races, ages, ethnicities, and social classes. After the war, she continued to provide sex-education lectures to women while also working to establish a foundation of support for her work, which involved extending the idea of social-hygiene advocacy beyond disease prevention to include family planning and birth control. With the war behind her, Yarros went on to help build and run eight birth-control clinics in Chicago (the highest number in any U.S. city at the time), to teach numerous sex-education courses to audiences of mixed-gender medical students, and to convince Chicagoland physicians and professors to publish a credo that supported providing women with sex education.[2] Until her death in 1946, Yarros worked diligently with (and as a member of) government-supported organizations such as the ASHA to ensure that women, immigrants, minorities, and the working classes were consistently included, both as students and as teachers, in the movement toward public sex education.

The previous chapter demonstrated that, although there was extensive support for sex education targeting white soldiers during World War I, government-sponsored organizations such as the ASHA devoted few resources to providing sex education to women, immigrants, minorities, and the working classes at this time. The present chapter demonstrates how, during and directly after the war, Yarros worked to alleviate the resulting gap in health care by convincing social-hygiene advocates of the value in offering more inclusive public sex education. She modeled rhetorical strategies that helped her to build support for accessible sex-education programs aimed at a variety of different audiences. Her primary discursive technique for garnering such support involved urging leaders to empathize with women, the working classes, immigrants, and people of color. As a social-hygiene advocate, doctor, immigrant, and woman, Yarros was positioned at the intersections of a number of different communities that did not often overlap. As the historian Maureen A. Flanagan puts it, Yarros "crossed the boundaries of class and ethnicity," and her intersectionality, in this case, created opportunities and constraints for her as a persuasive speaker.[3] Her unique social positioning helped her to structure discourse in ways that helped audiences see the world from new perspectives and thus consider alternative ideas and ideologies. At the same time, however, her intersecting identity as both a leader in the social-hygiene movement and as an immigrant and a woman, as well as her position as someone appealing to eugenic advocates on behalf of immigrant and minority women, compelled her to speak in favor of women's access to sex education by endorsing women's subordination.

In 1918, Yarros delivered a keynote address before the ASHA at its annual conference entitled "Experiences of a Lecturer"; she published it the following year in the ASHA's journal, *Social Hygiene*.[4] This address survives as a pivotal example of how Yarros repeatedly worked to constitute multiple constructions of subjectivity for those in power and thereby encourage them to support sex-education initiatives targeted at women, immigrants, minorities, and working-class populations. The publication of the address in *Social Hygiene* assured that its circulation went well beyond its original audience. Its historical positioning, in which it preceded the creation of ASHA-led social-hygiene poster campaigns (for which Yarros served as a consultant) that explicitly and aggressively targeted traditionally overlooked populations, suggests the significant role that this speech (and others like it, also by Yarros) played in helping to establish public sex-education initiatives for women in the United States.

In "Experiences of a Lecturer," Yarros argued that providing women with public sex education would further the aims of the social-hygiene movement and benefit society at large. She drew from popular arguments concerning World War I as a justification for educating white soldiers about sex, and she altered those arguments so they could be applied to women as well. She formatted her address as a speech within a speech, a stylistic choice that helped her to situate social-hygiene advocates in the subject positions of the women in her sex-education lectures and encourage them to see the world through women's eyes. This structure also allowed her to represent her sex-education lectures for women in ways that appealed to her social-hygiene audience, whether or not that was how she really gave the lectures to women. (Transcripts of Yarros's addresses to women do not survive, so it is especially important to analyze what *is* still available: her representation of those addresses.) These discursive moves aided Yarros in persuading social hygienists to support her initiatives and alter normative assumptions concerning who should be targeted by sex-education programs. In this light, the rhetorical strategies Yarros utilized in her "Experiences of a Lecturer" address, as well as the appeals she made in her other early writings and lectures, helped her to connect wartime social-hygiene efforts with postwar social-hygiene efforts and to expand such initiatives to reach diverse audiences.

Yarros and the American Social Hygiene Association

As World War I drew to a close, Dr. Rachelle Slobodinsky Yarros delivered "Experiences of Lecturer" before the ASHA, a professional organization that formed in 1913 when the American Vigilance Association and the American Federation for Sex Hygiene (formerly Dr. Prince A. Morrow's American Society for Sanitary and Moral Prophylaxis) merged to champion public sex education and stop the spread of venereal diseases.[5] Its members consisted mainly of doctors and other health-care professionals, philanthropists, educators, and social workers.

In 1914, the organization published the first issue of *Social Hygiene*. The issue began with the transcript of a speech delivered by Dr. Charles Eliot, president of the ASHA, at an organizational meeting in New York City. Eliot used the address to lay out the organization's goals, which were to regulate vice in U.S. cities, to encourage the American public to establish healthy behaviors to improve the state of public health, and to create and facilitate public sex-education programs, thereby slowing the spread of venereal diseases.[6] In its early years, the ASHA also focused on diagnosing and treating those infected with venereal diseases, funding scientific research on venereal diseases, and upsetting the "conspiracy of silence" by publicizing the potential harms of pre- and extramarital sex. As the ASHA's general secretary Dr. William F. Snow explained in a 1916 pamphlet, the organization worked to promote "sex education, the establishment of the single standard of morality, and the repression of prostitution and its associated evils—venereal disease, mental and moral degeneracy, and economic waste."[7]

During the war, the ASHA focused almost all of its efforts on partnering with the CTCA to provide white soldiers with sex-education programs. Once the war ended, many organization members became dedicated to bringing wartime sex-education programs to civilians. They worried, however, that demobilization, decreases in government funding, and lessening public support for social-hygiene programs would inhibit their ability to maintain the programs they had created during the war. Thus, they redoubled their original efforts, hoping to transfer the pro-sex-education momentum from the war to the postwar era.[8]

Unfortunately, their concerns about maintaining existing social-hygiene programs made ASHA members less likely to focus on new programs that would target populations that had been traditionally overlooked by the organization. That being the case, when Yarros spoke before the ASHA in

1918, the organization's priorities did not include sex education for women. Instead, the ASHA was "naturally" focusing foremost on "the education and treatment of young men, first, who were eligible for the Army; and, second, whose industrial efficiency, quite as much as the fighting ability of the soldier, depended upon their physical condition."[9] Women's health and contributions to society were framed as secondary to those of men.

The ASHA had a number of female members—including Yarros, the social reformer Jane Addams, and the philanthropist Grace H. Dodge—who played central roles in building the organization and expanding its influence. However, many of its recognized "leaders" were male professionals who tended to see public-policy decisions through their own gendered experience. The social hygienist Charles Clarke's 1961 book *Taboo: The Story of the Pioneers of Social Hygiene* celebrated the work of over ten male social hygienists and only one female and upheld these individuals as the movement's pioneers. More recently, the historian Jeffrey P. Moran identified three male scientists as the "builders" of the social-hygiene movement. Even the contemporary American Social Health Association deems Dr. Prince A. Morrow the "father" of social hygiene and points to men such as Drs. Edward L. Keyes, Thomas N. Hepburn, and Charles W. Eliot as his fellow "founders" of the ASHA.[10] Early issues of *Social Hygiene* reflected the organization's emphasis on maintaining men's, and especially soldiers', sexual health. The issue that included Yarros's speech transcript also included articles discussing the drop in venereal diseases among soldiers during the war, efforts to protect soldiers from vice who had been sent to military camps in Puerto Rico, and the role of the "social-hygiene sergeant" in training camps.[11]

The journal largely mentioned women in one of three ways: as potential allies in the fight to uphold chastity and morality, as prostitutes who needed to be "dealt with" by law-enforcement officers, or as bearers of children. Several *Social Hygiene* articles discussed women's role in the fight against venereal diseases, particularly during the war, but these articles tended to focus on the CTCA's American Plan and not at all on providing basic public sex education to women.[12] Other articles outlined plans for creating detention and industrial homes for prostitutes, shutting down red-light districts, and apprehending women who were having sex outside of marriage.[13] The article that directly followed Yarros's speech was entitled "Adequate Reproduction"; its author, Roswell H. Johnson, framed "superior" women as a "resource" who should be encouraged to have more children for the sake of racial progress. According to Johnson, the "superior" woman who had few children was particularly offensive to society "when her husband is highly mentally superior."[14] Johnson's framing of women as a means to an end for men and society, as well as his appeal to eugenic philosophy, was not unusual for early issues of *Social Hygiene*. Even the ASHA president, Dr. Charles Eliot, used *Social Hygiene* as a venue to argue that the organization was dedicated to ensuring that "the civilization of the white race" survived.[15] Eliot, like many of his social-hygiene contemporaries, was an active member of the eugenics movement and therefore dedicated to ensuring that "fit" whites reproduced at a rate that would prevent "race suicide."[16]

In this respect, Yarros's keen interest in women's health and the health of immigrants, minorities, and the working classes made her an atypical member of the ASHA. Nonetheless, she was a founding member of the organization, a widely recognized social-hygiene "pioneer" for involving Chicago women's clubs in the social-hygiene movement, and secretary and education director of the ASHA's Chicago chapter, the Illinois Social Hygiene League, for over twenty years. Yarros's dedication to social hygiene emerged from her experience as an obstetrician/gynecologist. Women began earning medical degrees in the United States in the mid-to-late nineteenth century, and by 1900 they made up almost a fifth of the total number of American physicians.[17] Yarros was one of these early "hen medics," as they were often called, with more than a note of derision. After immigrating to the United States from Russia in her late teens, she worked for several years doing factory work before fellow Russian immigrants offered to help fund her medical education. In 1893, she graduated with distinction from the Philadelphia Women's Medical College. Following graduation, she interned at hospitals in Massachusetts and New York, did postgraduate work in Vienna, and set up an obstetrical and gynecological practice in Chicago. In 1898 Yarros became the first woman on the faculty at the University of Illinois College of Medicine and subsequently a leader in Chicago's fight for public sex education. She lived in Jane Addams's settlement house, Hull-House, from 1907 to 1927, working as an in-house physician, running her practice, and teaching courses at the university.[18]

In an article published in the *Medical Women's Journal* in 1926, Yarros recalled her time interning at the Tewksbury (Massachusetts) State Hospital caring for women infected with venereal diseases. She explained that the experiential knowledge she gained there inspired her to dedicate herself to providing women with sex education. Yarros told her readers that "ignorance on the subject of sex and sex behavior played a very conspicuous part in the spread of venereal diseases. And I was impressed more and more by the heavy penalty paid for this ignorance."[19] She learned from the confidences of her female patients that many of them were drained of vitality because they never learned how to protect themselves from venereal diseases and/or because they were misinformed about family-planning practices. According to Yarros, if someone had provided these women with information about sex, their lives would have improved immeasurably. This being the case, Yarros informed her readers, "I consider it the duty of an enlightened and conscientious physician to face these problems."[20] Yarros took this duty seriously, and she noted that when she was not teaching or seeing patients individually, she was giving social-hygiene lectures in Chicago and throughout the United States. She claimed that she often spent "long nights and days" with her obstetrical students "in the homes of poor people" seeing to their health problems and informing them about contraception, reproduction, and sexual health.[21] During the war, she increased her lecturing duties so she could ensure that as many people as possible knew about "the problems of venereal disease and their relation to health and welfare."[22]

When Yarros spoke before the ASHA in 1918, she did so from the unique position of a person who had established herself as a leader within the professional social-hygiene community and who had personal and professional ties to working-class and immigrant women. She hoped to bring these interests together by demonstrating how they could benefit each other: individual women could use information about sex to protect themselves from venereal diseases and unwanted pregnancies, and members of the ASHA could better attempt to halt the spread of venereal diseases and create a state of public health if the organization extended its programs to women. But to unite these interests, Yarros needed to convince an audience that was led largely by male professionals, preoccupied with maintaining existing sex-education programs for white men, and ideologically sympathetic to eugenics that it would be well served to dedicate some of its sparse resources to educating women from diverse races and classes about sex. Yarros's "Experiences of a Lecturer" address had to cater to and earn the support of this audience, and she worked to do so by speaking in ways that introduced ASHA members to a range of diverse subject positions and perspectives.

The Arguments of a Lecturer

With the ASHA's focus on men's health and tradition of male leadership in mind, Yarros used her "Experiences of a Lecturer" address to make three arguments that emphasized men's honor and the ways that sex-education programs for women would benefit men and society at large. Although she was using the direct language about sex education for men that had become increasingly common during the war, she had to adjust that language and its accompanying logic to include women. Yarros argued that public sex education for women would help with the war and postwar social-hygiene effort. She expanded the idea of war as a justification for men's sex education to argue that the war was also an exigency for women's sex education. If male soldiers had to learn about sex because of the war, Yarros claimed that it was women's patriotic duty to learn about sex as well. According to Yarros, sex education lectures and materials encouraged men to avoid the activities that led to venereal diseases, diseases that ultimately kept them from the battlefield. Sex education, in this light, served as a first line of defense against venereal diseases for the men who would protect the country from defeat. Yarros reasoned that sex education for women would form "a strong second line of defense."[23] If women also received information about the dangers of venereal diseases and the importance of premarital chastity, they would act as yet another barrier to venereal disease transmission. In this sense, women who were educated about sex would help to fortify national security. Women may not have been able to fight physically for democracy, but by learning about the dangers of venereal diseases, they could fight to end the spread of sexually transmitted diseases.

Yarros also argued that sex education for women would keep them from exploiting men's "sensitivity" to sexual excitation and other sexual weaknesses. She maintained that because men are more sexually driven than women, sex education would inform women about how their own actions might drive men to have illicit sex. Yarros explained that man's "nature has made him different" because "his sex urge is more direct and manifests itself in a distinctly conscious feeling in his genital organs. He is much more sensitive, much more susceptible to every stimulus of sex feeling."[24] This was a common physiological argument from this time among social-hygiene advocates. For instance, the ASHA member Katherine Bement Davis argued that women must be careful that their "dress, conduct, and personal influence" was "patriotic" (i.e., modest) so that vulnerable men could keep their bodies and minds under control.[25]

Like Davis, Yarros argued that "the sex temptation is not so great in [women]."[26] She reiterated the widespread idea that women naturally longed to receive attention from men, to be held, kissed, and adored, but that they generally did not desire to engage in premarital sexual activity. Then she reasoned that, because women did not experience the same intense feelings of sexual desire that men experienced, they often did not realize how difficult it was for men to keep their sexual desires in check. Women, according to Yarros, were oblivious to the effect that their "come-on stares" had on men. They had no idea that it was "hard for [a man] after many hours of courtship to dismiss the whole thing from his mind. He usually tosses backward and forward and longs definitely for the sex act, and consequently may seek a way for this gratification."[27] Yarros maintained that sex education aimed at women would alleviate this problem by helping women to "learn to play a fair game with boys."[28]

In addition, Yarros argued that sex education for women was necessary because mothers had to know how to inform their children about sex. She explained that by teaching their young children about sex, mothers "would not only help to carry on the government program but make a permanent contribution toward the solution of intricate social hygiene problems, thus insuring greater happiness and making it possible to look forward to a better race."[29] She created a directional argument that began with sex-education instructors supplying women with information about sex, went on to have those women become mothers and teach their children "in matters of sex," and concluded with the creation of a happier, healthier society. In this way, Yarros identified sex-education programs for women as a necessary step in the process of developing a "better race" of citizens. At the same time, she implied that because women from all races and classes became mothers, all women needed to be prepared to provide their children with sex education. She argued that sexually informed women would be better at steering their children away from premarital sexual behaviors from early ages. Teaching women about sex would enlist them in the social-hygiene movement and allow the movement to reach further into the citizenry than it ever had in the past.

Yarros interspersed these major arguments throughout her speech, wherein she explained how she gave sex-education talks to four different audiences of girls and women (club women, school girls, prostitutes, and immigrant mothers) during the war. She began by describing talks she gave "to club women and other organizations of women," leading her social-hygiene audience through

a specific lecture she gave to this group. Yarros explained how social hygienists should encourage club women to spread the word about social hygiene to
other women and to their children. When she introduced a second talk she
had given to this group, Yarros switched from speaking to her social-hygiene
audience to directly addressing a hypothetical audience of club women. She
noted, "I proceeded somewhat as follows: 'Children must be taught very early
to know that continued life of any living thing is impossible unless there is a
way to reproduce it,'" and concluded that "'every mother, therefore, should
learn how to tell simple stories of the various forms of reproduction.'"[30] At
this point, she spoke as if she were giving one of the lectures she presented
during the war, telling club women why they needed to teach their children
about reproduction and how they should go about that process. Not only did
Yarros address an audience other than the one to which she was speaking, at
one point she took this tactic one step further. Later in this section of the
speech, she addressed her hypothetical audience's hypothetical children to
show the club women how they should talk to them about sex. In this moment, Yarros was giving a speech within a speech within a speech, because
she was still speaking before her original audience of ASHA members. The
ASHA members were thus listening to the talk as themselves but also as club
women and as the club women's children, a position that allowed them to
step outside of their own subjectivity to view these issues from different and
intersectional perspectives.

Eventually, Yarros switched back to directly addressing the social-hygiene
audience so she could provide justification and explanation for her appeals.
At this point, most of her sentences were framed with phrases such as, "I
tell them," "I explain," and "I directly ask them," highlighting her rhetorical
strategies as a sex-education instructor of women. She was modeling for
her ASHA audience the ways to address women on these topics, probably
because many ASHA members had little experience talking with women
about social hygiene. In addition, some ASHA leaders believed that only
women could successfully teach other women about sex.[31] Although Yarros
did not directly refute this idea, by carefully explaining how her mostly male
audience should give social-hygiene lectures to women, she implied that
they were capable of doing so successfully.

Yarros also described talks she gave "to groups of young women and
girls" in secondary school. She spent the majority of her speech dealing with
a series of three lectures she targeted at this group, frequently alternating
between addressing the social-hygiene audience and addressing hypotheti-

cal audiences of young women and girls. She positioned herself within the broader community of social hygienists by explaining to the young women that "we bring [these facts] to you because we feel that the time has come for a change, and we see clearly what can be done to eliminate these diseases."[32] At one point while Yarros was describing one of these lectures, she spoke as if she were one of her gynecological patients who had passed away from an untreated gonorrhea infection. Yarros brought the woman and her story to life for both her real and her hypothetical audiences by speaking in the voice of the woman herself during her last hours of life. She explained that after she became ill, "I got steadily worse, and here I am now, an invalid, in pain most of the time, unable to walk even an ordinary distance."[33]

Beyond talks given to club women and high school girls, Yarros also described a talk she gave "to a group of prostitutes made up of girls and women from fourteen to forty—all types and classes—Mexicans, colored and white, most of them shabby and highly painted and powdered."[34] This was a topic she discussed again in 1919 at the National Conference of Social Work, where she claimed that prostitutes were "generally victims of conditions" and thus in need of the training and education that would help them to rise above those conditions.[35] Taking a similar stance in her ASHA address, Yarros explained how she convinced audiences of prostitutes to trust her, assuring them "that I was not there to scold them or even preach to them; that I was there as a friend to tell them some of the things they would like to know."[36] She then spoke directly to the hypothetical prostitutes, telling them, "I came to tell you that the life of prostitution is not an easy life," and claiming that prostitution eventually left a person in "the gutter."[37] She appealed to the inner desires of the women she addressed, arguing that "in your hearts you know you crave for real things at your best moments, but you shut your eyes and try to forget in despair, because you see no other way."[38] She informed them that they could take part in government programs that would help them to start a new life. At this point, Yarros switched back to addressing her social-hygiene audience, instructing ASHA members to teach prostitutes that they should abandon their trade because "their country needs them to help in this great struggle for democracy."[39] Yarros assured the social hygienists that "there is a way of appealing to the best in the worst of us" and implied that if they followed her directions for teaching prostitutes about social hygiene, they would successfully make such an appeal. Yarros's idea that prostitutes could be rehabilitated went against the idea common among social hygienists that the best way to handle prostitutes was to use law enforcement to punish them and keep them off the streets. One postwar ASHA pamphlet argued that "prostitution must be suppressed" and implied that prostitution would never be eradicated because "fallen women" were incapable of reform and thus a perpetual problem.[40] But even before her 1918 address to the ASHA, Yarros had publicly argued that, with the proper education, prostitutes could be "saved."[41]

The final talk Yarros described was one she gave to a group of "Mexican mothers." For this discussion, Yarros spoke only to her social-hygiene audience, perhaps because she used an interpreter when she gave the speech to Spanish-speaking mothers. She referenced other lecturers who gave talks on social hygiene during the war, and she noted that their lectures ensured that "thousands and thousands of women and girls will never again be indifferent" to issues such as venereal diseases, prostitution, promiscuity, and reproduction.[42] For the most part, the major arguments featured in Yarros's early speeches and writings did not differ greatly from arguments presented by several other speakers and texts of the time, which seemed to help build little support for public sex education. In this light, I contend that taking a closer look at the structure of her rhetoric—as it presented its content to immediate and former or hypothetical audiences—will offer a clearer picture of how Yarros worked to build support for sex-education initiatives targeting women.

Representing Rhetoric, Other, and Self

The structure of Yarros's "Experiences of a Lecturer" speech allowed her an additional degree of control in positioning her audience members as subjects. When Yarros switched from speaking directly to ASHA members to speaking to hypothetical audiences of women, she constituted social hygienists as women in need of sex education. In this way, Yarros encouraged male social hygienists to see sex education through women's eyes, to confront the world as, for instance, a club woman determined to protect her children from disease, a girl approaching puberty without preparation, a working prostitute suffering from a venereal disease, or an immigrant mother hoping to build a prosperous life for her family's next generation. By casting social hygienists as women attending sex-education lectures, Yarros provided them with the opportunity to consider issues of social hygiene anew. Her speech created an opportunity for social hygienists to identify with women's concerns and to experience why it was so important for all women to have access to public sex-education programs. From that vantage point, they could see that many women were desperate for information about sex because they wanted to protect themselves, their families, and their peers from disease, poverty, and despair.

It should be noted, however, that subjects who are constituted within narratives can be constrained by the very language that creates them.[43] In this respect, they may lack the agency to act outside of the narrative into which they have been interpellated. Yarros sidestepped this conundrum by only temporarily positioning social hygienists in disempowered subject positions and thus not permanently rescinding their more privileged agency. She constituted social hygienists as women in need of sex education *and* as the social hygienists they considered themselves to be. The first position temporarily robbed them of the agency to act as ASHA members but allowed them to see through women's eyes. The second position restored their privileged agency and their ability to support Yarros's sex-education initiatives. When Yarros addressed them as themselves, later in the speech, she did so with the knowledge that they had become more than themselves because they had the experience of being constituted as women in need of sex education. In this sense, they were more likely to back her initiatives to educate women about sex because they had considered women's struggles anew. Persuasive speakers in general aim to encourage identification among different people, but identification was particularly central to Yarros's mission as she attempted to get social hygienists to understand women's needs in a very personal way.[44] She worked to make social hygienists feel that, because they had shared a subject position with women in need of sex education and potentially identified with their interests, they had a responsibility to see that women's needs were met. In this way, Yarros's speech helped to make women who had once seemed separate and strange to social hygienists seem increasingly connected and familiar.

In the process of placing social hygienists in the positions of women, Yarros's speech structure gave her control over the representation of the lectures themselves, the women who heard the lectures, and her own representation. Because Yarros reproduced the lectures she originally gave to audiences of women during the war, she could represent the lectures to social hygienists in ways that appealed to them and thereby alleviate their concerns about sex-education programs for women.

Representation of Rhetoric

No transcripts of Yarros's wartime sex-education lectures survive. The only account of the content of her lectures appears in her representation of them in "Experiences of a Lecturer." Thus, there is no concrete way to compare what Yarros actually said with what she told ASHA members she said in her lectures. Nevertheless, analyzing how she represented her rhetoric sheds light on how she worked to convince social hygienists that they should support sex-education initiatives for women. Yarros represented her lectures as discourse that supported existing social-hygiene programs and as communication that did not blame men for women's sexual-health problems. Representing the lectures in these ways helped her to assure social hygienists that her goal to educate women about sex and their goal to stop the spread of venereal diseases and protect the health of soldiers and other men were complementary.

Throughout this speech and others that she gave around this time, Yarros found ways to assure social hygienists that the lectures she was endorsing were designed to build off of and work with existing social-hygiene programs. She tried to quell any fear among ASHA members that by supporting sex-education programs for women, they would be abrogating elements of existing sex-education programs for men. Before introducing each of the lectures she gave to different groups of women, Yarros applauded the work of the ASHA, emphasizing "the fact that in this new government program, we have the strongest backing for a single standard of morals and the possibility of a definite change in the attitude of man toward the problem of promiscuous sex indulgence."[45] By using the pronoun "we," Yarros positioned herself as a fellow social hygienist who was proud of the ASHA's work up until that point and wanted it to continue. Similarly, in her 1919 speech at the National Conference of Social Work, she spoke of the "courageous war program" that ensured that "between three and four million boys in our army and navy" were "taught in detail" about sex and venereal diseases.[46]

Beyond celebrating the ASHA's existing programs and past successes, Yarros emphasized the role these lectures could play in informing women about the social-hygiene movement and converting them to the cause. She explained that because many women she talked with during the war did not know about the ASHA or its programs, the lectures she gave them were important simply because they publicized the social-hygiene movement. Before settling into the lectures themselves, Yarros noted how she used them to outline "the government social hygiene program, so different from anything which the other warring nations had attempted."[47] Once she was speaking directly to the women themselves, Yarros spent quite a bit of time informing them about the work of the movement. In this way, she showed, rather than simply told, ASHA members that her lectures were designed to inform women about ongoing social-hygiene efforts and to encourage them to join the movement as much as they were designed to teach women information about sex.

In addition, Yarros represented the lectures as opportunities to guide prostitutes and other "wayward" women toward existing rehabilitation programs. She told an audience of hypothetical prostitutes that "the government of our country is anxious to protect our girls, not only those who have not sinned, but those who have fallen," noting that "there are all over the country now what we call Committees (under government supervision) for the protection of girls, to which any girl can go and appeal, and she will be given a chance to begin all over again."[48] In this case, Yarros was showing social hygienists how the lectures could encourage women to turn themselves in to detention and rehabilitation centers. Perhaps not surprisingly, this was a task ASHA members and other "rescue workers" were struggling to get women to do.[49] Similarly, Yarros appealed to the eugenic goals at the heart of the ASHA movement by telling white women in her hypothetical audiences how they could use the tenets of social hygiene to "improve the race." Ultimately, Yarros set up and performed the lectures in ways that demonstrated they would work for the ASHA rather than against it.

Yarros also represented her lectures as rhetoric that did not blame men for women's sexual problems. Members of the ASHA, at this point, were largely concerned with protecting soldiers and other young men from venereal diseases. Thus, messages that focused on protecting (and venerating) men would have appealed to them in ways that rhetoric focused on blaming men would not. Yarros repeatedly recognized the work soldiers and other men had already done for the sake of the country and the social-hygiene movement. She noted how "keen and willing they [were] to make sacrifices for this cause."[50] She used the lectures she gave to hypothetical women to show that she did not endorse the idea that men purposefully cause women's sexual problems. Yarros guaranteed her hypothetical audiences that only extraordinarily "vicious" men would use women to "satisfy [their] cravings."[51] According to Yarros, most men were honorable and wanted only to protect their country and their families.

To demonstrate the horror men generally felt when their loved ones were hurt by venereal diseases, Yarros relayed the story of a young husband who unintentionally gave his new wife a deadly venereal disease. After providing her audience with details about the woman's symptoms and painful death, she turned her attention to "the poor husband, who I am sure loved her more than he did his own life."[52] This man "suffered tortures" and "had a complete breakdown and recovered only after many months."[53] According to Yarros, he contracted his venereal disease after his fraternity brothers dragged him to a house of prostitution during his college years. After that fateful night, he made an appointment with an "old-fashioned doctor" who gave him some useless medicine and told him "'not to be a goose'" by worrying about venereal diseases.[54] Yarros portrayed this man as a victim, rather than a perpetrator, in the battle against venereal diseases. By conveying this story, Yarros assured her immediate audience that the sex-education programs she was endorsing would not blame men for women's sexual-health problems and that she valued the "modern," scientific perspective of the social-hygiene movement. She made analogous appeals in a 1916 article about "the future of women in medicine," wherein she encouraged female physicians to "recognize the justice and the appreciation that men have shown personally for good work that women have done in college and medical work" rather than to view men as subverting women's efforts to advance in medicine. No matter the context or topic, Yarros was always careful to position those in power in a favorable light, even when it would have been easy for her to criticize them for their faults.[55] All in all, she represented her lectures as rhetoric that could publicize the social-hygiene movement, generate new social-hygiene converts, and further existing social-hygiene programs and goals without blaming men for the country's venereal-disease epidemic.

Representation of the Other

Because Yarros switched back and forth between speaking to ASHA members and speaking to hypothetical audiences of women in her 1918 speech, she could control not only the representation of the lectures but also women's reactions to them. Her representations of female audience members and their reactions were designed to move ASHA members from identification with them (the result of taking on their subject positions) to action on their behalf. In this situation, Yarros seemed to speak with the understanding that getting those who are already sympathetic to a cause to act in favor of that cause can sometimes be surprisingly difficult and thus may require extensive rhetorical attention and effort.[56] Her speech represented women from a variety of races and classes to social hygienists who were already "converted" to the sex-education movement but who did not necessarily identify with women (especially immigrant, minority, or working-class women) or their situation. Because social hygienists tended to be preoccupied with social hygiene as it related to white men and the war, they were often not familiar with the struggles many women faced because of a lack of information about sex. They did not necessarily realize how desperate women were to learn about sex, and they were unsure about how women would respond to sex education. "Experiences of a Lecturer" allowed social hygienists to view a representation of women's reactions to sex-education lectures. This representation helped to alleviate social hygienists' implicit concerns that women who had access to information about sex would seek to overthrow existing structures of gender and power. In this way, Yarros's representations of women learning about sexual information functioned to encourage social hygienists to move from being sympathetic to her cause to being active supporters of her initiatives.

According to Yarros, what originally inspired her to give her "Experiences of a Lecturer" speech was the "wonderful response" she got from audiences of women during the war. She wanted social hygienists to know how excited women were to hear about the social-hygiene movement and how grateful they were to gather information about sex. She told them, for instance, that she found the club women to be "exceedingly responsive and very earnest in trying to learn what they could do."[57] She also showed the social hygienists how committed women were to getting sex education. When Yarros spoke as if she were her patient dying from gonorrhea, she embodied the desperation of a woman who had never learned about venereal diseases and was suffering as a result of her ignorance. According to Yarros, sex education was a life-or-death subject for the women in her audiences, and they were passionately interested in hearing what she had to say about it.

Furthermore, Yarros wanted social hygienists to know that privileged white women were not the only women who were eager to hear her sex-education lectures. Immigrant, minority, and working-class women, those who were truly Other to the social hygienists, sought sex education too. In general, individuals and communities tend to create their identities by comparing themselves with others. They articulate who they are not so they can better understand who they are.[58] Dominant groups within a population use what the sociologist Stuart Hall calls "repertoires of representation" to construct Others—people who have traits and characteristics that members of the dominant group do not see (or do not want to see) in themselves.[59] In "Experiences of a Lecturer," Yarros represented Othered individuals to a dominant group, and she did so in a way that highlighted the Other as unusual but also as innocuous and in need of assistance. For instance, she claimed that prostitutes who had "just been interned," many of whom were infected with venereal diseases, found her lectures valuable. She confessed that it was difficult, at first, to get prostitutes to calm down and listen to her speak. But once she got started and introduced her topic, Yarros realized that her "audience was eager" to hear what she had to say.[60] By the end of that speech, Yarros explained that even she was surprised by the prostitutes' positive responses to her lectures.

Yarros spent the most time discussing "Mexican mothers" and their responses to her lectures, perhaps to demonstrate that even those women who seemed the furthest removed from the ASHA members in front of her—women who could not even speak English—appreciated the lectures and responded to them intelligently. Her reasoning on this front would have been consistent with her reasoning in 1916's *International Abstract of Surgery*, where she argued that "the bulk of our population needing the [sex-related] knowledge most has remained absolutely ignorant," concluding, therefore, that government agencies and organizations had to target previously overlooked populations with educational initiatives.[61] In her speech to the ASHA, Yarros acknowledged the concerns her audience members probably had about the degree of difference they perceived in Mexican women by noting, "Their own customs and ideas were so different from the American ones that it was difficult to know just how they would take my speech."[62] But Yarros claimed that, despite her concerns, the women "listened with such intense interest that it almost seemed as if they understood what I said" before her words were translated for them by an interpreter.[63] Yarros maintained that they were elated to learn how to teach their children to protect themselves from diseases. She added, "At the end of the meeting, I was surprised at the vigor and fluency with which these mothers bombarded me with the most intelligent questions."[64] Although Yarros portrayed the women's faces as "strange" and "interesting," a statement that may have mirrored the thoughts of her ASHA audience members, she portrayed their responses to the talks as just as excited and smart as those of any other person. If anything, Yarros portrayed the Mexican mothers as more desperate than others to hear the lectures, noting that they "begged me to tell them how to give children the facts of life."[65] In this way, although she did not critique negative stereotypes about Mexican women as Others, she demonstrated that Othered women needed information about sex and responded well to that information upon hearing it.

Even though they were "excited" and "eager" to obtain information about sex, Yarros was careful to represent women in ways that demonstrated they were not eager to overthrow existing structures of gender and power. According to Yarros, women may have wanted to know about sex to protect themselves and their families from harm, but it was also painful for them to do so because it upset their feminine sensibilities. After providing her hypothetical audiences with facts about sex, she confronted them on a personal level: "You now know facts that you have not known before, and some of them are very disagreeable and almost shocking for young people to face."[66] She argued that, despite their inherently feminine sensibilities, girls and women "must learn the scientific facts about venereal diseases and face the situation frankly" to make "the world safe for democracy."[67] Yarros told women that, if they did not feel up to the task of learning information about sex, they should "think of those young soldiers and sailors, full of life, desiring and longing to live and to get the most out of life, yet ready to sacrifice life itself for the sake of a great ideal!"[68] She repeatedly compared females' "sacrifice," their willingness to learn about sex despite their inclinations to remain innocent of such knowledge, with the soldier's sacrifice of life for his country. For instance, she reminded her hypothetical audience, "Our boys are already showing how keen and willing they are to make sacrifices for this cause, and the women of this country must not fall behind. They, too, must be ready to make sacrifices."[69] Women, after all, "must not be slackers."[70] Yarros assured social hygienists that by learning about sex, women would be doing their duty to help the social-hygiene effort and sacrificing their natural inclinations to avoid discussions about sex. She wanted social hygienists to believe that women had no desire to subvert existing gender roles by rejecting feminine ideals of modesty and propriety. Thus, she represented women as seeking to learn about sex to protect existing ways of life in the United States.

Representation of Self

The rhetorical structure Yarros utilized allowed her to represent herself in distinctive ways and to lead ASHA members in her audience with her through each subject position. Not only did ASHA members experience being in Yarros's audience as women in need of sex education, they also experienced themselves as social hygienists (those with the power to support Yarros's program) and as sex-education lecturers (those who were actively helping to carry out her initiatives). One of the first goals Yarros seemed to have been trying to accomplish in "Experiences of a Lecturer" was to establish herself as a credible member of the social-hygiene community. She began the speech by reiterating the narrative that social-hygiene advocates often used to justify their work. She recalled that "when the United States entered the great world war we already knew from the experience of other warring nations that venereal disease and prostitution were a great menace to the armies and navies," and "it was stated on good authority that many hundred thousand soldiers were incapacitated for service as the result of these diseases."[71] Yarros thus demonstrated that she understood the problems the ASHA was attempting to thwart and was supportive of wartime programs to protect soldiers from harm. She went on to further emphasize her membership and authority in the social-hygiene community by maintaining that those of "us who had been studying and working in the social hygiene movement in America for many years knew that something more fundamental than diagnosis and treatment would have to be supplied if we were to keep our boys fit,"[72] and that "something" was sex education. In this case, Yarros was representing herself as one of the earliest social hygienists who, like her audience, wanted to use education to halt the spread of venereal disease and vice among the "boys." She wanted social hygienists to know that she shared their history, that she "enjoyed the privilege of being among the first to whom the opportunity was given to do such intensive work."[73] She wanted them to see her as one of the people who, when the war began, "felt the time had come to make an intensive social hygiene campaign under the most favorable conditions—with the wonderful and effective backing of a strong government program."[74] Yarros represented herself as a member of the social hygiene collective, and in doing so she encouraged social hygienists to trust her, identify with her, and take her initiatives seriously.

On that same note, she also represented herself as an experienced physician, a position she would have shared with many other ASHA members and that carried with it a certain amount of esteem. She peppered her lectures with stories from the examining room to "illustrate the danger of abortions, miscarriages, locomotor ataxia, sterility, ophthalmia neonatorum, etc."[75] In using these specialized terms, Yarros was performing her expertise for ASHA members. This performance may have served to enhance her credibility within the social-hygiene community and prepare her to adopt yet another subject position: social-hygiene instructor.

Yarros represented herself as a person experienced in teaching women about sex and eager to train others to follow her lead. After emphasizing the number of lectures she gave to women during the war, Yarros provided ASHA members with instructions for giving their own sex-education lectures to women. She conveyed how she established credibility with audiences of women so her social-hygiene audience members could do so as well. She noted, "I explain to the mothers that I speak from experience, having told the story to many children."[76] Yarros advised ASHA members about exactly what topics to cover in speeches to specific audiences, noting in one case that instruction should develop by discussing the following subjects in order: "Description of organs of reproduction, maturing follicles, menstruation, awakening of sex as manifested in boys and girls, the sex urge in the male, the attitude of girls toward boys, right companionship, right habits of study, reading and thought."[77] Throughout her speech, Yarros explained what each lecture was intended to accomplish before giving the lecture herself and thus performing the kinds of rhetoric she wanted to see performed by others. She provided social hygienists with guidelines for better reaching audiences, and she would occasionally interrupt a lecture directed at hypothetical audiences of women to explicate why a particular aspect of the lecture would appeal to women. In this sense, Yarros was acting on the assumption that the social hygienists in her audience not only supported her initiatives but were willing to be trained so they could become lecturers in their own right. Her discourse positioned social hygienists as those moving into the action stage of support.

Perhaps the most interesting aspect of Yarros's self-representation was how she did *not* represent herself. Nowhere in "Experiences of a Lecturer" did Yarros mention her immigration from Russia or her experiences working in a factory when she first came to the United States. By omitting key elements of her intersectional identity—her working-class background and nation of origin—she chose not to represent the ways that oppressions intersected in her own life and encouraged her to fight for diverse women's access to information and health care.[78] Her discourse suggests that she wanted her audience to see her as a peer, not as one of the Othered women she was trying to represent. This point is especially interesting given her attempts to constitute social hygienists in the subject positions of immigrant and minority women. Perhaps Yarros felt that by highlighting the aspects of her history that made her different from other social hygienists she might undermine her credibility within that community. While most social hygienists would have been able to escape the narrative that constituted them as immigrant women during the speech, Yarros may have found herself caught in the immigrant narrative by admitting her own real experiences in that position. And, once she was caught, social hygienists may have found it more difficult to identify with Yarros and follow her lead, especially given the eugenic ideology that pervaded the social-hygiene community. Thus, Yarros positioned herself as someone who had witnessed the hardships of working-class, immigrant women but not as a person who had personally experienced those hardships. Her address's unique structure made this rhetorical choice possible.

Speaking for Others

Yarros's early addresses and writing shed light on how she worked to generate support for sex-education programs targeting women from a variety of races and classes at the end of World War I and directly thereafter. The structure of her "Experiences of a Lecturer" speech, in particular, promoted social hygienists' identification with women from a variety of subject positions, assured the male leadership of the social-hygiene movement that Yarros's initiatives did not blame men for women's ills or seek to upset existing hierarchies of power, and taught social hygienists how to promote and teach sex-education programs targeted at women. From this vantage point, Yarros's appeals for public sex education helped to expand their sense of who should be targeted by national sex-education initiatives. Moreover, her speech modeled and endorsed an accessible and relatively straightforward style of sex-education instruction.

Although Yarros confronted an audience that was used to fairly direct talk about sex education for men, audience members were not as familiar with discussions about sex education for women. Therefore she had to communicate her ideas in ways that would force her audience to consider the issue from a new angle. Her speech structure provided her with an added degree of control over the audience's perspective on their own subject positions, the lectures, the women who originally attended the lectures, and herself. The structure also allowed Yarros to constitute her audience in particular subject positions without permanently rescinding their agency and, with it, their ability to support her cause.

But a structure of this nature is not without complication, as there are some inherent problems with speaking on behalf of others. Perhaps most importantly, speaking for or about others can foster misrepresentation and/

or remove individuals' ability or willingness to speak on their own behalf. In some cases, speaking for or about others can constitute an act of violence against them by reiterating existing hierarchies of race, class, and gender.[79] Indeed, Yarros represented women in ways that assured ASHA members that she did not intend to overthrow existing structures of gender, race, and power, and she appealed explicitly to their penchant for eugenic ideology. In this way, her rhetoric undeniably functioned as a form of violence against the women she was trying to help.

There are times, however, when speaking for or about others is the best possible option because the represented parties are not able (or allowed) to speak for themselves.[80] Most of the women Yarros represented did not have access to members of the social-hygiene community, nor did they have the resources or ability to communicate their needs. In this sense, Yarros's representational rhetoric may have been justified because it alerted ASHA members to women's tribulations, made their problems salient, and encouraged them to take action on behalf of women. And Yarros's appeals regarding gender and racial hierarchies may have been attempts at audience adaptation that she felt she needed to earn ASHA members' trust. In many cases, garnering support for an issue involves establishing common ground with an individual about other issues the person embraces.[81] Yarros represented her female students by pairing positive statements about their intelligence and interest with what some ASHA members saw as their strangeness. She could have used herself as an example of an immigrant woman who had flourished as a result of her education, but in doing so she risked startling audience members out of their new sense of perspective.

Beyond the politics of representation, some critics might question whether Yarros was successful at providing women with the information about sex they truly needed, especially given her representation of the sex-education lectures in her ASHA address. Many of Yarros's appeals for sex education mirrored the appeals the CTCA used in its wartime propaganda aimed at girls and women. Like members of the CTCA, Yarros argued that women should have access to information about sex because it would benefit other people, not because women needed the information in their own right. She also argued that women who were informed about sex would serve as a "second line of defense" against venereal diseases among the troops, learn how to avoid actions that could excite men's "sensitive" sexual drives, and teach children about the dangers of venereal diseases and other sexual problems.

But although Yarros's appeals resembled many of the CTCA's arguments, she utilized the support she garnered from using those arguments to accomplish very different material results. The CTCA created pamphlets, films, and posters for women that focused primarily on the importance of chastity and, with only a few exceptions, glossed over details about sex. For instance, audiences generally received no information about the actions that they could take to keep from catching a venereal disease or becoming pregnant beyond abstaining from sex entirely. The CTCA also sponsored the American Plan, which punished "suspicious-looking" women found near army and military camps by subjecting them to invasive physical examinations and then shipping them off to detention centers. CTCA officials did not provide detainees with sex education, nor did they attempt to punish the men with whom they may or may not have had sex. Yarros, in contrast, created sex-education programs for women from a variety of backgrounds, "prostitutes" included, and she went beyond warning women against having sex by, for instance, helping to set up and run birth-control clinics and providing women with fairly detailed information about venereal diseases in sex-education campaigns (these campaigns are the focus of the subsequent chapter). Although Yarros may have appropriated some of the CTCA's arguments and strategies to win support from ASHA members, the programs she championed with the help of that support demonstrated that she did not share the CTCA's penchant for keeping women uninformed about sex.

Yarros's rhetoric in support of sex education for women was and is situated within a tradition of health communication that seeks to alleviate disparities in medical care. Elsewhere Yarros claimed that she was initially driven to speak about sex education for women when she became aware of societal health-care gaps, gaps delineated by sex, race, and class.[82] Her work as a physician, an activist, and a Hull-House resident showed her that, while many white men might have been getting better access to sex-education programs during the war, girls and women generally were not getting such access. Sex education was becoming more common when she gave her speech before the ASHA, but it had yet to target both sexes on a consistent basis. Yarros attempted to identify and address such public health disparities, and she did so long after the war had ended by serving as a consultant on public sex-education campaigns targeted at women and minorities in the 1920s.

FIVE

Campaigning for "Separate but Equal"

Directly after World War I, the U.S. Public Health Service, in cooperation with state boards of health and the American Social Hygiene Association, developed and publicized several sex-education campaigns. In 1919, they released "Keeping Fit: An Exhibit for Young Men and Boys." In 1922, they released "Youth and Life: An Exhibit for Girls and Young Women." In that same year, they also released "Keeping Fit: For Negro Boys and Young Men."[1] Each campaign was part of the postwar effort to redesign sex-education programs for white soldiers so they could be used to reach civilians.

What immediately stands out about these campaigns is that they featured sex-education messages tailored to distinct segments of the population. Rather than create one general civilian campaign, social-hygiene advocates targeted their messages specifically at white males, white females, and African American males, respectively. In this way, they represented increasing acceptance of the inclusive models of public sex education that Margaret Sanger, Ella Flagg Young, and Rachelle Slobodinsky Yarros advocated during the Progressive Era. During the war, government-sponsored sex-education campaigns tended to cater primarily to white males. But at war's end, Yarros's appeals in particular started to correspond with changes in practice as public health officials acknowledged that maintaining a general state of public health would require that they provide diverse populations with information about sex.[2]

Thus, they created different campaigns to target distinct populations and, in this way, demonstrated a modern sensitivity to disparities in health care.

Although it is only implicit in her "Experiences of a Lecturer" speech, Yarros argued that not only did all people need to receive information about sex, all people needed to receive approximately the *same* information about sex. When she recalled her experiences giving social-hygiene lectures to different audiences during the war, she concluded that "the question as to what should be taught to different groups, which has been so much discussed, is in reality a simple one." She noted that while she was traveling "from group to group, with but a short interval in between, I found myself relating practically the same facts, merely emphasizing different aspects of the questions according to the type of audience."[3] Yarros's idea that all people should be given the "same facts" in sex-education courses, with some variations in presentation and emphasis to target specific populations, differed markedly from ideas of the past. Many people who supported sex education for white men in the early twentieth century did not support sex education for women, immigrants, or minorities. Some argued that the best policy for "dealing with" the sexuality of Othered individuals was not education but a eugenically driven focus on sterilization for the "unfit" and "feeble-minded." With almost no exceptions, those labeled thusly were minorities, immigrants, and/or working-class women and men.[4] Others argued that if individuals from these groups did receive information about sex, it should be less technical and detailed than the information offered white men.[5] They felt that giving information to diverse audiences would be acceptable *if* the information those audiences received was censored more or less according to variables such as sex, race, and class.

The PHS campaigns, however, put some of Yarros's ideas into practice by providing all three audiences with approximately the same sex-education information, but they did so covertly by also emphasizing the differences among the campaigns. Campaign authors utilized variations in visual images and text to target their audiences; and, in the process, they made it easy for potential critics to assume the campaigns were providing white men, white women, and African American men with *different* information about sex. Ultimately, the PHS campaigns targeted different audiences in a way that drew attention away from the campaigns' similarities and thus helped to make them increasingly socially acceptable. This form of top-down, postwar public sex education was groundbreaking in the United States, not only because it targeted different segments of the populations with different appeals but because it provided diverse populations with equivalent and accessible information about sex. Despite the campaigns' superficial dissimilarities, they were a step forward in sex education in that they worked to alleviate disparities in health care. But they were also problematic because, in the process of targeting difference, they reiterated common assumptions about traditional gender roles and racial hierarchies to the point where groups of African American women, those who were neither white nor male, were overlooked almost entirely by campaigners.

The Public Health Service Sex-Education Campaigns

Catalyzed by high rates of syphilis and gonorrhea among active soldiers, Congress passed the Chamberlain-Kahn Act on July 9, 1918, thereby setting aside four million dollars to fight the spread of venereal diseases, 20 percent of which was to go directly to public sex-education initiatives.[6] The act also established the Venereal Disease Division of the U.S. Public Health Service. Headed by the Assistant Surgeon General of the United States, C. C. Pierce, who was an active member of the Committee on Training Camp Activities, the division oversaw the design, creation, and circulation of social-hygiene educational materials. In a 1919 article published in *Social Hygiene*, Pierce explained that the division was dedicated to disseminating "information by leaflets, lectures, and other means for the purpose of warning *everyone* of the serious nature of the venereal diseases."[7] "Keeping Fit" was created by male division officers (women could not serve as PHS officers at this time), including Pierce, Clark Hagenbuch, and J. A. Van Dis.[8] The campaign consisted of forty-eight different posters or lantern slides. Advances in printing and mass circulation during the Progressive Era helped to make posters a prominent part of everyday life in the United States. Health advocates developed visually stimulating poster campaigns to educate the American public about tuberculosis, immunization, and disease eradication. During World War I, the U.S. government created a Division of Pictorial Publicity, which produced thousands of propaganda posters to build support for the war effort and encourage soldiers and civilians to behave in ways that would promote public health. These included sex-education posters and pamphlets from the "Keeping Fit to Fight" venereal-disease campaign, a precursor of the "Keeping Fit" campaign.[9]

Upon arriving at the "Keeping Fit" exhibit's location, attendees would experience a "silent lecture": each attendee would walk quietly through the exhibit to take in the campaign's messages without "unnecessary" discussion.[10] In rural areas where the exhibits themselves did not travel, community leaders distributed pamphlets featuring each of the different forty-eight frames. Pierce described the illustrated pamphlet as discourse "for older boys and men . . . telling how they may keep themselves in prime physical condition; information regarding sex hygiene and venereal disease is included."[11] The historian Alexandria M. Lord maintains that over two million people saw "Keeping Fit" in a period of just three years, as it was featured in at least thirteen thousand different settings, ranging from school auditoriums to YMCA gymnasiums, as well as factory break rooms where high school dropouts were likely to find employment.[12] "Keeping Fit" was designed to reach heterogeneous audiences ranging from "rural and urban boys, to native-born and immigrant boys, to Southerners and Midwesterners, to Christians and Jews, and to working boys and boys still in school."[13] "Keeping Fit" was originally created for and presumably seen by a fairly broad, although still primarily white, group of young men from diverse religious and cultural backgrounds.

The CTCA distributed the pamphlet for "Keeping Fit"'s predecessor, "Keeping Fit to Fight," to all enlisted men during the war. The pamphlet began by promising a straightforward presentation: "This is a man-to-man talk, straight from the shoulder without gloves. It calls a spade a spade without camouflage."[14] It went on to argue that soldiers could be masculine and chaste simultaneously and to inform them about the dangers of venereal diseases. "Keeping Fit" retained its predecessor's appeals to manliness and chastity, but it was less straightforward about issues such as venereal disease and vice. No matter how strenuously members of the PHS and the ASHA worked to transfer wartime support for social-hygiene programs to post-war society, they could not overcome the public's general reticence during peacetime to deal publicly with issues of sex.[15] Thus, they started returning to their prewar strategies of using ambiguous language to discuss sex and public education. In this case, the organizations billed "Keeping Fit" as a "physical fitness program," with the inclusion of sex education as a mere afterthought. They assured the public that leading educators "have been enthusiastic about it and heartily endorse this method of reaching the older boys of the United States with a message of physical fitness."[16] Audiences could interpret the organization's reference to teaching "physical fitness" narrowly as an exercise program or broadly as a body-maintenance program that might include information about sex. By enveloping sex education within a program to promote physical fitness, campaign creators were using a rhetorical strategy similar to that used by Dr. Ella Flagg Young when she framed the Chicago Experiment as just another effort to improve students' health. PHS officials promised parents, educators, and community leaders that the campaign's "reference to sex is brief, simple and direct," and "the subject of venereal diseases, although limited to four cards (any of which may be omitted), is handled adequately and in a dignified, constructive way."[17] They wanted readers to know that although issues of social hygiene may have been included in "Keeping Fit," the campaign's major appeals concerned the much less controversial topics of health, fitness, and general hygiene.

In keeping with this theme, the first posters in the "Keeping Fit" exhibit (the posters were numbered consecutively from one to forty-eight) discussed hygiene in general. The posters' sequencing introduced audiences to the most divisive content about venereal diseases and sex outside of marriage only after easing them into the discussion with some seemingly innocuous posters about maintaining bodily health. Audiences were instructed in the proper ways to bathe, sleep, eat, exercise, stand, and study. In this way, the posters fostered organized, disciplined bodies, bodies that behaved in normalized, "healthy" ways.[18] Then, they assured audiences that an athletic or "outdoor life" would protect them from falling victim to unhealthy practices such as masturbation because it would use up their nervous energy and teach them to develop their will power. The next few posters encouraged audiences to keep their minds clean and not to worry if they experienced seminal emissions. Other posters introduced audiences to the biology of sex by picturing and narrating the reproductive processes as they occurred in fish, chickens, rabbits, and plants. Posters toward the end of the exhibit discussed the harms of venereal diseases to the individual and the family.

"Keeping Fit" served as a model for the social-hygiene campaigns that came later, including "Youth and Life" and "Keeping Fit: For Negro Boys and Young Men," for which Pierce hired Yarros and several other health workers to serve as consultants. The title "Youth and Life" highlighted the gendered lens through which many people at this time viewed health: men worked to become "fit," while women worked to maintain a youthful, innocent appearance and approach to life. Men set out to develop their bodily strength, and women set out to look attractive to others. As "Keeping Fit" focused on teaching its male readers about "physical fitness," "Youth and Life" worked to inspire "a better womanhood based on physical and mental fitness."[19] Writers framed the campaign as not "just" about sex, assuring audiences that references to "the reproductive organs and their functions" and to

"venereal diseases" were "handled adequately and in a dignified, constructive way that helps to build up the larger health ideal which is maintained
throughout."[20] The strategically fragmented nature of the discussion about
sexual health in these campaigns is also reminiscent of Young's argumentation style in favor of the Chicago Experiment.

The posters of "Youth and Life" were organized similarly to those of
"Keeping Fit," dealing first with issues of general health and cleanliness,
then reproduction as it occurred in plants and animals, and finally venereal diseases and their consequences. According to Lord, "Youth and Life"
was intended to reach audiences just as diverse as the target audiences for
"Keeping Fit," "including girls and women in rural and urban areas, girls
from the middle and working classes, and girls from immigrant and native-
born communities."[21] Unfortunately, PHS officials did not track how many
people saw the exhibit or its accompanying pamphlet. Lord surmises that
because "Youth and Life" was released to the public after funding for the
Chamberlain-Kahn Act had been reduced by more than half, "Youth and
Life" reached far fewer individuals than did "Keeping Fit."[22] But regardless
of the number of people who saw "Youth and Life," the fact that the PHS
created a sex-education campaign specifically for girls and women (albeit
only white girls and women) denoted a desire to inform women about social
hygiene that the organization rarely communicated before or during the war.
That the campaign was targeted specifically at females also implied that the
"Youth and Life" campaign was providing girls and women with different
information about sex than the "Keeping Fit" campaign was providing boys
and men, a point to which I will return shortly.

Beyond "Keeping Fit" and "Youth and Life," the PHS created a third
campaign targeting African American males entitled "Keeping Fit: For Negro
Boys and Young Men." After the war, many members of the PHS remained
convinced that African American men were at a high risk for contracting
syphilis and gonorrhea and therefore were in need of social-hygiene campaigns targeting them specifically. In 1923, an ASHA pamphlet argued that
"an adequate program in any phase of public health must include all races.
Disease and vice draw no racial line." Therefore, organization leaders announced that "the American Social Hygiene Association has included in its
general program efforts to create a public health consciousness among all
races—especially among Negros—and in both white and colored an understanding of their mutual dependence in the community."[23] This statement
reveals the social-hygiene community's emerging attention to African Ameri-

cans as an underserved health population, driven, ultimately, by a desire to protect the health of whites, as well as its assumption that African Americans were "especially" likely to contract venereal diseases.

The PHS described "Keeping Fit: For Negro Boys and Young Men" as an adaptation of the original campaign "for colored boys and men."[24] And as in the original, physical fitness was framed as the campaign's focus. The title page of the exhibit read: "Fitness—physical, mental, moral—depends fundamentally on health. This means not only the avoidance of disease and defects, but positive, abundant health—prime condition of mind and body."[25] Unfortunately, only twelve of the campaign's forty-eight posters survive, but the PHS's description of the campaign provides evidence that the differences between "Keeping Fit" and "Keeping Fit: For Negro Boys and Young Men" were fairly minimal. The PHS noted that the campaign

> consists of illustrations and reading matter on the physical and social factors affecting health, namely: physical exercise and training, physical and mental hygiene, biology and physiology, the nature, control and direction of the sex impulse, the causes and results of the venereal diseases, and the appeal for clean living as exemplified in the lives of representative men and inspired by the girl, the wife, the mother, and the home and family life.[26]

Like "Youth and Life," no statistics exist about how many people saw this exhibit, but the PHS reported that it traveled around the United States and was featured in churches, schools, community centers, and "colored" branches of YMCAs. And given the central role that African American women were playing in racial-uplift initiatives through organizations such as the YWCA during this time, it is quite possible that some African American women not only saw this campaign but helped to shape its content.[27]

The publicity for all three campaigns emphasized their visual appeals and the role of the visual in reaching audiences. A pamphlet introducing "Keeping Fit: An Exhibit for Young Men and Boys" to the public prominently featured the phrase, "Every projection makes its impression."[28] Another pamphlet encouraged parents, educators, and community leaders to "help him to keep fit. Let him *see* 'Keeping Fit.'"[29] Campaign organizers drew from the argument that images are especially likely—often more likely than text—to impress a person's memory. They then used this reasoning to argue that getting audiences to view the posters and take in their images would be the key to getting them to follow the advice offered therein.[30] The posters' images would serve as a sterile lens through which audiences could consider their environments. According to one pamphlet, the ASHA was interested in "cleaning the windows through which children view the world" by replacing glass dirtied with "vulgar distortion of sex facts" and "low standards of living" with glass made clear by featuring "correct information and a sound view point on sex matters," as well as "sympathetic guidance."[31] In this case, the glass metaphor had a literal meaning because lantern slides were made out of glass.[32] Thus, the campaigns were actually providing audiences with glass windows featuring "clean" messages to frame their perceptions of right and wrong.

Several posters within the campaigns called attention to the way people's mental images could affect the health of their bodies. For instance, a "Youth and Life" poster featured a drawing of a woman with a thought bubble coming from her head encircling images of food and drink. According to the poster's text, the woman's mental pictures caused her to feel hunger and thirst because "the sight or thought of food often causes a flow of gastric juices in the stomach." The hunger for food served as an analogy for the hunger for love, and females were reminded that "thoughts aroused by day-dreams of love tend to mold character. Let your daydreams be fine and ennobling, not cheap and degrading." These appeals emerged from the common belief that people who thought about sexual ideas and acts would be able to think of nothing else and become useless to society. In *What Every Girl Should Know*, Margaret Sanger expressed this idea, explaining to her readers the dangers of "mental masturbation," which "consists of forming mental pictures, or thinking of obscene or voluptuous pictures. This form [of masturbation] is considered especially harmful to the brain, for the habit becomes so fixed that it is almost impossible to free the thoughts from lustful pictures."[33] The social-hygiene posters, then, were framed as an antidote to "obscene" mental pictures, providing audiences with pictures of health, vitality, and productivity that they could store in their brains and mirror in their daily lives.

Not only could the posters' images supposedly inspire audiences to think and act in "clean," virtuous ways, their creators argued that images could be especially useful in targeting specific populations. For instance, promotions for "Keeping Fit: For Negro Boys and Young Men" explained that the campaign had been adapted for African American males by "selection for picturization of the best examples of negro educators, athletes, and statesmen."[34] The idea, according to the promotion, was "to make the appeal and challenge for physical fitness more personal" for African American men by showing them images of people who shared their race and sex acting in culturally acceptable ways and engaging in PHS- and ASHA-endorsed activities such as exercising, reading wholesome books, and marrying before becoming sexually active.[35] In this light, the posters demonstrated "healthy" behavior for audiences inhabiting gendered and raced subject positions. At the same time, they also called attention to the fact that "the best examples of negro" leaders did not appear in the campaign aimed at white audiences, a point that ties into the broader cultural narrative of "separate but equal" working throughout these campaigns that I discuss more specifically later in this chapter.

Targeting Difference

The obvious differences among the campaigns performed several functions. They helped to make each campaign socially acceptable, as each one contained a number of unique visual images and text tailored to specific groups' norms and expectations. In this way, campaign creators demonstrated to potential critics, as well as targeted audiences, that they supported and respected existing social hierarchies of gender and race—a rhetorical practice that Yarros in particular had been using for years. The differences among the campaigns also functioned to draw attention away from the similarities, specifically the similarities in how each of the campaigns educated audiences about sex.

"Keeping Fit"

The "Keeping Fit" exhibit served as a model for the campaigns that came later, so a general analysis of its unique claims and appeals will act as a starting point for comparison with "Youth and Life" and "Keeping Fit: For Negro Boys and Young Men." Many posters in "Keeping Fit" featured white males doing and saying things that generally were valued by members of that population (e.g., achieving athletics feats or competing in business) and were promoted by the social-hygiene movement (e.g., staying chaste outside of marriage or supporting a family). Posters encouraged target audiences to identify with the individuals featured in the posters and to imitate the activities promoted therein. For instance, posters worked to ensure audiences that "real men" follow the basic tenets of social hygiene. Viewers walking through the "Keeping Fit" exhibit were exposed to images and narratives about men achieving physical fitness and self-control, variables that social hygienists worked to develop in young people so they would be less likely to have sex outside of marriage and spread diseases. When attendees reached the last three posters, they witnessed these characteristics personified as ideal masculinity in the portraits of the adventurer Robert Falcon Scott and the former presidents Theodore Roosevelt and Abraham Lincoln. The historian Alan Trachtenberg argues that photographic portraits of the rich and famous during the 1800s displayed "the ideology of American success" and instructed viewers about how to become model citizens.[36] Vestiges of that tradition remained in the 1900s. In the last posters of "Keeping Fit," the captions focused on the strength, courage, and will-power of these famous men and encouraged viewers to imitate their beliefs and behaviors.

The poster of Roosevelt is a clear example of this appeal at work. Roosevelt was an especially vocal proponent of male strength and courage, and his views helped to inspire popular early-twentieth-century models of masculinity.[37] In this sense, the poster featuring Roosevelt illustrated how young men might mold themselves after him. The following caption appeared at the bottom of the poster: "Sickly and frail when a boy, Roosevelt by faithful training achieved the vigor of manhood." Viewers saw Roosevelt staring with determination into the camera and read about his journey from tremulous boyhood to virile manhood. According to the historian Linda Gordon, after Roosevelt charged white American women with committing "race suicide" in 1905, he became a literal poster boy for eugenic ideology.[38] Beginning in the mid-nineteenth century, northern European-Americans' fertility rates steadily declined chiefly because women were using contraceptive devices and techniques to control their reproductive lives. Roosevelt worried that immigrants, nonwhites, and the poor would soon outnumber the white, middle-to-upper-class population. He argued that Americans of the best "stock" should have the largest families to pass on their fine genes to future generations, and his portrait worked to cue viewers into this cultural discourse. Similarly, several "Keeping Fit" posters referred to children's right to be "well-born" and the importance of improving the "race." In these posters, masculinity was associated with exercising sexual self-control before marriage to avoid passing a "sex disease" to future generations. Portraying Roosevelt as an ideal male citizen in "Keeping Fit," then, worked to celebrate the achievement of his vigorous manhood, to indirectly endorse eugenic ideology, and to underscore the many captions in the campaign arguing for generational improvement of the race.

Although the ideal white male was clearly represented as physically strong in "Keeping Fit," his outward appearance seemed to be of less importance than how he felt and the state of his overall health. In one poster, the young man was encouraged to stand tall because such posture was attractive but also because it communicated confidence and aided in digestion. In another poster, a man was shown scrubbing his skin, and viewers were assured that "pimples do not indicate any serious defect." At the most, acne might prove to be an "inconvenience," but it was no sign of infirmity or moral depravity. There was no mention in these posters of men primping to appear handsome to others, but there was an emphasis on upholding traditional codes of chivalry when in the company of women. Young men's romantic prospects were framed as more dependent on their actions than on their physical appearances.

While picturing and describing the "ideal" white male, "Keeping Fit" posters included explicit messages communicating the importance of marriage to the young man, his future family, and the community at large. Although the posters plainly framed sexual expression outside of marriage as immoral, they implied that the "directed" sex instinct could be put to good use within marriage. Several "Keeping Fit" posters featured images of blushing brides coming down a church aisle and happy nuclear families dining together. Other posters informed audience members that a man could safely direct his sex instinct toward endeavors such as business and sports to help him achieve a fulfilling life. The model white male redirected his sexual energies to compete in the arenas of capitalism and athleticism. He triumphed at work so he could support his family, and he prevailed at play so he could assert his physical masculinity to society at large. His sexual impulse, and the sexual activity that was its result, was symbolized in one poster by a bucking horse that needed to be controlled and trained to best serve the needs of its "rider." Entitled "The Spirited Horse and the Sex Impulse," the caption read that a "spirited horse is a great prize. It is a joy to ride him, to feel his strength and boundless energy under one's control. The sex instinct, when directed, is the source of power and of a richer, fuller life." This poster highlighted the dialectic of wildness and control that social hygienists wanted men to identify in themselves and learn to balance. The poster implied that men's inherent sexuality was what made them men, but their ability to control that sexuality was what made them civilized and successful. In essence, harnessing the wildness of their sex impulse in marriage, capitalistic ventures, and stereotypically masculine activities such as sports would, according to this poster, allow men to triumph over the competition and then gallop contentedly into the sunset.

Other "Keeping Fit" posters used fear appeals to communicate that deviance from the traditional model of marriage and reproduction would eventually be punished. Viewers learned that having sex outside of marriage put one at risk for catching harmful diseases such as syphilis and gonorrhea. When a sexually experienced individual eventually got married, he could infect his wife, and she would then give birth to deformed children or children who would pass on diseases to future generations. One staple of early sex-education propaganda was the use of photographs to illustrate the physical damage caused by venereal diseases, especially in those who were considered "innocent victims."[39] "Keeping Fit" included one poster labeled "Inherited Syphilis" featuring a young boy with a cleft palate and severely deformed nose. The boy's nose seems to have been altered to make his physical appearance especially shocking. Yet because the image was a photograph rather than a drawing, viewers may have been more likely to accept what they saw as reality. In this sense, this poster drew from widespread assumptions about photography's realism or naturalism to make its appeal.[40] The poster's caption claimed, "A man may transmit syphilis to his children. His children's children may pay the penalty of his mistake" (see figure 6).

The text did not specifically label the child as a person suffering from congenital syphilis, but audiences saw his deformity, his abnormality, and probably assumed as much. The poster's argument—that a person with syphilis would have children who would be marked as abnormal—was enthymematic in that audience members had to reach a conclusion on their own. The authors of "Keeping Fit" seemed to be saying that men could—and maybe even should—express their sexuality, but they put themselves and their families at risk if they did so outside of marriage.

The authors of "Keeping Fit" depended heavily on scientific evidence and appeals to validate their claims about the dangers of pre- and extramarital sex. This theme in the social-hygiene poster campaigns appealed to the modern sensibilities of the early twentieth century. According to the historian Nancy Tomes, after the emergence of germ theory in the 1870s, Americans tended to see the scientist as their all-knowing guide in the fight to attain and maintain a state of health.[41] One poster in "Keeping Fit" featured a male scientist hovering over a microscope. The scientist and the microscope were early-twentieth-century symbols of scientific authority and the "medical gaze" generally associated with almost superhuman powers.[42] In this poster, audiences were led to believe that the scientist was looking at something equivalent to the drawing of a syphilis germ, which was also

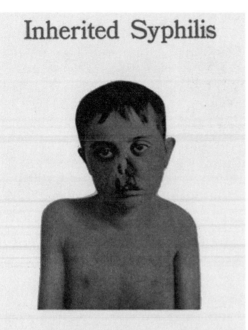

Inherited Syphilis

A man may transmit syphilis to his children

His children's children may pay the penalty of his mistake

Figure 6. "Inherited Syphilis," from "Keeping Fit: An Exhibit for Young Men and Boys" (1918). Courtesy Social Welfare History Archives, University of Minnesota.

featured in this and other "Keeping Fit" posters. The caption listed how the germ could negatively affect the body and how important it was that infected individuals be treated early. The caption directly under the drawing claimed, "The syphilis germs are the spiral-shaped objects seen in the above diagram" (see figure 7).

Viewers saw the male scientist fashioned in a white lab jacket, looking absorbed in his complicated work, and probably assumed that the simple diagram and captions next to him were accurate. They, after all, were not scientists, and so they did not have the background to question the poster's claims. They found themselves in a similar position when they encountered claims about the dangers of masturbation and/or the dangers of simply thinking about sex. "Keeping Fit" was not aimed at scientific audiences, and

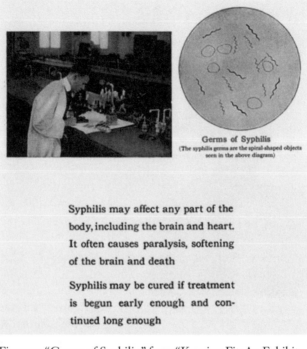

Figure 7. "Germs of Syphilis," from "Keeping Fit: An Exhibit for Young Men and Boys" (1918). Courtesy Social Welfare History Archives, University of Minnesota.

the drawings of syphilis strains would not have impressed the scientifically trained. Rather, the campaign's scientific appeals functioned to validate its claims to the lay public.

In sum, the "Keeping Fit" posters specifically targeted white males, framing ideal white males as self-controlled, chivalrous, and sympathetic to eugenic ideology. They also framed white males as naturally sexual but capable of limiting the expression of their sexual desire to marriage, and they portrayed the potential horrors of venereal diseases by featuring images of deformed children. "Keeping Fit" bolstered the credibility of its claims by appealing to scientific modernity and featuring scientific cues such as lab coats and microscopes. The campaigns that followed "Keeping Fit"—"Youth and Life" and "Keeping Fit: For Negro Boys and Young Men"—used some unique visual images and text to target different audiences and align with norms considered socially acceptable for those groups.

"Youth and Life"

Many of the images and text in "Youth and Life" drew from popular ideas about what it meant to be a "respectable" woman in the early-twentieth-century United States and paired those ideas with lessons about social hygiene and public sex education. "Youth and Life" audiences were encouraged to perform their gender in traditional ways, get married and raise healthy children, and have faith in science and modernity. The female ideal, as presented in the poster campaign "Youth and Life," had several characteristics in common with the male ideal as presented in "Keeping Fit": she was a hard worker, self-controlled, clean, well-educated, physically fit, and light-skinned. This last characteristic was central to the definition of an "ideal" woman, as common language practices, media representations, and mythology contrasted respectable, moral woman with black, sexually promiscuous "Jezebels."[43] But unlike her white, male counterpart, the female ideal was most importantly philanthropic, attractive, and instinctively maternal, characteristics that set her apart from men and highlighted her ability to make others' lives easier and more enjoyable.

The last two posters in "Youth and Life" featured the "ideal" woman personified in portraits of the educator and women's suffrage advocate Dr. Anna Howard Shaw and the opera singer Louise Homer. In contrast to the portraits of Scott, Roosevelt, and Lincoln in "Keeping Fit," which emphasized individual achievement, these women were not featured alone. Shaw was an interesting choice for the exhibit, as rumors about her lesbianism followed her in life and death, although she was often careful to conform to aesthetic and cultural gender norms when she was in public.[44] Featured in "Youth and Life," she seemed to be the picture of the era's New Woman, wearing a cap and gown, waving her diploma in the air, and displaying the three stripes of a Ph.D. on her shoulder, thereby communicating the campaign's support for women in higher education earning the highest degree possible. Yet she shared the page with a list of the names of twelve other well-known women who were also living "worthwhile lives" by giving back to their communities, drawing from their creative talents or their dedication to helping others.[45] Homer, too, shared her frame with others, her five daughters, and was featured atop the caption: "Such a woman gives richly to the world and its future through her work and her personality as well as through her children." The ideal woman's accomplishments, in other words, were dependent on her ability to give of herself and cooperate with others. She went to school chiefly as a means to better help those around her. The photographs and illustrations featured in "Youth and Life" functioned to lay out normative relationships and demonstrate who can do what and under what conditions.[46] They articulated the belief that ideal white women spent their time tending to others and that their doing so benefited the social body as a whole. Viewers of the exhibit saw that, although these women had impressive individual achievements, the posters celebrated them first and foremost for being helpful and dedicated to the well-being of those around them.

Men in "Keeping Fit" were hailed for developing their natural vigor and individual skills and talents. Women in "Youth and Life," in contrast, were often described and pictured as helpmates to the ever-striving male. A woman could aspire to be a "doctor's assistant," a homemaker, and/or, most importantly, a mother. Maintaining her health allowed her to "devote herself to the wellness of humanity" and to cultivate her grace, beauty, and overall attractiveness. Health, it seemed, was less about how a woman felt than how she looked to others. The art historian John Berger notes that images of males and females tend to illustrate that "men *act* and women *appear*."[47] In "Youth and Life," several posters featured women looking off into the distance or gazing at themselves in a mirror. In some cases, images of women looking into mirrors can symbolize their own compliance with or sense of the male gaze.[48] One poster, titled "Beauty Comes from Within," claimed, "Most girls could be prettier than they are because most girls could be healthier." Early-twentieth-century women were inundated with this "democratic rhetoric of beauty," which implied that any woman could be beautiful with a healthy regimen and a positive outlook.[49] Conventionally unattractive women, in this light, were framed as unhealthy and ultimately to blame for their unconventional appearances. The argument in "Beauty Comes from Within" depended on audience members caring enough about being pretty to change their health habits. The poster's text accompanied a drawing of a young girl holding onto her hat in the wind and gazing at a bird in a tree. She was posing for the sake of the viewer's gaze. The viewer was witness to her beauty, which served as evidence of her overall health and worth. The image on this poster was similar to images of women used in print advertisements at this time, many of which promoted beauty products by featuring an attractive woman staring off into the distance whose image had been captured by the "gaze of passing men."[50]

In the process of referencing ideal femininity, "Youth and Life" high-lighted the importance of marriage to women with an emphasis on enacting the values of republican motherhood.[51] According to one poster, a woman must eventually "take her place in the world as a mother and a useful citizen." In fact, several of the posters implied that to be a "useful citizen," a woman must mother healthy future citizens. For instance, the central focus of one poster was a drawing of a woman's body without arms or legs. The illustration depicted and labeled "glands" that were responsible for her reproductive capabilities, as well as her genitalia and several internal organs. Her biological ability to reproduce was what identified her as a woman in this drawing. By contrast, although "Keeping Fit" described the male reproductive functions, drawings of these processes were not included in the "Keeping Fit" posters. The male's identity was defined by decidedly more than his ability to reproduce, and hence there was no need to see his genitalia. In the case of the female, however, her identity was so synonymous with her reproductive capabilities, especially in the wake of Roosevelt's concerns about "race suicide," that the authors of "Youth and Life" omitted her appendages to allow viewers a clear look at her body. Viewers probably understood that they were learning about the female body so that they could one day fulfill their destinies as mothers and wives.

To highlight the campaigns' support for marriage and family, both "Youth and Life" and "Keeping Fit" featured a famous Norman Rockwell painting of a mother, father, and small daughter studying architectural plans for their new house. The family members were clearly white and middle-class. The historian Carolyn Kitch notes that this particular painting, entitled "Planning the Home," was also featured on the covers of several popular magazines, such as the *Literary Digest*. "Planning the Home" was one of many images featured in 1920s mainstream media depicting the ideal modern American family. In 1905, Americans averaged four magazine subscriptions per household, and the covers of those magazines were designed to feature an idealized version of the intended reader.[52] Magazine editors placed Rockwell's painting on their covers because many Americans saw the family it illustrated as a perfected rendering of their own families and were drawn to such a representation.

In the social-hygiene campaigns, Rockwell's painting was also used to represent an idealized version of the American family, but it was presented to women and men for different reasons. For women, the accompanying caption focused on the importance of building a home, establishing a partnership between spouses, and the creation of a "finer" race. The campaign's use of the term "race" was ambiguous because it could stand for the human race or the white race. Given that all individuals featured in these posters were light-skinned, as well as the fact that "race" was often used as a code during this time for eugenic ideology, the implication was in favor of the latter. The reference to marriage as a partnership was an homage to the women's movement, as was the image of the young girl playing on the floor with blocks rather than a doll. She was in training to one day build a home, but the painting also implied that she would not follow through with her plans until she was safely entrenched within marriage. For the men, the caption accompanying the Rockwell painting was reworded with no explicit mention of building or maintaining a home. Men should spend time with their families and contribute to the reproduction of the race, but their wives, sitting in the center of the painting, were the people responsible for keeping the family together.

In "Youth and Life," women who skirted their jobs as respectable home-maker, wife, and mother, like men who skirted their responsibilities as self-controlled breadwinner, athlete, and adventurer, were punished for their deviance. She who allowed a male companion to steal kisses or otherwise take advantage of her was "cheap." Cheap girls often adopted the lifestyle of what, in a few years, would be popularly known as a "flapper." The term "flapper" was never used in these social-hygiene campaigns, but, according to Kitch, it was a concept circulating throughout American society as an alternative model of femininity in the 1920s. To be a flapper was to wear short skirts and makeup, spend time in jazz clubs, and consume cigarettes and liquor. Such a life, according to "Youth and Life," put one at risk for contracting a disease or garnering the shame of an out-of-wedlock pregnancy.[53] When the supposedly sex-crazed, ultra-thin flapper finally came to her senses and got married, she risked giving birth to a "defective" child.

Yet the "defective" children portrayed in "Youth and Life" looked nothing like the startling boy without a nose in "Keeping Fit," perhaps because campaign writers worried that such an image would overwhelm women's sensibilities rather than persuade them to act according to the tenets of social hygiene. This idea would have emerged from the Victorian ideal of women as too fragile and sensitive to be exposed to violence, injury, sexual references, or other generally upsetting information. One poster, for instance, featured a drawing of a seemingly helpless, pretty little girl with her hands held out in front of her because she was blind. The caption began with the statement, "If the mother has gonorrhea, the child may be blinded at birth" (see figure 8).

Blinded by gonorrhea

If the mother has gonorrhea, her child may be blinded at birth

    Simple medical treatment at time of birth will prevent such blindness

Men who think themselves cured sometimes infect their wives with gonorrhea. Chronic ill-health and inability to have children are often caused by gonorrhea. Many serious operations on married women are due to this disease

Figure 8. "Blinded by Gonorrhea," from "Youth and Life: An Exhibit for Girls and Young Women" (1922). Courtesy Social Welfare History Archives, University of Minnesota.

Given that the "defective" child was represented by a drawing rather than a photograph, the sense that she was "real" was less apparent than it might have been for viewers of the photograph of the syphilitic boy. The girl's attractive appearance, although obviously not real, was symbolic of the ideal child and therefore invoked audiences' pity and sadness rather than their gruesome horror. In an era when healthy, middle-class children were often viewed as a commodity and women tended to identify themselves first and foremost as dedicated mothers, a woman who gave birth to a blind child could be viewed as a less-than-exemplary citizen.[54] In this light, it would be less important that the drawing of the girl actually resembled a real person and more significant that the poster served as a symbolic reminder of the consequences of selecting a mate infected with a venereal disease or of engaging in "cheap" behavior.

The creators of "Youth and Life" balanced appeals designed to invoke viewers' anxiety with appeals to the same sort of scientific knowledge used in "Keeping Fit." Women, like men, were exposed to drawings of the newly discovered syphilis and gonorrhea germs, as well as images of the male scientist in his white lab coat. Yet the posters' authors also used science in a new way for this second campaign. In an effort to legitimate homemaking as an enviable skill, "Youth and Life" framed housekeeping and child rearing scientifically. One poster was titled "Home-making a Science" and included a list of the business skills required to efficiently run a home. The image accompanying these words featured a mother serving bread and tea to two small girls seated at a child-sized table (see figure 9).

The room was decorated with intricate wallpaper, a well-set table, and expensive curtains; the mother had gone to great effort to keep the children and the playroom spotlessly clean. She seemed to be following the advice of domestic sanitarians and health officials by keeping her family safe from contamination and therefore proving herself to be what the historian Lynne Curry and others have called a "modern" or "scientific" mother.[55] Although she was wearing a ruffled dress rather than a lab coat, she approached homemaking and child rearing scientifically by meticulously keeping her home in order. Her tools were kitchen appliances rather than microscopes; her objects of study were her children and her home rather than syphilis spirochetes; and her research agenda involved planning dinner and bathing babies rather than discovering a cure for venereal diseases. Nevertheless, "Youth and Life" assured audiences that homemaking, the activity many of them had been reared to adopt, could be just as scientific as chemistry or physics.

Ultimately, "Youth and Life" targeted white women by drawing from established characterizations of femininity. The posters equated femininity with self-sacrifice, cooperation, and middle-to-upper-class whiteness, a representation that was reiterated by early-twentieth-century culture in general and by the social-hygiene community in particular. While viewing the posters, audiences were reminded of the popular idea that health and beauty were interconnected: to be healthy was to be beautiful to others, and to be beautiful to others was to be healthy. In this way, they were encouraged

Home-Making A Science

A real home is no accident. Efficient house-keeping increases home comfort. It requires knowledge and skill

Learn

To care for the house	. . .	*Business efficiency*
To spend wisely	. . . . .	*Budget system*
To feed the family	. . . .	*Food values*
To care for the baby	. . .	*Child hygiene*

Figure 9. "Home-Making a Science," from "Youth and Life: An Exhibit for Girls and Young Women" (1922). Courtesy Social Welfare History Archives, University of Minnesota.

to follow the posters' advice about health, if only so they could improve their appearance. Viewers learned that exemplary women were able to produce healthy, white children and maintain clean, attractive homes where their husbands could find refuge from the masculine world of competition. These women may have received a higher education, but they did so primarily so that they could better give of themselves to others and society at large. According to "Youth and Life," women who were "cheap" would eventually regret their decisions when they could not find a husband or their children were congenitally blind. The campaign's appeals to science granted these claims credibility and framed homemaking and child rearing as scientific and therefore comparable in importance to traditionally scientific endeavors.

"Keeping Fit: For Negro Boys and Young Men"

The twelve campaign posters that remain today from "Keeping Fit: For Negro Boys and Young Men" shed light on the ways this particular campaign used visual images and text to target African American men and provide them with information about sex. The major difference between these posters and the posters from the other two campaigns was that all but one of them featured images of African American characters. Clearly, the campaigns' creators felt that African American men would be more likely to pay attention to and identify with posters that featured characters who shared their race and, in many cases, their sex. The ASHA attributed its success in reaching "colored populations in the United States" largely "to the fact that the [ASHA] has been the pioneer national agency in the public health field to employ a trained colored worker for Negro groups."[56] Indeed, in the early 1920s the ASHA sponsored a series of sex-education lectures given by a "colored representative" at African American colleges and universities, summer schools, fraternities, and social agencies such as the National Urban League. These lectures were sponsored and sometimes given by Franklin O. Nichols, an African American "field representative" for the ASHA. Speaking before the Methodist Conference of Colored Social Workers in 1922, Nichols encouraged audience members to support social-hygiene lectures and exhibits targeting African Americans in order to improve the health conditions "among our people."[57] Nichols and other ASHA leaders argued that African Americans would be far more likely to take messages of sex education seriously if they could see themselves in the message, whether the "message" was delivered by an African American lecturer or posters that featured African American characters.

Many posters in this campaign encouraged African American males to perform their gender in traditional ways. African American men were shown boxing, jumping hurdles, running races, and playing baseball. The posters instructed readers to keep their bodies fit so they could "get in the game," a phrase that was also used in the "Keeping Fit" campaign. In this case, the reference to sporting opportunities for African American men appealed to the era's popularization of sports and African Americans' increasing participation in those sports.[58] However, the major models of African American masculinity in this campaign were not athletic icons; they were Frederick

Douglass and Booker T. Washington, two African American community leaders who were celebrated in these posters for their physical fitness, cleanliness, and industriousness.

As in the other two poster campaigns, this campaign encouraged audiences to get married before having sex and to have healthy children. One poster featured the photograph of a young, conservatively dressed African American woman and read, "Somewhere the girl who may become your wife is keeping pure. Will you take to her a life equally clean?" (see figure 10).

An equivalent poster in "Keeping Fit" featured the same text with a different image: a colorful painting of a young white girl holding a school book and looking playfully back at the viewer. By contrast, the African American girl in the "Keeping Fit: For Negro Boys and Young Men" poster was featured in profile, her face blending into the blurry black-and-white background.

Somewhere the girl who may become your wife is keeping pure

Will you take to her a life equally clean?

Figure 10. "Keeping Pure," from "Keeping Fit: For Negro Boys and Young Men" (1922). Courtesy Social Welfare History Archives, University of Minnesota.

While the painting of the white girl presented her as fun-loving and hopeful about her future, the photograph of the African American girl presented her as comparatively serious. To the African American men who viewed this woman's image, she may have represented health and a family without promising racial integration. At the same time, the woman's light skin and slicked-back hair, characteristics that manufacturers of African American beauty products tended to frame as commodities,[59] represented an ideal of African American female beauty during the 1920s that was predicated on a model of whiteness.

One of the posters available from this campaign revealed the tension in the social-hygiene movement's attempt to communicate to African American men about eugenics and fathering healthy children. This poster was the only one of the surviving twelve that did not feature an obviously African American character. Instead, the poster featured the photograph of a light-skinned baby (whose racial makeup was ambiguous) sitting in a wash basin with the caption, "Every child has the right to be well born. Will you give your children healthy bodies and a fair start in life?" (see figure 11).

The same caption appeared in a "Keeping Fit" poster, and a similar caption appeared in a "Youth and Life" poster. In all cases, the text functioned to encourage audiences to keep themselves and, by extension, their children "clean" by remaining chaste until marriage. However, this poster's placement within a campaign targeting African American males communicated an added degree of tension. By featuring a light-skinned baby, the poster implicitly equated cleanliness with light skin. Thus, the poster potentially functioned as a reminder that lighter-skinned African Americans suffered less discrimination than those with darker skin because they could "pass" as white and therefore as "clean" and "pure."[60]

The light-skinned baby also alluded to the eugenic philosophy that maintained that African Americans were genetically inferior to whites and therefore could never truly give their children a "fair start in life." This poster implied that African Americans could only do so much for their children but also that the things that they could do for them (e.g., not passing on venereal diseases, keeping them physically clean and well-fed, providing them with a traditional nuclear family) were worthwhile. The placement of the image in this poster within the larger African American campaign visually communicated some of the era's normative assumptions about race and reproduction. That the posters in this campaign implicitly acknowledged these norms may have made them seem more credible to

Every child has the right to be well born

Will you give your children healthy bodies and a fair start in life?

Figure 11. "Right to Be Well-Born," from "Keeping Fit: For Negro Boys and Young Men" (1922). Courtesy Social Welfare History Archives, University of Minnesota.

audiences because of their candor. Perhaps even more importantly, the reproduction of these assumptions functioned to assure potential critics that the campaign was offering African American males a lesser version of sex education, suited to their supposed inferiority.

None of the surviving twelve posters from this campaign directly mentioned science, but the PHS's description of the campaign implied that several posters that are no longer available included the same discussion about venereal diseases (complete with accompanying lab coats, microscopes, and syphilis germs) featured in the other two campaigns. What distinguished the remaining posters of this campaign from the other two campaigns was that audiences were encouraged to "think no further" about science-based topics such as seminal emissions and other biological processes. Although audience members were told, in another poster, to "keep [their] mind[s] occupied with good books," they were assured that "no attention need be given to" issues of science and biology beyond developing a basic understanding of how the body works. In a discussion about the campaign, PHS officials told community leaders, educators, and health advocates, "Though the exhibit is a scientific presentation, the subject matter is simple enough to be easily understood."[61] They worked from the assumption, documented by the historian James H. Jones, that audiences of African American men would not be smart enough to follow complicated scientific arguments, either because they lacked the educational background or because they were inherently less intelligent than audiences of whites.[62] Yet the surviving twelve posters, along with the description of the campaign as a whole, provided little evidence that campaign's authors simplified the content because, as they suggested, the campaign was already "simple enough." Ultimately, none of the campaigns required audiences to know much about science; they required only that audiences understand visual cues such as lab coats and microscopes as proof of credibility. In this respect, the posters that focused on science did not necessarily differ much from one campaign to the next because they required so little from their audiences.

"Keeping Fit: For Negro Boys and Young Men" framed its intended audience of African American men as stereotypically masculine in their love for sports and their desire to find a wife with whom they could start a family. But the campaign also framed African American men as deferential to whites and willing to work within existing systems of racial inequality and segregation. The campaign encouraged audience members to see themselves through the eyes of whites and the white-led culture at large and thus served as a reminder that African Americans were considered by many to be inferior members of society.

In summary, the PHS and the ASHA framed "Keeping Fit," "Youth and Life," and "Keeping Fit: For Negro Boys and Young Men" as very different campaigns. In describing the campaigns to the public, representatives from these organizations focused on how the original "Keeping Fit" campaign had been altered so that it would be appropriate for audiences of white women and audiences of African American men. Curious onlookers needed only to glance at images in either of the later campaigns to see that they seemed to be targeting white women and African American men by featuring characters who corresponded in terms of sex and race. And some text in each campaign played off of stereotypical understandings of white women as maternal, attractive, and self-effacing and of African American men as unintelligent and generally inferior to whites. This rhetoric of difference provided those who might criticize the campaigns for their similarity to "Keeping Fit" with enough evidence of variance to support, or at least ignore, their release to the public.

Similarity within Difference

While many of the differences among the campaigns discussed thus far may not seem surprising, those differences were probably the aspects of the campaigns that viewers noticed or heard about first. Public health officials repeatedly justified their decision to target women and minorities separately from white men by framing those audiences as unique and therefore best targeted with distinct appeals.[63] They argued, often implicitly, that women and minorities could not be grouped together with white men because they were so different from white men. White women were framed as generally more interested in their appearance than men and more sensitive to gruesome imagery. Similarly, African American men were framed as less intelligent and civilized than white men. Given the belief among some sex-education advocates that women and minorities should receive less and/or different information about sex than white men, the PHS's focus on the differences among the campaigns helped organization leaders build support for those initiatives. At the very least, the emphasis on difference helped the PHS to avoid some of the criticism that might have resulted if critics had realized that, in fact, the campaign targeting white women and the campaign targeting African American men provided those audiences with much of the same information about sex that was provided to white men.

Before I lay out how these campaigns worked toward Yarros's idea that all people should have access to the same information about sex, I want to note that all three campaigns were grounded in the assumption that health was the product of personal choices. Each campaign framed health largely as something that people accomplished individually. These posters implied that if people followed the steps laid out for them in these exhibits (i.e., exercising, eating wholesome foods, getting sufficient sleep, keeping clean, waiting to have sex until marriage), they would be rewarded with an abundance of energy, a body free of disease, and a joyful life. There were exceptions to this rule in that the campaigns sometimes framed women and children as innocent victims of venereal diseases that they contracted from a dishonest husband/father. But, for the most part, none of the campaigns accounted for the environmental or societal factors that affected an individual's health, factors that play a key role in the creation of health disparities. They assumed that all viewers would have the resources to, for example, breathe clean air or get adequate rest—resources that were often not available to those in the working classes. In this sense, the PHS ignored the claims of people like W. E. B. Du Bois, who argued in 1906 that "the negro death rate and sickness are largely matters of condition and not due to racial traits and tendencies," or Mary Ross, a writer for *The Survey*, who concluded in 1923 that health disparities were often the result of "grossly unequal" conditions.[64]

Despite the many problems inherent in the campaigns' assumption that health was the result of personal effort and choices, the logical conclusion to such an assumption was that all people, regardless of race, sex, or social class, needed approximately the same information about issues like sex so that they could make informed decisions about their health. The campaigns may have been most obviously defined by the different audiences they targeted, but they provided each of their audiences with similar and at times identical information about marriage, reproduction, and venereal diseases. All three campaigns framed marriage as the key to a happy, healthy life. They argued that young people should act in ways that would position them as attractive marriage partners. In the context of these campaigns, young people's efforts to exercise, read approved books, and perform other "healthy" activities were framed as steps that would lead, one day, to marriage and a family. Although the campaigns targeted different sexes and races, they all utilized fairly traditional understandings of gender roles within the context of marriage, framing the man as the breadwinner and the woman as the children's caretaker and the homemaker. According to these campaigns, the most important action that young people could take to secure their marriage prospects was to remain chaste in body and mind. The campaigns promoted what social purists of the nineteenth century labeled a "single standard of purity" because they encouraged everyone, not only women, to limit their sexual activity to marriage.[65] One "Keeping Fit" poster highlighted this standard, as well as the campaign's framing of marriage as a life goal, by asking audiences, "Have you a right to go to the marriage altar demanding honor and purity in the girl you marry, unless you are willing to offer her a clean life?" The image accompanying this text was a drawing of young bride, illuminated in light, walking ceremoniously toward her groom. Regardless of individuals' demographics, these campaigns encouraged them to exercise sexual self-control and see a blissful, healthy marriage as their reward for so doing.

The campaigns framed reproduction as the natural and happy conse-quence of marriage. All three campaigns used the same basic "birds and bees" narrative to describe the process of reproduction. For example, men and women, white and African American audiences were shown diagrams of the sex organs in a plant. Similarly, they viewed posters that featured the growth of a fertilized egg, which culminated in the hatching of a chick, and the growth of fetal rabbits within a female rabbit's body. Accompanying text described the coming together of the sperm and the egg in conception and noted that the same process occurred in human reproduction. In both "Keep-ing Fit" and "Youth and Life" (and perhaps in the sections of "Keeping Fit: For Negro Boys and Young Men" that no longer exist), audiences learned that, although the biological processes of reproduction in humans often mirrored those of plants and animals, humans brought cognitive abilities beyond "animal instinct" to reproduction and child rearing. Unlike animals, humans could make deliberate choices about their marriage partners, decid-ing on those who were healthy and had desirable hereditary traits to pass on to future generations.

Beyond marriage and reproduction, all three campaigns provided audi-ences with information about venereal diseases. They featured the same drawings of gonorrhea and syphilis germs under a microscope and ex-plained that the diseases, in the words of "Youth and Life," "may be passed from a diseased person to another diseased person through sexual inter-course." Despite the PHS's attempts to account for women's feminine sensibilities throughout the "Youth and Life" campaign, the campaign was surprisingly blunt with women about the connection between venereal diseases and sex. The campaigns spared female audiences few details about venereal diseases that they did not also spare to male audiences, assuring them, for example, that the diseases could "usually be cured if treatment is given early enough by a reputable physician or in a clinic." And, as I noted previously, the campaigns did not simplify scientific information about sex for audiences of women or African American men any more than they had for audiences of white men, even though some of the discussions about the campaigns implied as much.

In reviewing the similarities in content about sex among these campaigns, I am not making an overarching qualitative statement about that content. My point is not that the PHS's campaigns offered their audiences "good" or "bad" information about sex but that they offered their audiences approximately the same information about sex. For the most part, whatever these campaigns taught to white male audiences, they also taught to white female audiences and African American male audiences. In this sense, the campaigns were a step forward in that they provided traditionally under-served populations with more information about sex than those populations had received from public health organizations in the past. It should be noted, however, that the campaigns did not present exactly the same sexual infor-mation to each audience. For example, a discussion of seminal emissions was included in both versions of "Keeping Fit" but not in "Youth and Life," and a discussion of menstruation was included in "Youth and Life" but not in "Keeping Fit." This practice of providing audiences of one sex with little information about the other sex's reproductive functions is still evident in some contemporary sex-education programs, and such differences provide fodder for those who argue that separate educational programs can never truly be equal.

Sex Education in an Era of Separate but Equal

In 1892, Homer Plessy, a light-skinned, thirty-year-old male of mixed racial heritage, was arrested for refusing to leave the "whites only" car for the "colored" car of a train traveling through Louisiana. In 1890, Louisiana had passed the Separate Car Act, prohibiting African Americans from rid-ing in railway cars reserved for whites. The Supreme Court's 1896 ruling in *Plessy v. Ferguson* upheld the constitutionality of providing "separate but equal" facilities for white and African American citizens.[66] Speaking for the majority, Justice Henry Billings Brown reasoned:

> The object of the [Fourteenth] Amendment was undoubtedly to enforce the absolute equality of the two races before the law, but in the nature of things it could not have been intended to abolish distinctions based upon color, or to enforce social, as distinguished from political equality, or a commingling of the two races upon terms unsatisfactory to either. Laws permitting, and even requiring, their separation in places where they are liable to be brought into contact do not necessarily imply the inferiority of either race to the other.[67]

Brown held that the Louisiana Separate Car Act did not violate the Four-teenth Amendment's promise to provide all citizens with "equal protection of the laws" because separation did not necessarily produce inequality. Despite Plessy's complaints to the contrary, Brown implied that both whites and African Americans often wanted to be separated from one another and that integration was not a necessary element of egalitarianism. The *Plessy v. Ferguson* ruling explicitly authorized practices of racial segregation that had been transpiring since Reconstruction. The idea that whites could legally restrict African Americans from places like schools, restaurants, and doctor's offices if they provided them with separate but equal facilities permeated society in the form of Jim Crow laws. And the PHS poster campaigns demonstrated that performances of separate-but-equal ideology were also evident in arenas such as public sex education, manifesting themselves in instances of race, as well as gender, segregation.

Perhaps the most obvious example of the separate-but-equal ideology in the PHS campaigns was the use of different health icons in each campaign, Abraham Lincoln and Theodore Roosevelt to Frederick Douglass and Booker T. Washington. The parallels between the white icons and the African American icons suggest that the PHS was attempting to supply African American audiences with literally separate but equal role models. Indeed, the historian Nancy Marie Robertson argues that even interracial organizations from this time, such as the YWCA, publicly supported racial segregation, especially in matters of social-sexual relationships, as well as traditional representations of gender roles.[68] In this respect, it was probably no coincidence that Washington, for example, supported the white power structure and, in many ways, encouraged African Americans to accommodate that structure. Similarly, the female icons in "Youth and Life" such as Anna Howard Shaw and Louise Homer were framed in ways that suggested that they supported conventional understandings of women as caring accommodators, understandings that often positioned women as separate from men physically and mentally.

Not until the 1954 Supreme Court decision in *Brown v. Board of Education* was the separate-but-equal ruling overturned. The majority opinion held that separate but equal educational facilities deprived African American citizens of equal protection under the law. Chief Justice Earl Warren argued that segregation of white and African American children often fixed African American children with a sense of inferiority, and he claimed that facilities for African American children were generally of lesser quality than facilities for white children.[69] Warren acknowledged that segregation and inequality were often linked, and his decision legitimated long-standing concerns about the separate-but-equal ideology. As Justice John Marshall Harlan recognized in his dissent of the *Plessy v. Ferguson* case in 1896, the separate-but-equal clause was a "thin disguise" for discrimination.[70]

The argument that separation can easily disguise or create inequality is especially problematic for public health advocates attempting to overcome health disparities by targeting specific populations. In the case of the PHS campaigns, for instance, "Youth and Life" and "Keeping Fit: For Negro Boys and Young Men" were signs of progress in U.S. public sex-education efforts because they not only provided women and minorities with information about sex, they provided them with much of the same straightforward information about sex that they provided white males. At the same time, however, in singling out target populations of women and African American men and focusing on their socially accepted differences, these campaigns reiterated common assumptions about traditional gender roles and racial hierarchies and actively reinforced stereotypes that continually fueled those hierarchies. Women, for instance, were encouraged to pay attention to health because doing so would make them look more attractive to others. And African American men viewed images that suggested their inferiority to whites.

Being neither white nor male, African American women were the target of none of these campaigns. Although I found a brief reference to a PHS campaign targeted at African American women in the Social Welfare History Archives at the University of Minnesota, there exists little evidence that this campaign ever reached the public or, for that matter, existed at all.[71] Minority women have long dealt with a double dose of discrimination.[72] The lack of parallelism in the PHS campaigns (a campaign for white men, white women, and African American men but no campaign for African American women) highlighted the ways that individuals who were neither white nor male tended to be overlooked, even by those who were attempting to reach overlooked populations. The challenge for public sex-education programs, then and now, is to ensure that attempts to target difference by segmenting audiences do not also foster inequality, discrimination, or misrepresentation.

In many ways, the Progressive Era and post–World War I years were about compromise among individuals championing public policies and governmental programs without sacrificing cultural norms and economic stability. The rhetoric of the PHS campaigns is a reflection of those types of compromises in that its instigators seemed to realize that to provide underserved populations with accessible information about sex, they would need to build their campaigns around the expected and the normative; they would need to surround what was similar among the campaigns with what was different and culturally accepted. The campaigns' rhetoric of difference functioned as a cover for their similarities regarding sexual information. What may have initially appeared to be a clear effort to inform diverse individuals about health and hygiene was actually a radical undertaking in the sphere of early-twentieth-century sex-education initiatives.

Making the Case in the
Twenty-First Century

In the second decade of the twentieth century, Dr. Ella Flagg Young's strategically fragmented argumentation strategy helped her to garner support for the first sex-education program in U.S. public schools. She integrated arguments in favor of public sex education into other conversations and used the ideologies undergirding those conversations to convince people of their rationality. Because Young never gave speeches or wrote essays exclusively about sex education, choosing instead to advocate for public sex education in more understated ways, she granted audiences the space to consider her appeals without immediately realizing that they were so doing. By the time they focused on the issue at hand, they were likely to see public sex education as rational rather than as scandalous. At that point, they were also more open to educational programs that offered students increasingly direct discussions about sex. Although Young's Chicago Experiment did not last beyond its inaugural year (perhaps because the argumentation strategy she used to build support for her initiative could not withstand direct attack), the program's pro-sex-education vocabulary created an infrastructure for the proliferation of an inclusive model of public educational programs that influenced programs in the years to come.

Several years after Young's Chicago Experiment debuted, social hygienists identified the First World War as an exigency demanding public sex
education for soldiers. Their justification for such education—that the army
would need to stay free of venereal disease to triumph in Europe—led to
widespread support for social-hygiene propaganda targeting the enlisted.
While more straightforward discourse about sex and education circulated
during this time, women, African American soldiers, and many others generally did not have access to such discourse. In fact, as part of their sex education, white soldiers were trained to identify women as either safe or unsafe,
a characterization that implied that women were already either ruined or
inherently innocent and thus did not require sex education in their own
right. Most sex education targeting women also played into a dichotomous
depiction of women as virtuous or wicked and provided readers with vague
lessons offering little content. By the end of the war, the effort to provide
women, African American men, and other underserved populations with
access to sexual information lacked visibility and support.

Fortunately, Dr. Rachelle Slobodinsky Yarros focused her attention
during and after the war on supplying women with accessible information
about sex and building public support for sex-education programs targeting
women from a variety of races and classes. She stood at the intersection
of the professional world of social-hygiene advocacy and the day-to-day
hardships of immigrant and minority women. This position allowed her
to experience her subjectivity as fluid and to draw attention to disparities
in sexual-information delivery. In a 1918 address before the ASHA, Yarros
constituted the association's members in the subject positions of women in
need of sex education. The speech structure framed her arguments about
why women should be targeted by ASHA educational efforts and allowed
her to represent lectures targeted at women, the women who heard the
lectures, and herself in ways that would appeal to ASHA members in her
immediate audience. With this speech, as well as other early speeches and
writings, Yarros played a major role in the movement to make sex education in the United States truly "public" by framing immigrant, minority,
and working-class women as important sex-education audiences.

After the war, organizations such as the U.S. Public Health Service,
influenced by the appeals and direct consultation of Yarros, created several
sex-education poster campaigns. These campaigns included "Keeping Fit,"
"Youth and Life," and "Keeping Fit: For Negro Boys and Young Men."
Today, they exemplify the work that sexual-health advocates did in the post-

war years to negotiate the discursive reticence about sex that many citizens adopted once the "war as exigency" argument was moot. The most obvious feature of these campaigns was that they targeted different audiences, featuring different text and images aimed at white men, white women, and African American men, respectively. But underneath this rhetoric of difference was concealed a surprisingly egalitarian ideology concerning access to public sex education. This unique instantiation of the separate-but-equal philosophy offered more people information about sex than before and during the war, but it also traded in traditional understandings of gender and race to target distinct audiences and appease societal norms. These campaigns serve as examples of early health-disparity work and, by excluding African American women entirely, highlight the fallout health advocates often face when attempting to target specific populations.

The social-hygiene poster campaigns were part of a trend in which sex-education programs in schools and other public institutions became increasingly common. By 1922, the U.S. Bureau of Education found that almost half of all U.S. secondary schools provided male and female students with "social-hygiene education" discussing reproductive biology, venereal diseases, and chastity before marriage.[1] Not even a decade earlier, Young fought to get the first of such programs into a U.S. public-school system. The arguments, appeals, and pro-sex-education vocabularies that female leaders such as Sanger, Young, and Yarros introduced into the public sphere seemed to be taking hold. And with social-hygiene poster campaigns offering white women and African American men approximately the same information about sex that was offered to white men, the movement for public sex education appeared within reach.

Surprisingly, the words of Sanger, Young, and Yarros, as well as the visual messages of the U.S. Public Health Service posters, remain relevant more than eighty years after they were originally circulated. This is striking because unlike the turn of the century, when sex education was sparse, almost 90 percent of today's public secondary-school students in the United States will take at least one sex-education course before they graduate.[2] From this perspective, the public's access to sex education appears to have radically improved over time. But, although much has happened since the emergence of public sex education in the United States, including this growth in public sex-education availability, much has also stayed the same. Young people in the United States still suffer from high rates of venereal diseases (now sexually transmitted infections, or STIs), unintended pregnancies, and

abortions, comparatively higher than those in other developed countries. And racial minorities such as African Americans and Hispanics suffer from disproportionately higher rates of HIV/AIDS and other STIs.[3] There are more sex-education programs in schools today, but the sheer quantity of programs says little about their quality. Comparisons between historical and contemporary discourses indicate that rhetoric concerning public sex education still features many of the ideological foundations and rhetorical patterns that defined it at its emergence.

Public sex education remains a highly controversial topic in the United States, although the question is less about whether public institutions should offer sex education (an issue that was largely decided during World War I and the postwar era) and more about choosing a sex-education curriculum appropriate for students. Contemporary Comstockians, those who believe that public discussions about sex are inappropriate (unless those discussions concern the evils of nonmarital sex), exist. In a number of cases, these present-day vice reformers have found inadequate public support for their arguments, especially in light of mounting evidence that sex-education programs do not inadvertently encourage premarital sex.[4] Those against all forms of sex education in the schools sometimes choose to educate their children at home or in private schools rather than fight a seemingly interminable battle to remove sex-education curricula entirely from the public schools.[5]

Other manifestations of late-nineteenth-century ideologies concerning sex education persist as well, although the lines separating them blend and waver. If they were around today, Progressive Era social purists, those who tended to equate sex with danger, disease, and death, would probably endorse the use of abstinence-only-until-marriage curricula in the public schools. Beyond the practice of framing sex outside of marriage as dangerous and immoral, Progressive Era social purists would also identify with abstinence-only advocates because their programs have a history of being religiously oriented. Today, many of the major distributors of abstinence-only educational programs such as Respect, Inc., and Teen-Aid are developed in and remain connected to evangelical Christian churches.[6]

In contrast to social purists, social hygienists, those who tended to justify sex education by viewing it through the lenses of empiricism and science would probably support comprehensive sex-education programs. Their position would be grounded in research demonstrating that these programs have the most success in protecting young people from STIs and unplanned pregnancies.[7] Indeed, the American Social Health Association, the successor to the Progressive Era's American Social Hygiene Association, openly supports comprehensive sexuality education for grades kindergarten through twelve, specifically those programs that include "medically accurate and developmentally appropriate discussions of sexuality, reproduction, fertility, methods of contraception, decision-making, delaying first intercourse, abstinence, risk assessment and risk reduction, and sexually transmitted disease preventing, with special emphasis placed on the human immunodeficiency virus."[8] Comprehensive sex-education programs often emphasize the value of abstinence, but they also provide students with "scientific" information about contraception and safe sex outside of marriage. These programs are designed to respond to statistics demonstrating that many teens and unmarried people in the United States will not abstain from sex, will have more than one sexual partner, and will engage in oral and anal sex.[9]

Progressive Era free lovers would probably align themselves with today's sex-affirmative movement, whose supporters endorse an open, nonjudgmental attitude toward sexuality in its myriad forms of expression. Sex-affirmativists generally argue that a society that accepts a range of non-coercive sexual activities among individuals will foster healthier citizens and decrease sexual crime.[10] Progressive Era free lovers might also agree with the sociologist Janice Irvine that "comprehensive" has become a code word for "abstinence-plus" education, or programs that emphasize abstinence and teach students about contraception but offer them little to no information about topics such as homosexuality, abortion, sexual pleasure, or masturbation.[11] During a speaking tour in 1997, Leslie M. Kantor, the education director of the Sexuality Information and Education Council of the United States, claimed, "There is mainstream sex ed and there is right-wing sex ed. But there is no left-wing sex education in America. Everyone calls themselves 'abstinence educators.' Everyone."[12] Kantor's point is that only a discourse that, at some level, frames abstinence as the ideal for all young people, that discusses sexuality as something they should repress until marriage, will find an audience in contemporary American society. Similarly, Dr. Joycelyn Elders, who in 1994 was asked by President Bill Clinton to step down from her position as U.S. Surgeon General after publicly suggesting that masturbation might be a topic that should be taught in schools, recently argued that "our society remains unwilling to make sexuality part of a comprehensive health education program in the schools and anxious to the point of hysteria about young people and sex."[13] Given the free lovers' fight to abolish state-sponsored marriage and accept sexuality as a natural part of the human experience, they would almost certainly contest any program suggesting that people should abstain from sex until marriage. They might point out, like contemporary critics of abstinence-only and abstinence-plus curricula, that this instruction does not account for the experiences of gays, lesbians, and transsexuals who cannot legally marry and heterosexuals who reject state-sponsored marriage.

Contemporary discourse about public sex education includes numerous examples of ambiguity. This may come as no surprise in that many of the variables still exist that made it necessary for early sex-education advocates to use ambiguous language to communicate about sex education (e.g., societal taboos about discussing sex and children; laws censoring materials deemed obscene). One need look only as far as the titles of contemporary sex-education curricula for examples of strategic ambiguity. What is, after all, an "abstinence-only" sex-education program? One might argue that teaching only about abstinence is the opposite of providing sex education, in the same way that one might have argued in the late nineteenth century that "social-purity" programs, with titles seemingly promoting both sex and chastity, were nonsensical. Far from being nonsensical, however, abstinence-only sex-education programs, like social-purity programs of yore, seem to be so named to provide different audiences with distinct senses of their goals and meanings. On the one hand, the appeal to "abstinence-only" education resonates with the purveyors of government funds who require grantees to teach students to abstain from sex until they are married. On the other hand, the "sex education" aspect of the title assures concerned parents and educators that, although the program emphasizes abstinence, students are still learning what they need to know about sex to safely navigate their environments.

So-called abstinence-plus sex-education programs function in similar ways. Given that the "plus" in the title can brand a program as less deserving of certain kinds of federal support, one might wonder why these programs continue to include "abstinence" in their monikers. The answer most likely is that a focus on abstinence assures anxious parents, representatives of religious groups, and right-wing politicians that these programs are working, first and foremost, to encourage young people to abstain from sex outside of marriage. The "plus" functions to assure those in favor of "comprehensive" sex-education curricula that the programs provide students with more than a "just say no" message about sex.

To provide a more specific example of ambiguity at work in contemporary debates about public sex education, I turn to transcripts from the

2002 U.S. House of Representatives' hearing on abstinence-only education. During these hearings, Jacqueline Jones del Rosario, the executive director of the abstinence-only advocacy group Recapturing the Vision International, testified in support of renewing Title V of the 1997 Social Security Act. At one point, Rosario claimed that she supported "a comprehensive program."[14] When asked to clarify what she meant, she said, "I was saying 'comprehensive' in terms of holistic education. I just want to make that clear. . . . To make it clear [that programs that discuss more than abstinence and the dangers of sex outside of marriage] are called 'abstinence plus' or 'comprehensive sex education.' And I think we need to clarify our terms."[15] Rosario was implying that because she mentioned a "comprehensive" and not a "comprehensive sex-education" program, she was obviously referring to abstinence-only education. A more likely story, however, was that Rosario was using the term "comprehensive" to refer to abstinence-only curricula in an attempt to appeal to abstinence-only advocates and critics alike, which would mean that her emphasis on clarity was probably an attempt to obscure her strategically ambiguous language.

But abstinence-only advocates are hardly the only ones using ambiguous language to talk about sex education. As Kantor and Elders explain, increasing numbers of comprehensive-sex-education advocates are using the language of their abstinence-only counterparts to describe their curricula, implying that they offer students no more than an abstinence-plus educational program. Just as early debates over public sex education were built, by and large, upon a foundation of ambiguous language, the same seems to be the case for the contemporary debate over public sex-education curricula. Thus, those who are most straightforward when talking about sex education will suffer the most censure and have the least success in getting their programs into the classroom. But curricula packed with ambiguous phrases about, for instance, what it means to be sexually active will serve to confuse students more than to educate them. Such communicative patterns work to get certain programs approved by multiple audiences and then work against the programs' intended goal: education. From this perspective, one of the reasons behind the country's continued high rates of STIs and other sexual-health problems is the foundation of ambiguity that public sex-education discourses continue to utilize after all these years.

But while the ambiguous language of years past continues to linger in contemporary discourse about sex education, the creative strategies that Young and Yarros used to navigate ambiguous language and alleviate disparities in health care generally do not. Dr. Ella Flagg Young's efforts to insert arguments in favor of sex education into other conversations to convince audiences of her arguments' validity stand in stark contrast to most arguments about sex education today. According to the sociologist Janice Irvine, contemporary arguments about sex education are rarely subtle. Instead, debates often become shouting matches, complete with fainting participants, police escorts, angry protestors, and exaggerated news coverage.[16] Most debaters come to these disputes with an unwavering agenda, less interested in listening than in expressing their devotion to a single position. Their rhetoric tends to be hostile, pointed, focused specifically on public sex education, and emotional. That said, many debates about sex education from the Progressive Era were hardly rational, calm, orderly affairs either, and Young's strategically fragmented argumentation strategy helped her to sidestep the circus that was those debates and draw from other, more convincing, rhetorical resources. Young's experience demonstrates that an advocate does not have to, and sometimes is not wise to, author individual speeches dedicated to forcefully addressing a controversial topic. A strategically fragmented approach can sometimes prove to be more persuasive to audiences because it may catch them unawares. And, in an increasingly technological society that is far more mediated and fast-paced than that of the early twentieth century, strategically fragmented arguments about public sex education could allow rhetors to fit into existing patterns of information circulation.

Dr. Rachelle Slobodinsky Yarros's speech-within-a-speech structure is more than an obscure artifact from the past. Rhetoric formatted in this way could serve as a mediating strategy, which would be useful to those interested in moderating the heated contemporary battles over sex-education curricula. For instance, a contemporary health advocate with ties to both abstinence-only and comprehensive sex-education organizations could appropriate this structure and use it to convince each group that the other represents a potential ally in efforts to improve public health. The great degree of control that this structure grants a speaker could allow the speaker to, for instance, constitute comprehensive sexual educators in the position of abstinence-only educators, or vice versa. Probably one of the most important lessons that Yarros exemplified in her speech before the ASHA is that sex-education policy often moves forward or changes when those in power are convinced that changes in policy will work in their favor. Simply making sound, rational arguments about the benefits of sex-education programs for underserved populations will only go so far in bringing about change. The way arguments are presented is often more important than the arguments themselves.

As one would expect, the use of visual images in contemporary sex-education curricula has moved far beyond the posters, slides, and pamphlets of the early twentieth century, although those media are still common. Today, sex-education curricula and information take the form of films, Web sites, and even video games. Messages about safe sex practices and sexual risk are embedded into popular television shows,[17] and abstinence-only groups sponsor traveling concert series with motivational speakers, music, lighting, and performances. Over the last decade, several abstinence-only organizations have marketed a variety of consumer products, including t-shirts, hats, key chains, mugs, lollipops, stickers, and rings sporting messages such as "waiting until marriage," "abstinence is for virgins," and "pants, keep them on." Some of these visually oriented artifacts highlight the gendered narratives that, in many cases, still pervade contemporary attempts at public sex education. Not surprisingly, while the Silver Ring Thing Web site offers shoppers a "good girl" button, it does not offer a corresponding "good boy" button.[18] Just as women were dichotomized in social-hygiene materials circulating during World War I, the Silver Ring Thing buttons play off of characterizations of women as either safe or unsafe depending on their degree of sexual experience outside of marriage. Women today often have access to public sex education (as Sanger, Young, and Yarros worked so diligently to ensure years earlier), but that education may contain harmful, stereotypical accounts of women that are not conducive to their learning (a situation resembling that of the postwar social-hygiene campaigns targeting white women and African American men).

In *A. C. Green's Game Plan: Abstinence Program*, a program utilized in many public-school curricula throughout the country, students are encouraged to make a "game plan" for their lives that does not include premarital sex, a game plan very similar to the one that the former L.A. Lakers' basketball star A. C. Green supposedly made when he was in school.[19] The textbook's self-proclaimed theme is competitive sports, and many of the photographs featured in the book are of people playing sports or holding sporting equipment. The overwhelming majority of these photographs (seventeen out of twenty) feature males. Photographs of females in the textbook are more likely to show them laughing with friends, posing for the camera, or cheering from the sidelines. After viewing these photographs, students might assume that men, not women, are the target audience for this textbook. They might also conclude that men need a game plan to protect themselves from bad girls, the ones trying to whisper sweet, premarital nothings into their ears, and to save themselves for good girls, the ones cheering for them on the sidelines and waiting for their own game to begin in marriage. This conclusion provides audiences, regardless of sex, with a potentially damaging sense of self and others and a skewed perception of how to maintain sexual health.

The visual and textual rhetoric of targeting difference during the post–World War I era is evident today in the growing attention that public health scholars are devoting to alleviating health disparities among distinct segments of the population; but whether or not that rhetoric of difference is working to cover up other aspects of contemporary sex-education discourse remains to be seen. As the previous two examples demonstrate, the differences between sex-education messages aimed at girls and those aimed at boys are often explicit. Several contemporary sex-education programs like Silver Ring Thing and Project Reality, the distributor of *A. C. Green's Game Plan*, communicate different information and values about sex to audiences of different sexes. In this respect, contemporary sex-education messages may not be continuing the trend evident in the U.S. Public Health Service posters of offering women and men equivalent information about sex.

In some ways, assessing whether contemporary sex education offers different messages about sex to members of different races or classes is especially difficult because, unlike with gender, markers of race and class are not necessarily evident within language. Photographs featured in textbooks such as *A. C. Green's Game Plan* and on sex-education Web sites such as Sex, Etc., and Coalition for Positive Sexuality seem to be designed to speak to young people from a variety of racial and ethnic backgrounds by featuring African Americans, Asians, Hispanics, Indians, and Caucasians.[20] However, a recent study on sex education in public schools found that some regions with high numbers of non-English-speaking students did not provide adequate translated materials to accommodate that population. These findings indicate that some members of underserved populations do not have access to the information about sex that is available to their English-speaking peers. In this light, efforts to offer sex education to diverse publics will require new communicative approaches and growing support in the years to come.[21]

If they were alive today, Sanger, Young, and Yarros would be pleased to learn that public sex education is now offered in most public U.S. secondary schools—that is, until they began to review scholarly evaluations of existing programs. For example, researchers from Indiana University's Center for Sexual Health Promotion recently reported that sex-education programs in Florida's public schools were very short, offered later than students needed them, not accessible to every student, neither uniform in content nor in instructor training, and lacked quality-assurance or evaluation standards.[22] In this respect, the nation supports public sex education in only the most superficial sense. In the early 1900s, Young argued that schools needed to provide students with the training and information that would allow them to safely and successfully navigate their environments, and her reasoning on this front is still poignant. Today, young people's environments frequently include exposure to risky sexual activity, unintended pregnancies, and STIs. Federal funding policies that require instructors to deny students information about topics such as condoms, abortion, and homosexuality set the nation up for inheriting a generation of citizens who are unprepared to lead the country into the future.

Yarros's early attention to disparities in health care among underserved populations is also telling in the present situation. A nation that fails to provide adequate sex education to non-English-speaking and/or minority students invites negative repercussions for those students and the sexual health of society at large. Yarros's attempts to help those in power see the world through the eyes of those who needed information about sex but had no access to it would probably be just as eye-opening for many contemporary audiences as they were for early-twentieth-century ASHA members. And the social-hygiene poster campaigns for which Yarros served as a consultant offered publics a reasonably standardized, instructive discussion of sexual health, which, according to recent studies, is more than can be said for many sex-education programs in today's middle and high schools.[23]

So despite the country's rich history of public sex-education advocacy and the innovative rhetorical strategies advocates used to gain support for public sex education in the early twentieth century, discourse about public sex education in the contemporary United States is driven by ambiguous language and produces programs that fail to foster sexually healthy individuals. Like Sanger, Young, and Yarros, today's health advocates must utilize innovative discursive tools to create support for public sex-education programs. And these programs must be imbued with the infrastructure to allow educators the training and ability to answer students' questions about sex in an accessible manner. Ideally, there will come a time when people representing different factions in the public sex-education debates will communicate in ways that allow them to understand each other more clearly, not less; when the lines between abstinence-only, abstinence-plus, and comprehensive sex education will be easy to decipher; and when everyone will have access to the sexual information they seek regardless of their sex, race, or class. History demonstrates that the terms health advocates use, narratives they tell, and arguments they make will enable (or disable) that process.

Notes

INTRODUCTION

1. U.S. House of Representatives, Committee on Ways and Means, *Summary of Welfare Reforms Made by Public Law 104–196*, 76; Irvine, *Talk about Sex*, 191.

2. Guttmacher Institute, *Facts in Brief.*

3. For examples of such studies, see Brückner and Bearman, "After the Promise," 271–78; Guttmacher Institute, *Sex Education: Needs, Programs, and Policies;* Jemmott, Jemmott, and Fong, "Abstinence and Safer Sex HIV Risk-Reduction Interventions for African American Adolescents," 1529–36; Santelli, Ott, Lyon, Rogers, Summers, and Schleifer, "Abstinence and Abstinence-Only Education," 72–81.

4. Saussure, *Course in General Linguistics.*

5. Peters, *Speaking into the Air.*

6. D'Emilio and Freedman, *Intimate Matters,* 365; Dubois and Gordon, "Seeking Ecstasy on the Battlefield," 20.

7. Bailey, *From Front Porch to Back Seat,* 74; D'Emilio and Freedman, *Intimate Matters,* 242–43.

8. Foucault, *History of Sexuality,* 8.

9. Borda, "Woman Suffrage in the Progressive Era: A Coming of Age," 340.

10. Horowitz, *Rereading Sex,* 382; Reed, *From Private Vice to Public Virtue,* 37.

11. Tomes, *Gospel of Germs.*

12. Hogan, *Rhetoric and Reform of the Progressive Era,* xiii.

13. Ball, "Theoretical Implications of Doing Rhetorical History," 62.

14. Campbell, *Critical Study of Early Feminist Rhetoric.*

15. Leff, "Interpretation and the Art of the Rhetorical Critic," 339; Lucas, "Renaissance of American Public Address," 253.

16. McKerrow, "Critical Rhetoric," 101. See also McGee, "Text, Context, and the Fragmentation of Contemporary Culture"; Dow, "Response Criticism and Authority in the Artistic Mode."

17. Finnegan, "Review Essay." Finnegan argues that visual artifacts are inherently rhetorical and thus not in opposition to textual artifacts.

18. Benson, "Respecting the Reader." For a discussion of visual argumentation, see Birdsell and Groarke, "Toward a Theory of Visual Argument"; Blair, "Possibility and Actuality of Visual Arguments."

19. Crenshaw, "Mapping the Margins," 173.

20. Davis, "Intersectionality as Buzzword," 79.

21. Haslett, "Yarros, Rachelle Slobodinsky," 998–1001.

22. Yarros's roles as a social activist and physician are mentioned in passing in

Chesler, *Women of Valor,* 226–27, 344–45; and Kennedy, *Birth Control in America,* 174.

23. University of Minnesota Libraries, "Social Hygiene Poster Campaigns in the 1920s."

24. "Keeping Fit: An Exhibit for Young Men and Boys," 1918, box 171, folder 8, American Social Hygiene Association Records, Social Welfare History Archives, University of Minnesota; "Youth and Life: An Exhibit for Girls and Young Women," 1922, box 171, folder 10, American Social Hygiene Association Records, Social Welfare History Archives, University of Minnesota; "Keeping Fit: For Negro Boys and Young Men," 1922, unfiled, American Social Hygiene Association Records, Social Welfare History Archives, University of Minnesota. For mention of the poster campaign targeted at African American women, see "Catalog of Social Hygiene Motion Pictures Slides and Exhibits," n.d., box 171, folder 14, p. 12, American Social Hygiene Association Records, Social Welfare History Archives, University of Minnesota.

25. Sanger, *What Every Girl Should Know;* Sanger, *Family Limitation.*

26. Blount, "Ella Flagg Young and the Chicago Schools," 163; Moran, "Modernism Gone Mad."

27. *Plessy v. Ferguson,* 163 S. Ct. 537 (1896).

CHAPTER 1. ENGAGING AMBIGUOUS DISCOURSE

1. Morrow, *Social Diseases and Marriage,* 384.

2. Link and McCormick, *Progressivism,* 33; McGee, "Rhetoric and Race in the Progressive Era."

3. I use the term "white" to denote what, at this time, was considered the norm or the status quo. The "white identity," according to the historian David R. Roediger and others involved in the critical study of whiteness, is a constructed and constantly changing concept that depends less on race or ethnicity than it does on historically situated cultural hierarchies. For several examples of scholars who frame whiteness in this way, see Hale, *Making Whiteness;* Ignatiev, *How the Irish Became White;* Jacobson, *Whiteness of a Different Color;* Roediger, *Colored White;* Roediger, *Working toward Whiteness.*

4. D'Emilio and Freedman, *Intimate Matters,* 153.

5. Rodrique, "Black Community and the Birth Control Movement," 138–56.

6. The communication scholar Leah Ceccarelli defines "strategic ambiguity" as a form of polysemy (language with multiple denotative meanings) that is "planned by the author and result[s] in two or more otherwise conflicting groups of readers converging in praise of a text" (404). Strategic ambiguity often helps authors to increase their popularity among audiences because what appears to be a singular message can be interpreted in multiple ways, thus opening up the possibility for positive responses from diverse individuals. By contrast, Ceccarelli defines "resistive reading" as a form of polysemy that occurs when a communicator "no longer has control over the denotational meaning of the message" because an outside party interprets the message in a way that subverts his or her intended meaning (400).

Cases of resistive reading usually function so that the author and audience members "[diverge] in conflict over the text" (397). Ceccarelli, "Polysemy."

7. D'Emilio and Freedman, *Intimate Matters*, 56, 60, 183; Moran, "Modernism Gone Mad," 492; Bailey, *From Front Porch to Back Seat*, 78.

8. Dubois and Gordon, "Seeking Ecstasy on the Battlefield," 13; D'Emilio and Freedman, *Intimate Matters*, 181; Moran, *Teaching Sex*, 493.

9. Horowitz, *Rereading Sex*, 369–70.

10. Moran, *Teaching Sex*, 63.

11. For more information about Comstock's life from early-twentieth-century perspectives, see Trumbull, *Anthony Comstock, Fighter*; Broun and Leech, *Anthony Comstock*.

12. Comstock, *Traps for the Young*, 240.

13. Trumbull, *Anthony Comstock*, 233; see also Broun and Leech, *Anthony Comstock*.

14. Comstock, *Traps for the Young*, 240.

15. See Bates, *Weeder in the Garden of the Lord*; Beisel, *Imperiled Innocents*; Bennett, *Anthony Comstock*.

16. Beisel, *Imperiled Innocents*, 39.

17. Comstock, *Traps for the Young*, 245; Beisel, *Imperiled Innocents*, 53–57, 71.

18. Brodie, *Contraception and Abortion in Nineteenth-Century America*; Smith-Rosenberg, "Abortion Movement and the AMA."

19. Horowitz, *Rereading Sex*, 382; Reed, *From Private Vice to Public Virtue*, 37.

20. Brodie, *Contraception and Abortion*, 283, 288; Reed, *From Private Vice to Public Virtue*, 37.

21. *Queen v. Hicklin*, LR 3 QB 360 (1868), qtd. in Beisel, *Imperiled Innocents*, 91, and Bates, *Weeder in the Garden of the Lord*, 141.

22. Hopkins, "Birth Control and Public Morals."

23. Gordon, *Moral Property of Women*, 36.

24. Minor, "O Wicked Flesh."

25. Gordon, *Moral Property of Women*, 73–75.

26. Rosen, *Lost Sisterhood*, 11.

27. Gordon, *Moral Property of Women*, 73.

28. Willard, "White Cross Movement in Education," 171.

29. Comstock, *Traps for the Young*, 25.

30. D'Emilio and Freedman, *Intimate Matters*, 153; Pivar, *Purity and Hygiene*, 3, 48; Newman, *White Women's Rights*, 66–69.

31. Willard, "White Cross Movement in Education," 176.

32. Ibid., 177.

33. Ibid., 167.

34. D'Emilio and Freedman, *Intimate Matters*, 208.

35. Pivar, *Purity and Hygiene*, 120.

36. Ibid., 4; Bristow, *Prostitution and Prejudice*.

37. Brandt, *No Magic Bullet*, 34.

38. Pivar, *Purity and Hygiene*, 48.

39. Willard, "White Cross Movement in Education," 162.

40. Ibid., 173.

41. Horowitz, *Rereading Sex*, 267–68.

42. Ibid., 412; Heywood, *Cupid's Yokes*, 19; Broun and Leech, *Anthony Comstock*, 172.

43. D'Emilio and Freedman, *Intimate Matters*, 163.

44. Heywood, *Cupid's Yokes*, 16.

45. Woodhull, "And the Truth Shall Make You Free," para. 125.

46. Horowitz, *Rereading Sex*, 348.

47. Woodhull, "And the Truth Shall Make You Free," para. 120.

48. "Free Love," 5; "Free Love System," 2.

49. Munnell, "Beecherism and Legalism," 31.

50. Woodhull, "And the Truth Shall Make You Free," para. 86.

51. Ibid., para. 130.

52. Ibid., para. 86.

53. Following Woodhull's speech, her sister gave a lecture before the Cooper Institute claiming that Woodhull's free-love rhetoric outraged her sense of "virtue, honor, and decency." "Opposition to Free Love," 8.

54. Ceccarelli, "Polysemy," 402.

55. Comstock, *Traps for the Young*, 158.

56. Heywood, *Cupid's Yokes*, 19.

57. Woodhull, "And the Truth Shall Make You Free," para. 133.

58. Gordon, *Moral Property of Women*, 126; Gordon, "Voluntary Motherhood," 263.

59. Broun and Leech, *Anthony Comstock*, 107; Horowitz, *Rereading Sex*, 397.

60. Broun and Leech, *Anthony Comstock*, 212.

61. Beisel, *Imperiled Innocents*, 87, 89.

62. Ibid., 92.

63. Pivar, *Purity and Hygiene*, 26.

64. Ibid.; Brandt, *No Magic Bullet*, 40.

65. Brandt, *No Magic Bullet*, 204.

66. Kelves, *In the Name of Eugenics*, ix.

67. Pivar, *Purity and Hygiene*, 151; Kelves, *In the Name of Eugenics*, 20, 71.

68. Hasian, *Rhetoric of Eugenics in Anglo-American Thought*, 73.

69. Gordon, *Moral Property of Women*, 86, 89; Brandt, *No Magic Bullet*, 7; Brodie, *Contraception and Abortion in Nineteenth-Century America*, 261.

70. Roosevelt, "On American Motherhood."

71. Roosevelt, *Foes of Our Own Household*, 263.

72. Gordon, *Moral Property of Women*, 90; Kelves, *In the Name of Eugenics*, 92, 99–100; Pivar, *Purity and Hygiene*, 147.

73. Morrow, *Social Diseases and Marriage*, 331 (emphasis added).

74. Brandt, *No Magic Bullet*, 24; Moran, *Teaching Sex*, 26, 31.

75. Ceccarelli, "Polysemy," 407.

76. Morrow, *Social Diseases and Marriage*, 34.

77. Burnham, "The Progressive Era Revolution in American Attitudes toward Sex," 896. See also Carter, "Birds, Bees, and Venereal Disease."

78. Pivar, *Purity and Hygiene*, xi, 29

79. Moran, *Teaching Sex*, 32.

80. D'Emilio and Freedman, *Intimate Matters*, 205.

81. Moran, *Teaching Sex*, 35.

82. Eliot, "School Instruction in Sex Hygiene," 596. See also Brandt, *No Magic Bullet*, 27, 30.

83. Moran, *Teaching Sex*, 37.

84. Moran, "Modernism Gone Mad," 499.

85. D'Emilio and Freedman, *Intimate Matters*, 47.

86. The historian Judith Schwarz notes that Sanger spoke to the members of Heterodoxy and was disappointed at their lack of support for her sex-education and birth-control initiatives. Schwarz, *Radical Feminists of Heterodoxy*, 81–82; Sanger, *Margaret Sanger*, 108.

87. Sanger, "Comstockery in America," 48.

88. Reed, *From Private Vice to Public Virtue*, 77.

89. Ibid., 78.

90. Ibid., 106.

91. Chesler, *Woman of Valor*, 22, 39.

92. Sanger, *What Every Girl Should Know*, 80.

93. Haller, *Eugenics*, 89.

94. Gray, *Margaret Sanger*, 41.

95. Ibid., 43; Kennedy, *Birth Control in America*, 16.

96. D'Emilio and Freedman, *Intimate Matters*, 60; Gordon, *Moral Property of Women*, 24; May, *End of American Innocence*, 345.

97. Gray, *Margaret Sanger*, 45; Sanger, *What Every Girl Should Know*.

98. Johannessen, Preface, viii.

99. Gordon, *Moral Property of Women*, 143.

100. Johannessen, Preface, xiii; Boston Women's Health Book Collective, *Our Bodies, Ourselves*.

101. Sanger, *What Every Girl Should Know*, 1.

102. Ibid., 26.

103. Ibid., n.p.

104. Ibid., 62.

105. Ibid., 5.

106. Ibid., 5–6.

107. Ibid., 81.

108. Ibid., 3.

109. Ibid., 51.

110. Ibid., 21–22.

111. Ibid., 25.

112. Ibid., 80.

113. Ibid.
114. Ibid., 18.
115. Ibid., 28.
116. Ibid., 33.
117. Masel-Walters, "For the 'Poor Mute Mothers'?," 4.
118. Numerous authors discuss and interpret Sanger's shift in ideology. For examples of this scholarship, see Jensen, "Evolution of Margaret Sanger's 'Family Limitation' Pamphlet," 550; McClearey, "Tremendous Awakening," 185; Murphy, "To Create a Race of Thoroughbreds," 24; Murphy, "Margaret Higgins Sanger," 243.
119. Sanger, "The Aim," 1.
120. Sanger, "Comstockery in America," 46–49.
121. Broun and Leech, *Anthony Comstock*, 231, 243.
122. Sanger, *Family Limitation*.
123. Ibid., 46.
124. Sanger, "Comstockery in America," 49.
125. Jensen, "Evolution of Margaret Sanger's 'Family Limitation' Pamphlet," 548.
126. Sanger, *Family Limitation*, 3–4.
127. Jensen, "Evolution of Margaret Sanger's 'Family Limitation' Pamphlet," 564.
128. Qtd. in Broun and Leech, *Anthony Comstock*, 249.
129. Sanger, *Family Limitation*, 7.

CHAPTER 2. CHAMPIONING THE CHICAGO EXPERIMENT

1. Moran, "Modernism Gone Mad," 501.
2. Qtd. in "Attack Eugenics for High Schools," 8.
3. "Board Ousts Ella F. Young: John D. Sloop Heads Schools," 1; Moran, "Modernism Gone Mad," 507.
4. Keene and Wright, "Shall Sex Hygiene Be Taught in the Public Schools?" 698.
5. Ibid.
6. Moran, "Modernism Gone Mad," 481–513.
7. McKerrow, "Critical Rhetoric," 100. See also Sloop, *Disciplining Gender*, 18. Sloop makes the important point that, from a critical-rhetoric perspective, discursive meaning has a material presence in culture.
8. Chicago Public Library, "Timeline: Key Moments in Chicago Planning"; Herrick, *Chicago Schools*, 38; Boehm, *Popular Culture and the Enduring Myth of Chicago*, 31.
9. Miller, *City of the Century*, 144.
10. Smith, *Urban Disorder and the Shape of Belief*, 11–12.
11. Pierce, *Rise of a Modern City*, 20–63.
12. Ibid., 240.
13. Sinclair, *The Jungle*.
14. Grossman, *Land of Hope*.

15. Pierce, *Rise of a Modern City*, 53–55.

16. Clapp, *Mothers of all Children*.

17. Miller, *City of the Century*, 135; Pierce, *Rise of a Modern City*, 468–69.

18. Miller, *City of the Century*, 122.

19. Pierce, *Rise of a Modern City*, 55.

20. Ibid., 311, 321.

21. Boehm, *Popular Culture and the Enduring Myth of Chicago*, xv.

22. Stead, *If Christ Came to Chicago*; Miller, *City of the Century*, 17.

23. Boehm, *Popular Culture and the Enduring Myth of Chicago*, 80–85; Moran, "Modernism Gone Mad," 492.

24. Smith, *Urban Disorder and the Shape of Belief*, 121.

25. Boehm, *Popular Culture and the Enduring Myth of Chicago*, 69, 71.

26. Pierce, *Rise of a Modern City*, 465.

27. Herrick, *Chicago Schools*, 32.

28. Pierce, *Rise of a Modern City*, 384.

29. The Harper report was a 248-page document detailing the problems of the Chicago Public School system at the end of the nineteenth century. The report was the result of a year-long investigation by a commission established by Mayor Carter Harrison. Although many of the commission's suggestions for improvement were not immediately addressed, the report garnered increased public attention about the state of the schools and their need for reform. See Herrick, *Chicago Schools*, 83–86.

30. Pierce, *Rise of a Modern City*, 394, 397, 487.

31. "A Review of the First Year's Work of the Chicago Society of Social Hygiene," 1908, box 4, folder 1, American Social Hygiene Association Papers, Social Welfare History Archives, University of Minnesota.

32. Ibid.

33. "Sexual Hygiene: A Circular of Information for Young Men," 1908, box 4, folder 1, American Social Hygiene Association Papers, Social Welfare History Archives, University of Minnesota.

34. The historian Jeffrey P. Moran notes that the Chicago Experiment's personal-purity lectures offered girls less information about sex than they offered boys. However, none of the sources I have uncovered during my research provide evidence for this claim. See Moran, "Modernism Gone Mad," 507.

35. Young, "Report of the Superintendent of Schools" (1911), 87.

36. Ibid., 87–88.

37. Qtd. in Young, "Report of the Superintendent of Schools" (1912), 120.

38. Ibid., 121.

39. Ibid.

40. Qtd. in "Attack Eugenics for High Schools," 8.

41. Ella Flagg Young, in "Report of the Sex Education Sessions of the Fourth International Congress on Social Hygiene and the Annual Meeting of the American Federation for Sex Hygiene," 1913, box 2, folder 3, p. 74, American Social Hygiene Association Papers, Social Welfare History Archives, University of Minnesota.

42. "Chicago Teaches Sex Hygiene," 26.

43. Herrick, *Chicago Schools*, 81.

44. Dewey, *Moral Principles in Education*, 5.

45. Lagemann, "Experimenting with Education," 33.

46. Dewey, *Moral Principles in Education*, 6–7.

47. Young, *Isolation in the School.*

48. Qtd. in Fenner and Fishburn, *Pioneer American Educators*, 133.

49. Lagemann, "Experimenting with Education," 31–46.

50. Young, "Report of the Superintendent of Schools" (1911), 105.

51. Dewey, *Moral Principles in Education*, 6.

52. Dewey, *Democracy and Education.*

53. Young, "Review Essay," 6.

54. Young, *Isolation in the School*, 95, 94.

55. McManis, *Ella Flagg Young and a Half-Century of the Chicago Public Schools*, 46.

56. Young, *Ethics in the School*, 24.

57. Young, "Report of the Superintendent of Schools" (1911), 104.

58. Young, "Report of the Sex Education Sessions of the Fourth International Congress on Social Hygiene," 73.

59. Qtd. in "Sex Education in the Schools," 5.

60. "School Boards Scored as Bad for Teachers," 10.

61. Qtd. in "Sex Education in the Schools," 5.

62. Young, "Report of the Superintendent of Schools" (1912), 101.

63. Young, "Report of the Superintendent of Schools" (1911), 87.

64. "The Wrong Course and the Right," 6.

65. Qtd. in "Governor Opposes Teaching on Sex," 1.

66. "Sex Education in the Schools," 4.

67. Qtd. in ibid., 7.

68. Young, "Scientific Method in Education," 144.

69. "Sexual Hygiene: A Circular of Information for Young Men."

70. "A Review of the First Year's Work of the Chicago Society of Social Hygiene."

71. Bigelow, *Sex-Education*, 229.

72. Morrow, *Social Diseases and Marriage*, 345.

73. Ibid., 346.

74. "A Review of the First Year's Work of the Chicago Society of Social Hygiene."

75. Morrow, *Social Diseases and Marriage*, 360–61.

76. Moran, *Teaching Sex*, 31.

77. Young, "Report of the Superintendent of Schools" (1912), 120.

78. Young, "Report of the Sex Education Sessions of the Fourth International Congress on Social Hygiene," 72.

79. Qtd. in "Attack on Eugenics for High Schools," 8.

80. Blount, "Several Aspects of the Teaching of Sex Physiology and Hygiene," 138.

81. Qtd. in "Sex Education in the Schools," 5.

82. Moran, "Modernism Gone Mad," 490.

83. Keene and Wright, "Shall Sex Hygiene Be Taught in the Public Schools?" 695.

84. Qtd. in in Bigelow, *Sex-Education*, 213.

85. *Chicago Citizen*, May 17, 1913, 4; *Chicago Citizen*, July 20, 1912, 4; *Chicago New World*, June 28, 1913, 4; Moran, "Modernism Gone Mad," 504; "Sex Hygiene Teaching," 12.

86. "School Boards Scored as Bad for Teachers," 10.

87. Keene and Wright, "Shall Sex Hygiene Be Taught in the Public Schools?" 700.

88. Engs, *Progressive Era's Health Reform Movement*, 74.

89. Young, "Present Status of Education in America," 184.

90. Ibid., 183.

91. The American *School* Hygiene Association should not be confused with the American *Social* Hygiene Association, although both organizations have been referred to as the ASHA and originated during the Progressive Era. The former organization was dedicated to making physical exercise a standard element of public school curricula, and the latter organization was dedicated to championing scientific public sex-education programs for citizens across the country. ("ASHA" will refer to the American Social Hygiene Association throughout this study.)

92. Engs, *Progressive Era's Health Reform Movement*, 255–56.

93. Young, "Report of the Superintendent of Schools" (1913), 108.

94. Young, "Report of the Superintendent of Schools" (1911), 100.

95. Ibid., 99.

96. Young, "Present Status of Education in America," 184.

97. Young, "Report of the Superintendent of Schools" (1911), 98.

98. Qtd. in "Sex Education in the Schools," 5.

99. Young, "Report of the Sex Education Sessions of the Fourth International Congress on Social Hygiene," 74.

100. "School Boards Scored as Bad for Teachers," 10.

101. Young, "Report of the Sex Education Sessions of the Fourth International Congress on Social Hygiene," 74.

102. Keene and Wright, "Shall Sex Hygiene Be Taught in the Public Schools?" 697.

103. Ibid., 699.

104. "Sex Lectures Unmailable," 3.

105. Qtd. in "Sex Education in the Schools," 6.

106. Moran, "Modernism Gone Mad," 506–8.

107. "Board Ousts Ella F. Young," 1; Moran, "Modernism Gone Mad," 507.

108. "Chicago's New Head of Schools," 2.

109. Young's penchant for sex-education speeches rather than texts may have added to the indirect nature of her appeal because speeches that never appear in print tend to provide critics with less concrete ammunition for attack.

110. Condit, *Decoding Abortion Rhetoric*, 7.

CHAPTER 3. PROPAGATING WARTIME SEX EDUCATION

1. "Placard Exhibits," 1918, box 131, folder 8, American Social Hygiene Association Records, Social Welfare History Archives, University of Minnesota.

2. *Fit to Win: Honor, Love, Success*, 1918, box 131, folder 5, American Social Hygiene Association Records, Social Welfare History Archives, University of Minnesota.

3. Bristow, *Making Men Moral*, 137–78.

4. Brandt, *No Magic Bullet*, 54; Pivar, *Purity and Hygiene*, 9.

5. Clarke, "The Promotion of Social Hygiene in War Time," 189.

6. Spingarn, "The War and Venereal Diseases among Negros," 333.

7. *Fit to Win*, 8.

8. Bristow, *Making Men Moral*, 49.

9. "Women's Share in a National Service," 1918, box 132, folder 7, American Social Hygiene Association Records, Social Welfare History Archives, University of Minnesota.

10. Pivar, *Purity and Hygiene*, 211.

11. Falconer, "Part of the Reformatory Institution in the Elimination of Prostitution," 1.

12. Pivar, *Purity and Hygiene*, 210; Kunzel, *Fallen Women, Problem Girls*, 18.

13. "Army Educational Materials," 1918, box 131, folder 8, p. 12, American Social Hygiene Association Records, Social Welfare History Archives, University of Minnesota.

14. Ibid. .

15. Paul Strong Achilles, "The Effectiveness of Certain Social Hygiene Literature," 1923, box 171, folder 10, p. 13, American Social Hygiene Association Records, Social Welfare History Archives, University of Minnesota.

16. *A Few Facts about Syphilis*, 1918, box 131, folder 3, American Social Hygiene Association Records, Social Welfare History Archives, University of Minnesota; *A Few Facts about Gonorrhea*, 1918, box 131, folder 3, American Social Hygiene Association Records, Social Welfare History Archives, University of Minnesota; see also Achilles, "Effectiveness of Certain Social Hygiene Literature."

17. Bristow, *Making Men Moral*, 34.

18. Brandt, *No Magic Bullet*, 63–64; Bristow, *Making Men Moral*, 19–23.

19. *Fit to Win*.

20. Achilles, "Effectiveness of Certain Social Hygiene Literature," 12, 14.

21. *Fit to Win*.

22. *Colonel Care Says*, 1918, box 131, folder 6, American Social Hygiene Association Records, Social Welfare History Archives, University of Minnesota.

23. Ibid.

24. Ibid., 4.

25. Bristow, *Making Men Moral*, 115.

26. "Hello, Soldier Sport, Want to Have a Good Time?" 1918, box 131, folder 6, American Social Hygiene Association Records, Social Welfare History Archives, University of Minnesota.

27. Ibid.

28. *The Girl You Leave Behind*, 1918, box 131, folder 6, American Social Hygiene Association Records, Social Welfare History Archives, University of Minnesota.

29. Ibid.

30. *Fit to Win.*

31. *The Girl You Leave Behind.*

32. Ibid.

33. Katharine Bement Davis, "Social Hygiene and the War: Woman's Part in the Campaign," 1918, box 131, folder 9, p. 11, American Social Hygiene Association Records, Social Welfare History Archives, University of Minnesota.

34. Bristow, *Making Men Moral*, 114.

35. Ibid., 158–61.

36. Spingarn, "War and Venereal Diseases among Negros," 341.

37. Smith, *Sick and Tired of Being Sick and Tired*, 34; Rodrique, "Black Community and the Birth Control Movement"; Bristow, *Making Men Moral*, 160.

38. Gamble, *Germs Have No Color Line;* Terry, "The Negro, a Public Health Problem," 459.

39. Allen, "Negro Health Problem," 194.

40. Jones, *Bad Blood*, 24.

41. Gamble, *Germs Have No Color Line.* See also Haller, *Outcasts from Evolution*, 40–68.

42. Du Bois, *Philadelphia Negro*, 195–96.

43. Boas, "Relative Prevalence of Syphilis among Negros and Whites," 610.

44. Murrell, "Syphilis and the American Negro," 847. See also Jones, *Bad Blood*, 24–27.

45. Spingarn, "War and Venereal Diseases among Negros," 333.

46. Ibid., 343.

47. Bristow, *Making Men Moral*, 173.

48. Ibid., 139.

49. Barbeau and Henri, *Unknown Soldiers*, 21–26.

50. Bristow, *Making Men Moral*, 161.

51. Osborne, "The Law Enforcement Program Applied," 83.

52. Barbeau and Henri, *Unknown Soldiers*, 9; Du Bois, "Perpetual Dilemma," 270–71.

53. Ellis, *Race, War, and Surveillance*, 9.

54. Bristow, *Making Men Moral*, 139–44.

55. Robertson, *Christian Sisterhood, Race Relations, and the YWCA*, 52–53.

56. *Colonel Care Says*, 1.

57. Bristow, *Making Men Moral*, 151.

58. Brandt, *No Magic Bullet*, 116.

59. Bristow, *Making Men Moral;* Colwell, "End of the Road."

60. *The End of the Road*, 1918, box 131, folder 8, p. 14, American Social Hygiene Association Records, Social Welfare History Archives, University of Minnesota.

61. Bristow, *Making Men Moral*, 91–93.

62. Davis, "Social Hygiene and the War," 9.

63. "Any Soldier or Sailor," 1918, box 132, folder 7, American Social Hygiene Association Records, Social Welfare History Archives, University of Minnesota.

64. *The End of the Road,* 14.

65. See, for example, Campbell, *Critical Study of Early Feminist Rhetoric,* 46; Mattingly, *Well-Tempered Women,* 126; Zaeske, *Signatures of Citizenship,* 43.

66. *Do Your Part,* 1918, box 132, folder 7, American Social Hygiene Association Records, Social Welfare History Archives, University of Minnesota.

67. Davis, "Woman's Part in Social Hygiene," 527.

68. Mabel S. Ulrich, "For a New World: The Girl's Part," 1918, box 132, folder 7, p. 15, American Social Hygiene Association Records, Social Welfare History Archives, University of Minnesota.

69. Mabel S. Ulrich, "Mothers of America," 1918, box 132, folder 7, p. 15, American Social Hygiene Association Records, Social Welfare History Archives, University of Minnesota.

70. Ulrich, "For a New World," 7.

71. Smith, *Sick and Tired of Being Sick and Tired,* 34; Rodrique, "Black Community and the Birth Control Movement," 138–56.

72. *Fit to Win,* 3.

CHAPTER 4. SPEAKING FOR WOMEN AT WAR'S END

1. Yarros, "Experiences of a Lecturer."

2. "Dr. Rachelle S. Yarros"; Haslett, "Yarros, Rachelle Slobodinsky"; Ward, "Yarros, Rachelle Slobodinksy."

3. Flanagan, *Seeing with Their Hearts,* 118; Zinn and Dill, "Theorizing Difference from Multiracial Feminism"; Shields, "Gender."

4. Yarros, "From Obstetrics to Social Hygiene"; Yarros, "Experiences of a Lecturer."

5. Engs, *Progressive Era's Health Reform Movement,* 22–23.

6. Eliot, "American Social Hygiene Association."

7. William F. Snow, "Progress, 1900–1915," 1916, box 1, folder 1, p. 2, American Social Hygiene Association Records, Social Welfare History Archives, University of Minnesota.

8. American Social Health Association, *Celebrating Eighty Years,* 7–9.

9. Katharine Bement Davis, "Social Hygiene and the War: Woman's Part in the Campaign," 1918, box 131, folder 9, p. 6, American Social Hygiene Association Records, Social Welfare History Archives, University of Minnesota.

10. Clarke, *Taboo;* Moran, *Teaching Sex,* 40–41; American Social Health Association, *Celebrating Eighty Years,* 2–5.

11. Kleinschmidt, "Is Education a Worth-while Factor in the Control of Venereal Diseases?"; Goodman, "Puerto Rican Experiment"; Bradley, "Social Hygiene Sergeant."

12. Davis, "Woman's Part in Social Hygiene"; Rippin, "Social Hygiene and the War: Work with Women and Girls."

13. French, "Need for Industrial Homes for Women."

14. Johnson, "Adequate Reproduction," 226.
15. Eliot, "American Social Hygiene Association," 2.
16. Engs, *Progressive Era's Health Reform Movement*, 107, 115–16; Hasian, *Rhetoric of Eugenics in Anglo-American Thought*, 48–49.
17. Morantz-Sanchez, *Sympathy and Science*, 232.
18. Charles S. Bacon, "Rachelle Yarros, 1869–1946," *Proceedings of the Institute of Medicine of Chicago*, 1946, box 1, folder 4, pp. 257–58, Rachelle and Victor Yarros Collection, Special Collections Library, University of Illinois at Chicago; Haslett, "Yarros, Rachelle Slobodinsky," 998–1001; Patrician Spain Ward, "The Chicago Birth Control Debate: Dr. Rachelle Yarros of the University of Illinois at Chicago vs. Herman Bundesen Commissioner of Health," 1990, Patricia Spain Ward Papers, Special Collections Library, University of Illinois at Chicago.
19. Yarros, "From Obstetrics to Social Hygiene," 309.
20. Ibid., 308.
21. Ibid., 307.
22. Ibid., 309.
23. Yarros, "Experiences of a Lecturer," 211.
24. Ibid., 215.
25. Davis, "Social Hygiene and the War," 16.
26. Yarros, "Experiences of a Lecturer," 216.
27. Ibid., 215.
28. Ibid., 220.
29. Ibid., 208.
30. Ibid.
31. Davis, "Social Hygiene and the War," 15.
32. Yarros, "Experiences of a Lecturer," 213.
33. Ibid., 212.
34. Ibid., 218.
35. Yarros, "Prostitute as a Health and Social Problem," 222.
36. Yarros, "Experiences of a Lecturer," 218.
37. Ibid., 219–20.
38. Ibid., 220.
39. Ibid.
40. *Investing for the Future*, 1919, box 142, folder 11, American Social Hygiene Association Records, Social Welfare History Archives, University of Minnesota; Kline, *Building a Better Race*, 46–47.
41. "Steps to Save the Girls Taken by Clubwomen," 10.
42. Yarros, "Experiences of a Lecturer," 222.
43. Charland, "Constitutive Rhetoric," 140.
44. Burke, *Rhetoric of Motives*.
45. Yarros, "Experiences of a Lecturer," 208.
46. Yarros, "Prostitute as a Health and Social Problem," 221.
47. Yarros, "Experiences of a Lecturer," 207.
48. Ibid., 220.

49. Kunzel, *Fallen Women, Problem Girls,* 17.
50. Yarros, "Experiences of a Lecturer," 211.
51. Ibid., 219.
52. Ibid., 212.
53. Ibid.
54. Ibid.
55. Yarros, "Medical Women of Tomorrow," 148.
56. For example, Stephen H. Browne describes how Theodore Weld's 1839 book *American Slavery as It Is* represented the slave in ways that encouraged northerners, who were often sympathetic to antislavery causes, to join the abolitionist movement. Weld's book allowed people who generally did not have the opportunity to "see" slavery to witness its evils, and in this way it encouraged them to move from tacit support for abolition to actively putting an end to slavery as an institution. Browne, "Like Gory Spectres."
57. Yarros, "Experiences of a Lecturer," 207.
58. Burke, "Rhetoric of Hitler's 'Battle.'"
59. Hall, *Representation,* 225.
60. Yarros, "Experiences of a Lecturer," 219.
61. Yarros, "Some Practical Aspects of Birth Control," 605.
62. Yarros, "Experiences of a Lecturer," 221.
63. Ibid.
64. Ibid., 222.
65. Ibid.
66. Ibid., 213.
67. Ibid., 207–8.
68. Ibid., 214.
69. Ibid., 211.
70. Ibid., 220.
71. Ibid., 205.
72. Ibid.
73. Ibid., 206.
74. Ibid.
75. Ibid., 212–13.
76. Ibid., 209.
77. Ibid., 218.
78. Collins, *Black Feminist Thought,* 18.
79. Alcoff, "The Problem of Speaking for Others."
80. Ibid.
81. Burke, *Rhetoric of Motives,* 56.
82. For examples of Yarros implying she was driven to speak about public sex education because of gaps in health care delineated by class, race, and gender, see Yarros, "From Obstetrics to Social Hygiene," 305–9; Yarros, "Prostitution, Promiscuity, and Venereal Disease"; Yarros, "Women Physicians and the Problems of Women."

CHAPTER 5. CAMPAIGNING FOR "SEPARATE BUT EQUAL"

1. "Keeping Fit: An Exhibit for Young Men and Boys," 1918, box 171, folder 8, American Social Hygiene Association Records, Social Welfare History Archives, University of Minnesota; "Youth and Life: An Exhibit for Girls and Young Women," 1922, box 171, folder 10, American Social Hygiene Association Records, Social Welfare History Archives, University of Minnesota; "Keeping Fit: For Negro Boys and Young Men," 1922, unfiled, American Social Hygiene Association Records, Social Welfare History Archives, University of Minnesota. This last campaign was discovered during a visit I made to the archives in March 2006; the campaign had not yet been filed in the archive.

2. Lord, "Naturally Clean and Wholesome," 430.

3. Yarros, "Experiences of a Lecturer," 207.

4. Kline, *Building a Better Race*, 20–29.

5. Moran, *Teaching Sex*, 59–60.

6. U.S. Public Health Service, *Annual Report of the Surgeon General of the Public Health Service of the United States*, 234–35; Moran, *Teaching Sex*, 73; Lord, "Naturally Clean and Wholesome," 427.

7. Pierce, "The Public Health Service Campaign against Venereal Diseases," (emphasis added).

8. Lord, "Models of Masculinity," 129.

9. See National Library of Medicine, "Visual Culture and Health Posters"; and Gallo, *Poster in History*, 193; Stanley, *What Did You Do in the War, Daddy?* 7, 12.

10. Lord, "Models of Masculinity," 133; Gruenberg, *High Schools and Sex Education*, 81.

11. Pierce, "Public Health Service Campaign against Venereal Diseases," 432.

12. Lord, "Models of Masculinity," 146.

13. Ibid., 135.

14. Qtd. in Bristow, *Making Men Moral*, 31.

15. Lord, "Models of Masculinity," 134.

16. "Keeping Fit: An Exhibit for Young Men and Boys," 2.

17. Ibid.

18. Foucault, *Discipline and Punish*.

19. "Youth and Life."

20. Ibid.

21. Lord, "Naturally Clean and Wholesome," 430.

22. Ibid., 439.

23. "Social Hygiene and the Negro," 1923, box 177, folder 8, American Social Hygiene Association Records, Social Welfare History Archives, University of Minnesota.

24. "Catalog of Social Hygiene Motion Pictures Slides and Exhibits," n.d., box 171, folder 14, p. 11, American Social Hygiene Association Records, Social Welfare History Archives, University of Minnesota.

25. "Keeping Fit: For Negro Boys and Young Men."

26. Ibid.

27. Robertson, *Christian Sisterhood, Race Relations, and the YWCA*, 45–70.

28. "Keeping Fit: An Exhibit for Young Men and Boys," n.d., box 171, folder 8, p. 11, American Social Hygiene Association Records, Social Welfare History Archives, University of Minnesota.

29. "Help Him Keep Fit," 1921, box 171, folder 8, American Social Hygiene Association Records, Social Welfare History Archives, University of Minnesota (emphasis added).

30. The idea that images and mental pictures are especially likely to impress into a person's memory can be traced back to the writings of ancient orators. Quintilian, for example, argued that rhetoric "which makes us seem not so much to narrate as to exhibit the actual scene" causes audiences' emotions to "be no less actively stirred than if we were present at the actual occurrence." Quintilian, *Institutio Oratoria*, 434–37.

31. "Cleaning the Windows through which Children View the World," 1925, box 177, folder 7, American Social Hygiene Association Records, Social Welfare History Archives, University of Minnesota.

32. Leighton, "The Lantern Slide and Art History."

33. Sanger, *What Every Girl Should Know*, 32.

34. "Keeping Fit: For Negro Boys and Young Men," 11–12.

35. Ibid.

36. Trachtenberg, "Illustrious Americans," 38.

37. Bederman, *Manliness and Civilization*, 44; Hoganson, *Fighting for American Manhood*, 143–45.

38. Gordon, *Moral Property of Women*, 90; Haller, *Eugenics*, 46.

39. Eberwein, *Sex Ed*, 25, 42.

40. Savedoff, "Escaping Reality," 202.

41. Tomes, *Gospel of Germs*, 92.

42. Eberwein, *Sex Ed*, 5, 15.

43. Lerner, *Black Women in White America*, 163–71; Roberts, *Killing the Black Body*, 10–12.

44. Faderman, *To Believe in Women*, 41.

45. The list of twelve women accompanying the picture of Shaw includes the educator Alice Freedman Palmer, the Belgian nurse Edith Cavell, the actress Ethel Barrymore, the first U.S. female astronomer Maria Mitchell, the poet Elizabeth Barrett Browning, the novelist Mrs. Humphrey Ward, the novelist Mary Roberts Rinehart, the poet Margaret Deland, the opera singer Madame Schumann-Heink, the Polish scientist Madame Curie, the nurse Florence Nightingale, and the reformer Jane Addams.

46. Gallagher and Zagacki, "Visibility and Rhetoric," 178.

47. Berger, *Ways of Seeing*, 47.

48. Ibid., 51.

49. Banner, *American Beauty*, 205–6. See also Conor, *Spectacular Modern Woman*.

50. Conor, *Spectacular Modern Woman*, 133.

51. For scholarship on republican motherhood, see Kerber, *Women of the Republic;* Zagarri, "Morals, Manners, and the Republican Mother." Kerber coined the term "republican motherhood" to refer to the postrevolutionary idea that women could best contribute to society by supporting their husbands and raising healthy citizens. Zagarri builds off of and challenges Kerber's work by claiming that the concept of republican motherhood in America had a number of European antecedents.

52. Kitch, *Girl on the Magazine Cover,* 154–59, 4–5.

53. Ibid., 121.

54. Ibid., 136.

55. Curry, *Modern Mothers in the Heartland;* Apple, "Constructing Mothers"; Tomes, "Private Side of Public Health," 514–15.

56. "Social Hygiene and the Negro."

57. Nichols, "Some Public Health Problems of the Negro," 281.

58. Wiggins and Miller, *Unlevel Playing Field.*

59. Blackwelder, *Styling Jim Crow,* 18.

60. Hale, *Making Whiteness,* 40–41.

61. "Keeping Fit: For Negro Boys and Young Men."

62. Jones, *Bad Blood,* 26.

63. "Catalog of Social Hygiene Motion Pictures, Slides, and Exhibits," n.d., box 171, folder 14, American Social Hygiene Association Records, Social Welfare History Archives, University of Minnesota.

64. Du Bois, *Health and Physique of the Negro American,* 90; Ross, "Health Hazards of Being a Negro," 619.

65. Pivar, *Purity and Hygiene,* 139.

66. Medley, *We as Freemen;* Olsen, *Thin Disguise.*

67. *Plessy v. Ferguson,* 163 S. Ct. 537 (1896).

68. Robertson, *Christian Sisterhood, Race Relations, and the YWCA,* 64–66.

69. *Brown v. Board of Education,* 347 S. Ct. 483 (1954).

70. *Plessy v. Ferguson,* 163 S. Ct. 537 (1896). See also Olsen, *Thin Disguise,* 120.

71. See "Catalog of Social Hygiene Motion Pictures Slides and Exhibits," 12.

72. Collins, *Black Sexual Politics;* hooks, *Ain't I a Woman;* Lorde, *Sister Outsider.*

CONCLUSION. MAKING THE CASE IN THE TWENTY-FIRST CENTURY

1. Edson, *Status of Sex Education in High Schools;* Brandt, *No Magic Bullet,* 30–31.

2. Kaiser Family Foundation, *Sex Education in America.*

3. Guttmacher Institute, *Facts in Brief;* Centers for Disease Control and Prevention, *Eliminating Racial and Ethnic Health Disparities.*

4. Kirby, *Emerging Answers.*

5. Irvine, *Talk about Sex,* 104–5; Starkman and Rajani, "Case of Comprehensive Sex Education."

6. Levine, *Harmful to Minors,* 98–99.

7. Kirby, *Emerging Answers.* For studies that find abstinence-only-until-marriage programs to be ineffective in reducing premarital sex, STIs, and/or unplanned pregnancy, see Goodson, Pruitt, Buhi, Wilson, Rasberry, and Gunnels, *Abstinence Education*

Evaluation; Hauser, *Five Years of Abstinence-Only-until-Marriage Education;* Smith, Dariotis, and Potter, *Evaluation of the Pennsylvania Abstinence Education and Related Services Initiative.*

8. American Social Health Association, "ASHA Position Statements."

9. Centers for Disease Control and Prevention, "Youth Risk Behavior Surveillance"; Hoff, Greene, and Davis, *National Survey of Adolescents and Young Adults.*

10. Johansson, "Sex Negative, Sex Positive."

11. Irvine, *Talk about Sex,* 188.

12. Qtd. in Levine, *Harmful to Minors,* 90.

13. Elders, Foreword, ix; Putzel, "White House Forces Elders to Resign over Remarks," 1.

14. U.S. House of Representatives, Committee on Energy and Commerce, *Welfare Reform,* 87. See also Social Security Act, Title V, Section 510 (1997), Maternal and Child Health Bureau, U.S. Department of Health and Human Services.

15. U.S. House of Representatives, Committee on Energy and Commerce, *Welfare Reform,* 88.

16. Irvine, *Talk about Sex,* 141–43.

17. See Jensen and Jensen, "Entertainment Media and Sexual Health"; Kunkel, Eyal, Finnerty, Biely, and Donnerstein, *Sex on TV 4.*

18. Silver Ring Thing, "Good Girl Button."

19. Project Reality, *A. C. Green's Game Plan.*

20. Ibid.; Sex, Etc., "By Teens for Teens"; Coalition for Positive Sexuality, "Just Say Yes."

21. Bandiera, Jeffries, Dodge, Reece, and Herbenick, "Regional Differences in Sexuality Education on a State Level."

22. Dodge, Zachry, Reece, López, Herbenick, Gant, Tanner, and Martinez, "Sexuality Education in Florida."

23. Ibid.

Bibliography

PRIMARY SOURCES

Achilles, Paul Strong. "The Effectiveness of Certain Social Hygiene Literature." 1923. Box 171, folder 10. American Social Hygiene Association Records, Social Welfare History Archives, University of Minnesota.

Allen, L. C. "The Negro Health Problem." *American Journal of Public Health* 5 (1915): 194–203.

American Social Health Association. "ASHA Position Statements: Comprehensive Sexual Health Education," October 8, 2002; accessed February 27, 2009, http://www.ashastd.org/news/news_stmts_education.cfm.

———. *Celebrating Eighty Years*. Research Triangle Park, N.C.: ASHA, 1994.

"Any Soldier or Sailor." 1918. Box 132, folder 7. American Social Hygiene Association Records, Social Welfare History Archives, University of Minnesota.

"Army Educational Materials." 1918. Box 131, folder 8. American Social Hygiene Association Records, Social Welfare History Archives, University of Minnesota.

"Attack Eugenics for High Schools." *Chicago Daily Tribune*, June 26, 1913.

Bacon, Charles S. "Rachelle Yarros, 1869–1946." *Proceedings of the Institute of Medicine of Chicago*. 1946. Box 1, folder 4. Rachelle and Victor Yarros Collection, Special Collections Library, University of Illinois at Chicago.

Bigelow, Maurice A. *Sex-Education: A Series of Lectures Concerning Knowledge of Sex in Its Relation to Human Life*. New York: Macmillan, 1929.

Blount, R. E. "Several Aspects of the Teaching of Sex Physiology and Hygiene." In *The Child in the City: A Series of Papers Presented at the Conferences Held during the Chicago Child Welfare Exhibit*. Chicago: Manz Engraving Co., 1912. 136–38.

"Board Ousts Ella F. Young: John D. Sloop Heads Schools." *Chicago Daily Tribune*, December 11, 1913.

Boas, Ernst P. "The Relative Prevalence of Syphilis among Negros and Whites." *Social Hygiene* 1 (1915): 610–16.

Boston Women's Health Book Collective, eds. *Our Bodies, Ourselves*. New York: Simon and Schuster, 1976.

Bradley, William Aspenwall. "The Social Hygiene Sergeant." *Social Hygiene* 5 (1919): 193–204.

Broun, Heywood, and Margaret Leech. *Anthony Comstock: Roundsman of the Lord*. New York: Literary Guild of America, 1927.

Brown v. Board of Education. 347 S. Ct. 483 (1954).

"Catalog of Social Hygiene Motion Pictures Slides and Exhibits." N.d. Box 171, folder 14. American Social Hygiene Association Records, Social Welfare History Archives, University of Minnesota.

Chicago Citizen, May 17, 1913, 4; July 20, 1912, 4.

Chicago New World, June 28, 1913, 4.

"Chicago Teaches Sex Hygiene." *Vigilance* 26 (1913): 26.

"Chicago's New Head of Schools." *Chicago Daily Tribune*, December 11, 1913.

Clarke, Charles W. "The Promotion of Social Hygiene in War Time." *Annals* 79 (1918): 178–89.

"Cleaning the Windows through which Children View the World." 1925. Box 177, folder 7. American Social Hygiene Association Records, Social Welfare History Archives, University of Minnesota.

Coalition for Positive Sexuality. "Just Say Yes." Accessed January 3, 2009, http://www.positive.org/Home/index.html.

Colonel Care Says. 1918. Box 131, folder 6. American Social Hygiene Association Records, Social Welfare History Archives, University of Minnesota.

Comstock, Anthony. *Traps for the Young.* Ed. Robert Bremner. 1883; reprint, Cambridge, Mass.: Harvard University Press, 1967.

Davis, Katharine Bement. "Social Hygiene and the War: Woman's Part in the Campaign." 1918. Box 131, folder 9. American Social Hygiene Association Records, Social Welfare History Archives, University of Minnesota.

———. "Woman's Part in Social Hygiene." *Social Hygiene* 4 (1918): 525–60.

Dewey, John. *Democracy and Education: An Introduction to the Philosophy of Education.* New York: Macmillan, 1916.

———. *Moral Principles in Education.* Boston: Houghton Mifflin, 1909.

Do Your Part. 1918. Box 132, folder 7. American Social Hygiene Association Records, Social Welfare History Archives, University of Minnesota.

"Dr. Rachelle S. Yarros." *Journal of Social Hygiene* 32 (1946): 184.

Du Bois, W. E. B., ed. *The Health and Physique of the Negro American: Report of a Social Study Made under the Direction of Atlanta University.* Atlanta: Atlanta University Press, 1906.

———. *The Philadelphia Negro: A Social Study.* 1899; reprint, Philadelphia: University of Pennsylvania Press, 1996.

Edson, Newell W. *Status of Sex Education in High Schools.* Washington, D.C.: U.S. Bureau of Education, 1922.

Eliot, Charles W. "The American Social Hygiene Association." *Social Hygiene* 1 (1914): 1–5.

The End of the Road. 1918. Box 131, folder 8. American Social Hygiene Association Records, Social Welfare History Archives, University of Minnesota.

Falconer, Martha P. "The Part of the Reformatory Institution in the Elimination of Prostitution." *Social Hygiene* 5 (1919): 1–10.

A Few Facts about Gonorrhea. 1918. Box 131, folder 3. American Social Hygiene Association Records, Social Welfare History Archives, University of Minnesota.

A Few Facts about Syphilis. 1918. Box 131, folder 3. American Social Hygiene Association Records, Social Welfare History Archives, University of Minnesota.

Fit to Win: Honor, Love, Success. 1918. Box 131, folder 5. American Social Hygiene Association Records, Social Welfare History Archives, University of Minnesota.

"Free Love: Exposé of the Affairs of the Late 'Unitary Household.'" *New York Times*, September 21, 1860, 5.

"Free Love System: Origin, Progress, and Position of the Anti-Marriage Movement." *New York Times*, September 8, 1855, 2.

French, Allison T. "The Need for Industrial Homes for Women." *Social Hygiene* 5 (1919): 11–14.

The Girl You Leave Behind. 1918. Box 131, folder 6. American Social Hygiene Association Records, Social Welfare History Archives, University of Minnesota.

Goodman, Herman. "The Puerto Rican Experiment." *Social Hygiene* 5 (1919): 185–91.

"Governor Opposes Teaching on Sex." *Chicago Daily Tribune*, December 11, 1913.

Gruenberg, Benjamin C., ed. *High Schools and Sex Education: A Manual of Suggestions on Education Related to Sex.* Washington, D.C.: Government Printing Office, 1922.

"Hello, Soldier Sport, Want to Have a Good Time?" 1918. Box 131, folder 6. American Social Hygiene Association Records, Social Welfare History Archives, University of Minnesota.

"Help Him Keep Fit." 1921. Box 171, folder 8. American Social Hygiene Association Records, Social Welfare History Archives, University of Minnesota.

Heywood, Ezra H. *Cupid's Yokes; or, The Binding Forces of Conjugal Life: An Essay to Consider Some Moral and Physiological Phases of Love and Marriage, Wherein It Is Asserted the Natural Right and Necessity of Sexual Self-Government.* Princeton, Mass.: Co-operative Publishing Co., 1879.

Hopkins, Mary Alden. "Birth Control and Public Morals: An Interview with Anthony Comstock." *Harper's Weekly*, May 22, 1915; accessed January 16, 2006. http://www.expo98.msu.edu/people/Comstock.htm.

"Investing for the Future." 1919. Box 142, folder 11. American Social Hygiene Association Records, Social Welfare History Archives, University of Minnesota.

Johnson, Roswell H. "Adequate Reproduction." *Social Hygiene* 5 (1919): 223–26.

"Keeping Fit: An Exhibit for Young Men and Boys." 1918. Box 171, folder 8. American Social Hygiene Association Records, Social Welfare History Archives, University of Minnesota.

"Keeping Fit: For Negro Boys and Young Men." 1922. Unfiled. American Social Hygiene Association Records, Social Welfare History Archives, University of Minnesota.

Keene, Charles H., and Mabel M. Wright. "Shall Sex Hygiene Be Taught in the Public Schools?" *Journal of Proceedings and Addresses of the Fifty-Second Annual Meeting of the National Education Association* 52 (1914): 695–700.

Kleinschmidt, H. E. "Is Education a Worth-while Factor in the Control of Venereal Diseases?" *Social Hygiene* 5 (1919): 227–31.

McManis, John T. *Ella Flagg Young and a Half-Century of the Chicago Public Schools.* Chicago: A. C. McClurg and Co., 1916.

Minor, Robert. "O Wicked Flesh." *The Masses* (October/November 1912); accessed February 19, 2009, http://www.marxists.org/subject/art/visual_arts/satire/minor/minor4.htm.

Morrow, Prince A. 1909. Correspondence with Mary S. Cobb. Box 1, folder 4. American Social Hygiene Association Papers, Social Welfare History Archives, University of Minnesota.

———. *Social Diseases and Marriage.* New York: Lea Brothers and Co., 1904.

Munnell, Thomas S. "Beecherism and Legalism." *Christian Quarterly* 4 (1872): 31.

Murrell, Thomas W. "Syphilis and the American Negro: A Medico-Sociologic Study." *Journal of the American Medical Association* 54 (1910): 846–49.

Nichols, Franklin O. "Some Public Health Problems of the Negro." *Social Hygiene* 8 (1922): 281–85.

"Opposition to Free Love—Lecture by Mrs. Brooker." *New York Times*, March 8, 1872, 8.

Pierce, C. C. "The Public Health Service Campaign against Venereal Diseases." *Social Hygiene* 5 (1919): 415–39.

"Placard Exhibits." 1918, Box 131, folder 8. American Social Hygiene Association Records, Social Welfare History Archives, University of Minnesota.

Plessy v. Ferguson. 163 S. Ct. 537 (1896).

Project Reality. *A. C. Green's Game Plan: Abstinence Program.* Golf, Ill.: Project Reality, 2006.

Putzel, Michel. "White House Forces Elders to Resign over Remarks." *Boston Globe*, December 11, 1994.

Queen v. Hicklin. LR 3 QB 360 (1868).

Quintilian. *Institutio Oratoria.* Trans. H. E. Butler. Cambridge, Mass.: Harvard University Press, 1961–66.

"A Review of the First Year's Work of the Chicago Society of Social Hygiene." 1908. Box 4, folder 1. American Social Hygiene Association Papers, Social Welfare History Archives, University of Minnesota.

Rippin, Jane Deeter. "Social Hygiene and the War: Work with Women and Girls." *Social Hygiene* 5 (1919): 125–36.

Roosevelt, Theodore. "On American Motherhood." Keynote address, Washington, D.C., March 13, 1905; accessed January 13, 2009, http://www.nationalcenter.org/TRooseveltMotherhood.html.

———. *The Foes of Our Own Household.* New York: George H. Doran Co., 1917.

Ross, Mary. "The Health Hazards of Being a Negro." *The Survey* 50 (1923): 619–20.

Sanger, Margaret H. "The Aim." *Woman Rebel* 1 (1914): 1–2.

———. "Comstockery in America." *International Socialist Review* 16 (1915); accessed January 23, 2009, http://wilde.acs.its.nyu.edu/sanger/documents/show.php?sangerDoc=303242.xml.

———. *Family Limitation.* New York: Review Publishing Co., 1914.

———. *Margaret Sanger: An Autobiography.* New York: W. W. Norton, 1938.

———. *What Every Girl Should Know.* 1914; reprint, New York: Belvedere, 1980.

"School Boards Scored as Bad for Teachers." *Chicago Daily Tribune*, July 10, 1913.

"Sex Education in the Schools." *Vigilance* 26 (1913): 5.

Sex, Etc. "By Teens for Teens." Accessed January 3, 2009, http://www.sexetc.org/topic/guys_health.

"Sex Hygiene Teaching: Should be Done in Home, Not School, Says Catholic Worker." *New York Times*, September 24, 1912, 12.

"Sex Lectures Unmailable." *New York Times*, November 14, 1913.

"Sexual Hygiene: A Circular of Information for Young Men." 1908. Box 4, folder 1. American Social Hygiene Association Papers, Social Welfare History Archives, University of Minnesota.

Silver Ring Thing. "Good Girl Button." Accessed March 16, 2010, http://silver-ringthing.com/shopproductdetail.asp?prodID=618catID=15.

Sinclair, Upton. *The Jungle*. New York: Doubleday, Page, and Co., 1906.

Snow, William F. "Progress, 1900–1915." 1916. Box 1, folder 1. American Social Hygiene Association Records, Social Welfare History Archives, University of Minnesota.

"Social Hygiene and the Negro." 1923. Box 177, folder 8. American Social Hygiene Association Records, Social Welfare History Archives, University of Minnesota.

Social Security Act. Title V, Section 510 (1997). Maternal and Child Health Bureau, U.S. Department of Health and Human Services.

Spingarn, Arthur B. "The War and Venereal Diseases among Negros." 1918. Box 131, folder 2. American Social Hygiene Association Records, Social Welfare History Archives, University of Minnesota.

Stead, William T. *If Christ Came to Chicago! A Plea for the Union of All Who Love in the Service of All Who Suffer*. London: Review of Reviewers, 1894.

"Steps to Save the Girls Taken by Clubwomen." *Chicago Daily Tribune*, February 13, 1916, 10.

Terry, C. E. "The Negro, a Public Health Problem." *Southern Medical Journal* 7 (1915): 458–67.

Trumbull, Charles Gallaudet. *Anthony Comstock, Fighter*. New York: Fleming H. Revell Co., 1913.

Ulrich, Mabel S. "For a New World: The Girl's Part." 1918. Box 132, folder 7. American Social Hygiene Association Records, Social Welfare History Archives, University of Minnesota.

———. "Mothers of America." 1918. Box 132, folder 7. American Social Hygiene Association Records, Social Welfare History Archives, University of Minnesota.

U.S. House of Representatives, Committee on Energy and Commerce. *Welfare Reform: A Review of Abstinence Education and Transitional Medical Assistance*. Washington, D.C.: U.S. Government Printing Office, 2002.

U.S. House of Representatives, Committee on Ways and Means. *Summary of Welfare Reforms Made by Public Law 104–196: The Personal Responsibility and Work Opportunity Reconciliation Act and Associated Legislation*. Washington, D.C.: U.S. Government Printing Office, 1996.

U.S. Public Health Service. *Annual Report of the Surgeon General of the Public Health Service of the United States*. Washington, D.C.: Government Printing Office, 1919.

Willard, Frances E. "The White Cross Movement in Education." *National Education Association Journal of Proceedings and Addresses*. Saint Paul, Minn.: National Education Association, 1890.

"Women's Share in a National Service." 1918. Box 132, folder 7. American Social Hygiene Association Records, Social Welfare History Archives, University of Minnesota.

Woodhull, Victoria. "And the Truth Shall Make You Free: A Speech on the Principles of Social Freedom." Steinway Hall, New York, November 20, 1871; accessed February 17, 2009, http://praxeology.net/SPA-VCW-PSF.htm.

"The Wrong Course and the Right." *New York Times*, June 28, 1913, 6.

Yarros, Rachelle S. "Experiences of a Lecturer." *Social Hygiene* 5 (1919): 205–22.

———. "From Obstetrics to Social Hygiene." *Medical Women's Journal* 33 (1926): 305–9.

———. "Medical Women of Tomorrow." *Woman's Medical Journal* 26 (1916): 146–49.

———. *Modern Woman and Sex: A Feminist Physician Speaks.* New York: Vanguard Press, 1933.

———. "The Prostitute as a Health and Social Problem." In *Proceedings of the National Conference of Social Work.* Chicago: Rogers and Hall, 1919. 220–24.

———. "Some Practical Aspects of Birth Control." *International Abstract of Surgery* 23 (1916): 605–6.

———. "Women Physicians and the Problems of Women." *Medical Women's Journal* 50 (1943): 28–30.

Young, Ella Flagg. *Ethics in the School.* Chicago: University of Chicago Press, 1906.

———. *Isolation in the School.* Chicago: University of Chicago Press, 1901.

———. "The Present Status of Education in America." *Journal of Proceedings and Addresses of the National Education Association* 49 (1911): 183–86.

———. "Report of the Sex Education Sessions of the Fourth International Congress on Social Hygiene and the Annual Meeting of the American Federation for Sex Hygiene." 1913. Box 2, folder 3. American Social Hygiene Association Papers, Social Welfare History Archives, University of Minnesota.

———. "Report of the Superintendent of Schools." In *Fifty-Seventh Annual Report of the Board of Education.* Chicago: Board of Education, 1911. 85–105.

———. "Report of the Superintendent of Schools." In *Fifty-Eighth Annual Report of the Board of Education.* Chicago: Board of Education, 1912. 95–124.

———. "Report of the Superintendent of Schools." In *Fifty-Ninth Annual Report of the Board of Education.* Chicago: Board of Education, 1913. 101–28.

———. "Review Essay: Democracy and Education." *Journal of Education* 84 (1916): 6.

———. "Scientific Method in Education." *Decennial Publications of the University of Chicago First Series* 3 (1903): 143–55.

"Youth and Life: An Exhibit for Girls and Young Women." 1922. Box 171, folder 10. American Social Hygiene Association Records, Social Welfare History Archives, University of Minnesota.

SECONDARY SOURCES

Alcoff, Linda. "The Problem of Speaking for Others." *Cultural Critique* 20 (1991–92): 5–32.

Bailey, Beth L. *From Front Porch to Back Seat: Courtship in Twentieth-Century America.* Baltimore: Johns Hopkins University Press, 1988.

Ball, Moya Ann. "Theoretical Implications of Doing Rhetorical History: Groupthink, Foreign Policy Making, and Vietnam." In *Doing Rhetorical History: Concepts and Cases.* Ed. Kathleen J. Turner. Tuscaloosa: University of Alabama Press, 1998. 61–71.

Bandiera, Frank C., William L. Jeffries, Brian Dodge, Michael Reece, and Debby Herbenick. "Regional Differences in Sexuality Education on a State Level: The Case of Florida." *Sex Education* 8 (2008): 451–63.

Banner, Lois W. *American Beauty.* Chicago: University of Chicago Press, 1983.

Barbeau, Arthur E., and Florette Henri. *The Unknown Soldiers: African-American Troops in World War I.* 1974; reprint, New York: Da Capo Press, 1996.

Bates, Anna Louise. *Weeder in the Garden of the Lord: Anthony Comstock's Life and Career.* Lanham, Md.: University Press of America, 1995.

Bederman, Gail. *Manliness and Civilization: A Cultural History of Gender and Race in the United States.* Chicago: University of Chicago Press, 1995.

Beisel, Nicola. *Imperiled Innocents: Anthony Comstock and Family Reproduction in Victorian America.* Princeton, N.J.: Princeton University Press, 1997.

Bennett, De Robine M. *Anthony Comstock: His Career of Cruelty and Crime.* 1883; reprint, New York: Da Capo Press, 1971.

Benson, Thomas J. "Respecting the Reader." *Quarterly Journal of Speech* 72 (1986): 197–204.

Berger, John. *Ways of Seeing.* London: Penguin, 1973.

Birdsell, David S., and Leo Groarke. "Toward a Theory of Visual Argument." *Argumentation and Advocacy* 33 (1996): 1–10.

Blackwelder, Julia Kirk. *Styling Jim Crow: African American Beauty Training during Segregation.* College Station: Texas A&M University Press, 2003.

Blair, J. Anthony. "The Possibility and Actuality of Visual Arguments." *Argumentation and Advocacy* 33 (1996): 23–40.

Blount, Jackie M. "Ella Flagg Young and the Chicago Schools." In *Founding Mothers and Others: Women Educational Leaders during the Progressive Era.* Ed. Alan R. Sadovnik and Susan F. Semel. New York: Palgrave, 2002. 163–76.

Boehm, Lisa Krissoff. *Popular Culture and the Enduring Myth of Chicago, 1871–1968.* New York: Routledge, 2004.

Borda, Jennifer L. "Woman Suffrage in the Progressive Era: A Coming of Age." In *Rhetoric and Reform in the Progressive Era.* Ed. J. Michael Hogan. East Lansing: Michigan State University Press, 2003. 339–86.

Boyer, Paul S. *Purity in Print: The Vice-Society Movement and Book Censorship in America.* New York: Charles Scribner's Sons, 1968.

Brandt, Allan M. *No Magic Bullet: A Social History of Venereal Disease in the United States since 1880.* New York: Oxford University Press, 1985.

Bristow, Edward J. *Prostitution and Prejudice: The Jewish Fight against White Slavery, 1870–1939.* New York: Schocken Books, 1982.

Bristow, Nancy K. *Making Men Moral: Social Engineering during the Great War.* New York: New York University Press, 1996.

Brodie, Janet F. *Contraception and Abortion in Nineteenth-Century America.* Ithaca, N.Y.: Cornell University Press, 1994.

Browne, Stephen H. "'Like Gory Spectres': Representing Evil in Theodore Weld's *American Slavery as It Is.*" *Quarterly Journal of Speech* 80 (1994): 277–92.

Brückner, Hannah, and Peter Bearman. "After the Promise: The STD Consequences of Adolescent Virginity Pledges." *Journal of Adolescent Health* 36 (2005): 271–78.

Burke, Kenneth. *A Grammar of Motives.* Berkeley: University of California Press, 1945.

———. "The Rhetoric of Hitler's 'Battle.'" In *The Philosophy of Literary Form.* 3d ed. Berkeley: University of California Press, 1973. 191–220.

———. *A Rhetoric of Motives.* Berkeley: University of California Press, 1950.

Burnham, John C. "The Progressive Era Revolution in American Attitudes toward Sex." *Journal of American History* 59 (1973): 885–908.

Campbell, Karlyn Kohrs. *A Critical Study of Early Feminist Rhetoric, 1830–1925.* Vol. 1 of *Man Cannot Speak for Her.* Westport, Conn.: Praeger, 1989.

Carter, Julian B. "Birds, Bees, and Venereal Disease: Toward an Intellectual History of Sex Education." *Journal of the History of Sexuality* 10 (2001): 213–49.

Ceccarelli, Leah. "Polysemy: Multiple Meanings in Rhetorical Criticism." *Quarterly Journal of Speech* 84 (1998): 395–415.

Centers for Disease Control and Prevention. *Eliminating Racial and Ethnic Health Disparities.* Washington, D.C: CDC Office of Minority Health, 2006; accessed August 22, 2006, http://www.cdc.gov/omh/AboutUs/disparities.htm.

———. "Youth Risk Behavior Surveillance—United States, 2005." *Morbidity and Morality Weekly Report* 55 (2006): 1–108.

Charland, Maurice. "Constitutive Rhetoric: The Case of the *Peuple Québécois.*" *Quarterly Journal of Speech* 73 (1987): 133–55.

Chesler, Ellen. *Women of Valor: Margaret Sanger and the Birth Control Movement in America.* New York: Simon and Schuster, 1992.

Chicago Public Library. "Timeline: Key Moments in Chicago Planning." *One Book, One Chicago.* Accessed March 15, 2010, http://www.chipublib.org/eventsprog/programs/oboc/plan_of_chicago/timeline.php.

Clarke, Charles W. *Taboo: The Story of the Pioneers of Social Hygiene.* Washington, D.C.: Public Affairs Press, 1961.

Clapp, Elizabeth Jane. *Mothers of All Children: Women Reformers and the Rise of Juvenile Courts in Progressive Era America.* University Park: Pennsylvania State University Press, 1998.

Collins, Patricia Hill. *Black Feminist Thought: Knowledge, Consciousness, and the Politics of Empowerment.* 2d ed. New York: Routledge, 2000.

———. *Black Sexual Politics: African Americans, Gender, and the New Racism.* New York: Routledge, 2004.

Colwell, Stacie A. "The End of the Road: Gender, the Dissemination of Knowledge, and the American Campaign against Venereal Disease during World War I." In *The Visible Woman: Imagining Technologies, Gender, and Science*, Ed. Paula A. Treichler, Lisa Cartwright, and Constance Penley. New York: New York University Press, 1998. 44–82.

Condit, Celeste M. *Decoding Abortion Rhetoric: Communicating Social Change*. Urbana: University of Illinois Press, 1990.

Conor, Liz. *The Spectacular Modern Woman: Feminine Visibility in the 1920s*. Bloomington: Indiana University Press, 2004.

Crenshaw, Kimberlé. "Mapping the Margins: Intersectionality, Identity Politics, and Violence against Women of Color." In *Identities: Race, Class, Gender, and Nationality*. Ed. Linda Alcoff and Eduardo Mendieta. Oxford: Wiley-Blackwell, 2003. 175–200.

Curry, Lynne. *Modern Mothers in the Heartland: Gender, Health, and Progress in Illinois, 1900–1930*. Columbus: Ohio State University Press, 1999.

Davis, Kathy. "Intersectionality as Buzzword: A Sociology of Science Perspective on What Makes a Feminist Theory Successful." *Feminist Theory* 9 (2008): 67–85.

D'Emilio, John, and Estelle B. Freedman. *Intimate Matters: A History of Sexuality in America*. 2d ed. Chicago: University of Chicago Press, 1997.

Dodge, Brian, Kristina Zachry, Michael Reece, Ellen D. S. López, Debby Herbenick, Kristin Gant, Amanda Tanner, and Omar Martinez. "Sexuality Education in Florida: Content, Context, and Controversy." *American Journal of Sexuality Education* 3 (2008): 67–93.

Dow, Bonnie J. "Response Criticism and Authority in the Artistic Mode." *Western Journal of Communication* 65 (2001): 336–48.

Dubois, Ellen Carol, and Linda Gordon. "Seeking Ecstasy on the Battlefield: Danger and Pleasure in Nineteenth-Century Feminist Thought." *Feminist Studies* 9 (1983): 7–25.

Eberwein, Robert. *Sex Ed: Film, Video, and the Framework of Desire*. New Brunswick, N.J.: Rutgers University Press, 1999.

Elders, Joycelyn M. Foreword to *Harmful to Minors: The Perils of Protecting Children from Sex*, by Judith Levine. New York: Thunder's Mouth Press, 2002. ix–xii.

Ellis, Mark. *Race, War, and Surveillance: African Americans and the United States Government during World War I*. Bloomington: Indiana University Press, 2001.

Engs, Ruth Clifford. *The Progressive Era's Health Reform Movement: A Historical Dictionary*. Westport, Conn.: Praeger, 2003.

Faderman, Lillian. *To Believe in Women: What Lesbians Have Done for America—A History*. Boston: Houghton Mifflin, 2000.

Fenner, Mildred S., and Eleanor C. Fishburn. *Pioneer American Educators*. 1944; reprint, Port Washington, N.Y.: Kennikat Press, Inc., 1968.

Finnegan, Cara A. "Review Essay: Visual Studies and Visual Rhetoric." *Quarterly Journal of Speech* 90 (2004): 234–47.

Flanagan, Maureen A. *Seeing with Their Hearts: Chicago Women and the Vision of the Good City, 1871–1933*. Princeton, N.J.: Princeton University Press, 2002.

Foucault, Michel. *Discipline and Punish: The Birth of the Prison.* Trans. Alan Sheridan. London: Penguin, 1977.

———. *The History of Sexuality.* Vol. 1, *An Introduction.* Trans. Robert Hurley. New York: Vintage Books, 1978.

Gallagher, Victoria, and Kenneth S. Zagacki. "Visibility and Rhetoric: The Power of Visual Images in Norman Rockwell's Depictions of Civil Rights." *Quarterly Journal of Speech* 91 (2005): 175–200.

Gallo, Max. *The Poster in History.* 1974; reprint, New York: W. W. Norton and Co., 2001.

Gamble, Vanessa N. *Germs Have No Color Line: Blacks and American Medicine, 1900–1940.* New York: Garland Publishing, 1989.

Goodson, Patricia, B. E. Pruitt, Eric Buhi, Kelly L. Wilson, Catherine N. Rasberry, and Emily Gunnels. *Abstinence Education Evaluation: Phase Five Technical Report.* College Station: Texas A&M University Press, 2004.

Gordon, Linda. *The Moral Property of Women: A History of Birth Control Politics in America.* Urbana: University of Illinois Press, 2002.

———. "Voluntary Motherhood: The Beginnings of Feminist Birth Control Ideas in the United States." In *Women and Health in America: Historical Readings.* Ed. Judith Walzer Leavitt. Madison: University of Wisconsin Press, 1999. 253–68.

Gray, Madeline. *Margaret Sanger: A Biography of the Champion of Birth Control.* New York: Richard Marek, 1979.

Grossman, James R. *Land of Hope: Chicago, Black Southerners, and the Great Migration.* Chicago: University of Chicago Press, 1989.

Guttmacher Institute. *Facts in Brief: Teenagers' Sexual and Reproductive Health.* New York: Alan Guttmacher Institute, 2002.

———. *Sex Education: Needs, Programs, and Policies.* New York: Alan Guttmacher Institute, 2005.

Hale, Grace Elizabeth. *Making Whiteness: The Culture of Segregation in the South, 1890–1940.* New York: Pantheon Books, 1998.

Hall, Stuart. *Representation: Cultural Representations and Signifying Practices.* Thousand Oaks, Calif.: Sage, 1997.

Haller, John S. *Outcasts from Evolution: Scientific Attitudes of Racial Inferiority, 1859–1900.* New York: McGraw-Hill, 1971.

Haller, Mark H. *Eugenics: Hereditarian Attitudes in American Thought.* New Brunswick, N.J.: Rutgers University Press, 1963.

Hasian, Marouf A. *The Rhetoric of Eugenics in Anglo-American Thought.* Athens: University of Georgia Press, 1996.

Haslett, Diane C. "Yarros, Rachelle Slobodinsky." In *Women Building Chicago, 1790–1990.* Ed. Rima Luin Schultz and Adele Hast. Bloomington: Indiana University Press, 2001. 998–1001.

Hauser, Debra. *Five Years of Abstinence-Only-until-Marriage Education: Assessing the Impact.* Washington, D.C.: Advocates for Youth, 2004.

Herrick, Mary J. *The Chicago Schools: A Social and Political History.* Beverly Hills, Calif.: Sage Publications, 1971.

Hoff, Tina, Liberty Greene, and Julia Davis. *National Survey of Adolescents and Young Adults: Sexual Health Knowledge, Attitudes, and Experiences.* Menlo Park, Calif.: Henry J. Kaiser Family Foundation, 2003.

Hogan, J. Michael, ed. *Rhetoric and Reform of the Progressive Era.* East Lansing: Michigan State University Press, 2003.

Hoganson, Kristin. *Fighting for American Manhood: How Gender Politics Provoked the Spanish-American and Philippine-American Wars.* New Haven, Conn.: Yale University Press, 1998.

hooks, bell. *Ain't I a Woman: Black Women and Feminism.* Boston, Mass.: South End Press, 1981.

Horowitz, Helen Lefkowitz. *Rereading Sex: Battles over Sexual Knowledge and Suppression in Nineteenth-Century America.* New York: Alfred A. Knopf, 2002.

Ignatiev, Noel. *How the Irish Became White.* New York: Routledge, 1995.

Irvine, Janice M. *Talk about Sex: The Battles over Sex Education in the United States.* Berkeley, Calif.: University of California Press, 2002.

Jacobson, Matthew. *Whiteness of a Different Color: European Immigrants and the Alchemy of Race.* Cambridge, Mass.: Harvard University Press, 1998.

Jasinski, James. "Ambiguity (or Paradox) of Substance." In *Sourcebook on Rhetoric: Key Concepts in Contemporary Rhetorical Studies.* Thousand Oaks, Calif.: Sage Publications, 2001. 10–12.

Jemmott, John B., Loretta S. Jemmott, and Geoffrey T. Fong. "Abstinence and Safer Sex HIV Risk-Reduction Interventions for African American Adolescents: A Randomized Controlled Trial." *Journal of the American Medical Association* 279 (1998): 1529–36.

Jensen, Joan M. "The Evolution of Margaret Sanger's 'Family Limitation' Pamphlet, 1914–1921." *Signs* 6 (1981): 548–67.

Jensen, Robin E., and Jakob D. Jensen. "Entertainment Media and Sexual Health: A Content Analysis of Sexual Talk, Behavior, and Risks in a Popular Television Series." *Sex Roles* 56 (2007): 275–84.

Johannessen, Joy. Preface to *What Every Girl Should Know*, by Margaret Sanger. 1914; reprint, New York: Belvedere, 1980. 1–4.

Johansson, Warren. "Sex Negative, Sex Positive." In *Encyclopedia of Homosexuality.* Ed. W. R. Dynes. New York: Garland, 1990. 1182–83.

Jones, James H. *Bad Blood: The Tuskegee Syphilis Experiment.* New York: Free Press, 1981.

Kaiser Family Foundation. *Sex Education in America: A Series of National Surveys of Students, Parents, Teachers, and Principals.* Menlo Park, Calif.: Henry J. Kaiser Family Foundation, 2000.

Kelves, Daniel J. *In the Name of Eugenics: Genetics and the Uses of Human Heredity.* New York: Alfred A. Knopf, 1985.

Kennedy, David M. *Birth Control in America: The Career of Margaret Sanger.* New Haven, Conn.: Yale University Press, 1970.

Kerber, Linda K. *Women of the Republic: Intellect and Ideology in Revolutionary America.* Chapel Hill: University of North Carolina Press, 1980.

Kirby, Douglas. *Emerging Answers: Research Findings on Programs to Reduce Teen Preg-nancy.* Washington, D.C.: National Campaign to Prevent Teen Pregnancy, 2007.

Kitch, Carolyn. *The Girl on the Magazine Cover: The Origins of Visual Stereotypes in American Mass Media.* Chapel Hill: University of North Carolina Press, 2001.

Kline, Wendy. *Building a Better Race: Gender, Sexuality, and Eugenics from the Turn of the Century to the Baby Boom.* Berkeley: University of California Press, 2001.

Kunkel, Dale, Keren Eyal, Keli Finnerty, Erica Biely, and Edward Donnerstein. *Sex on TV 4: A Kaiser Family Foundation Report.* Menlo Park, Calif.: Henry J. Kaiser Family Foundation, 2005.

Kunzel, Regina G. *Fallen Women, Problem Girls: Unmarried Mothers and the Profes-sionalization of Social Work, 1890–1945.* New Haven, Conn.: Yale University Press, 1993.

Lagemann, Ellen Condliffe. "Experimenting with Education: John Dewey and Ella Flagg Young at the University of Chicago." In *Feminist Interpretations of John Dewey.* Ed. Charlene Haddock Seigfried. University Park: Pennsylvania State University Press, 2002. 31–46.

Leff, Michael C. "Interpretation and the Art of the Rhetorical Critic." *Western Journal of Speech Communication* 44 (1980): 337–49.

Leighton, Howard B. "The Lantern Slide and Art History." *History of Photography* 8 (1984): 107–19.

Lerner, Gerda, ed. *Black Women in White America: A Documentary History.* New York: Vintage Books, 1973.

Levine, Judith. *Harmful to Minors: The Perils of Protecting Children from Sex.* New York: Thunder's Mouth Press, 2002.

Link, Arthur S., and Richard L. McCormick. *Progressivism.* Wheeling, Ill.: Harlan Davidson, 1983.

Logue, Cal M., and John H. Patton. "From Ambiguity to Dogma: The Rhetori-cal Symbols of Lyndon B. Johnson on Vietnam." *Southern Speech Communication Journal* 47 (1982): 310–29.

Lord, Alexandra M. "Models of Masculinity: Sex Education, the United States Public Health Service, and the YMCA, 1919–1924." *Journal of the History of Medicine* 58 (April 2003): 123–52.

———. "'Naturally Clean and Wholesome': Women, Sex Education, and the United States Public Health Service." *Social History of Medicine* 17 (2004): 423–41.

Lorde, Audre. *Sister Outsider: Essays and Speeches.* Trumansburg, N.Y.: Crossing Press, 1984.

Lucas, Stephen E. "The Renaissance of American Public Address: Text and Context in Rhetorical Criticism." *Quarterly Journal of Speech* 74 (1988): 241–60.

Masel-Walters, Lynne. "For the 'Poor Mute Mothers'? Margaret Sanger and *The Woman Rebel.*" *Journalism History* 11 (1984): 3–10.

Mattingly, Carol. *Well-Tempered Women: Nineteenth-Century Temperance Rhetoric.* Carbondale: Southern Illinois University Press, 1998.

May, Henry F. *The End of American Innocence: A Study of the First Years of Our Own Time, 1912–1917.* New York: Alfred A. Knopf, 1959.

McClearey, Kevin E. "'A Tremendous Awakening': Margaret H. Sanger's Speech at Fabian Hall." *Western Journal of Communication* 58 (1994): 182–200.

McGee, Michael C. "Text, Context, and the Fragmentation of Contemporary Culture." *Western Journal of Speech Communication* 54 (1990): 274–89.

McKerrow, Raymie E. "Critical Rhetoric: Theory and Praxis." *Communication Monographs* 56 (1989): 91–111.

Medley, Keith Weldon. *We as Freemen: Plessy v. Ferguson*. Gretna, La.: Pelican Publishing Co., 2003.

Miller, Donald L. *City of the Century: The Epic of Chicago and the Making of America*. New York: Simon and Schuster, 1996.

Moran, Jeffrey P. "'Modernism Gone Mad': Sex Education Comes to Chicago, 1913." *Journal of American History* 83 (1996): 481–513.

———. *Teaching Sex: The Shaping of Adolescence in the Twentieth Century*. Cambridge, Mass.: Harvard University Press, 2000.

Morantz-Sanchez, Regina. *Sympathy and Science: Women Physicians in American Medicine*. New York: Oxford University Press, 1985.

Murphy, John M. "Margaret Higgins Sanger." In *Women Public Speakers in the United States, 1925–1993: A Bio-critical Sourcebook*. Ed. Karlyn Kohrs Campbell. Westport, Conn.: Greewood Press, 1994. 238–53.

———. "'To Create a Race of Thoroughbreds': Margaret Sanger and *The Birth Control Review*." *Women's Studies in Communication* 13 (1990): 23–45.

National Library of Medicine. "Visual Culture and Health Posters." Bethesda, Md.: National Institutes of Health, 1998; accessed March 7, 2009, http://profiles.nlm.nih.gov/VC/Views/Exhibit/narrative/history.html.

Newman, Louise M. *White Women's Rights: The Racial Origins of Feminism in the United States*. New York: Oxford University Press, 1999.

Olsen, Otto H., ed. *The Thin Disguise: Turning Point in Negro History*. New York: Humanities Press, 1967.

Peters, John Durham. *Speaking into the Air: A History of the Idea of Communication*. Chicago: University of Chicago Press, 1999.

Pierce, Bessie Louise. *The Rise of a Modern City, 1871–1893*. Vol. 3 of *A History of Chicago*. New York: Alfred A. Knopf, 1957.

Pivar, David J. *Purity and Hygiene: Women, Prostitution, and the "American Plan," 1900–1930*. Westport, Conn.: Greenwood Press, 2002.

Putzel, Michael. "White House Forces Elders to Resign over Remarks." *Boston Globe*, December 11, 1994, 1.

Reed, James. *From Private Vice to Public Virtue: The Birth Control Movement and American Society since 1830*. New York: Basic Books, 1978.

Roberts, Dorothy. *Killing the Black Body: Race, Reproduction, and the Meaning of Liberty*. New York: Vintage Books, 1997.

Robertson, Nancy Marie. *Christian Sisterhood, Race Relations, and the YWCA, 1906–46*. Urbana: University of Illinois Press, 2007.

Rodrique, Jessie M. "The Black Community and the Birth Control Movement." In

Passion and Power: Sexuality in History. Ed. Kathy Peiss and Christina Simmons. Chicago: Temple University Press, 1989. 138–56.

Roediger, David R. *Colored White: Transcending the Racial Past.* Berkeley: University of California Press, 2002.

———. *Working toward Whiteness: How America's Immigrants Became White.* New York: Basic Books, 2005.

Rosen, Ruth. *The Lost Sisterhood: Prostitution in America, 1900–1918.* Baltimore: Johns Hopkins University Press, 1982.

Santelli, John, Mary A. Ott, Maureen Lyon, Jennifer Rogers, Daniel Summers, and Rebecca Schleifer. "Abstinence and Abstinence-Only Education: A Review of U.S. Policies and Programs." *Journal of Adolescent Health* 38 (2006): 72–81.

Saussure, Ferdinand de. *Course in General Linguistics.* Trans. Roy Harris. 1915; reprint, LaSalle, Ill.: Open Court, 1986.

Savedoff, Barbara E. "Escaping Reality: Digital Imagery and the Resources of Photography." *Journal of Aesthetics and Art Criticism* 55 (1997): 201–14.

Schwarz, Judith. *Radical Feminists of Heterodoxy: Greenwich Village, 1912–1940.* Rev. ed. Norwich, Vt.: New Victoria Publishers, 1986.

Shields, Stephanie A. "Gender: An Intersectionality Perspective." *Sex Roles* 59 (2008): 301–11.

Sloop, John M. *Disciplining Gender: Rhetorics of Sex Identity in Contemporary U.S. Culture.* Amherst: University of Massachusetts Press, 2004.

Smith, Carl. *Urban Disorder and the Shape of Belief: The Great Chicago Fire, the Haymarket Bomb, and the Model Town of Pullman.* Chicago: University of Chicago Press, 1995.

Smith, Edward, Jacinda Dariotis, and Susan Potter. *Evaluation of the Pennsylvania Abstinence Education and Related Services Initiative: 1998–2002.* Philadelphia: Maternal and Child Health Bureau of Family Health, Pennsylvania Department of Health, 2004.

Smith, Susan L. *Sick and Tired of Being Sick and Tired: Black Women's Health Activism in America, 1890–1950.* Philadelphia: University of Pennsylvania Press, 1995.

Smith-Rosenberg, Carroll. "The Abortion Movement and the AMA, 1850–1880." In *Disorderly Conduct: Visions of Gender in Victorian America.* New York: Oxford University Press, 1985. 217–44.

Stanley, Peter. *What Did You Do in the War, Daddy? A Visual History of Propaganda Posters.* Melbourne: Oxford University Press, 1983.

Starkman, Naomi, and Nicole Rajani. "The Case of Comprehensive Sex Education." *AIDS Patient Care and STDs* 16 (2002): 313–18.

Tomes, Nancy. *Gospel of Germs: Men, Women, and the Microbe in American Life.* Cambridge, Mass.: Harvard University Press, 1998.

———. "The Private Side of Public Health: Sanitary Science, Domestic Hygiene, and the Germ Theory, 1870–1900." In *Sickness and Health in America: Readings in the History of Medicine and Public Health.* Ed. Judith Walzer Leavitt and Ronald L. Numbers. Madison: University of Wisconsin Press, 1997. 506–29.

Trachtenberg, Alan. *Reading American Photographs: Images as History, Mathew Brady to Walker Evans.* New York: Hill and Wang, 1989.

University of Minnesota Libraries. "Social Hygiene Poster Campaigns in the 1920s." Accessed February 21, 2009, http://special.lib.umn.edu/swha/exhibits/hygiene/essay.htm.

Ward, Patrician Spain. "The Chicago Birth-Control Debate: Dr. Rachelle Yarros of the University of Illinois at Chicago vs. Herman Bundesen Commissioner of Health." 1990, Patricia Spain Ward Papers, Special Collections Library, University of Illinois at Chicago.

———. "Yarros, Rachelle Slobodinsky." In *Biographical Dictionary of Social Welfare in America*. Ed. Walter I. Trattner. New York: Greenwood Press, 1986. 813–16.

Wiggins, David K., and Patrick B. Miller, eds. *The Unlevel Playing Field: A Documentary History of the African American Experience in Sport*. Urbana: University of Illinois Press, 2003.

Zaeske, Susan. *Signatures of Citizenship: Petitioning, Antislavery, and Women's Political Identity*. Chapel Hill: University of North Carolina Press, 2003.

Zagarri, Rosemarie. "Morals, Manners, and the Republican Mother." *American Quarterly* 44 (1992): 192–215.

Zinn, Maxine Baca, and Bonnie Thornton Dill. "Theorizing Difference from Multiracial Feminism." *Feminist Studies* 22 (1996): 321–31.

Index

scientific research: morality and, 55–59, 134; during the Progressive Era, 17–23, 34–35
Scott, Robert Falcon, 124
segregation of African Americans, 84–85, 144–47
self, the, 109–12
sexuality, xvi, xix, 9, 17, 22, 80, 125–26; of the other, 116; of youth, 25, 45–46, 153
Sexuality Information and Education Council of the United States, 153
sexually transmitted illnesses (STIs), xi, 18, 41, 96–97, 106, 109, 132–34, 151–52, 155, 159; "Keeping Fit" campaign, 117–23; tied to insanity, 74–75. See also post-war sex education; wartime sex education
Shaw, Anna Howard, 129, 145
Shaw, George Bernard, 30
Shoop, John D., 65
Snow, William F., 94
Social Diseases and Marriage, 1
Social Evil in Chicago, The, 43
Social Hygiene, 82, 93, 95, 96, 117
social-hygiene movement, the, 1–2, 34–35, 151; African Americans and, 81–86, 119, 120–21, 122, 136–41; in Chicago, 45–49; idealized families and, 131–32; the other and, 106–9; propaganda targeting women, 86–89, 95–96; Rachelle Yarros and, 94–97; representation of the self and, 109–12; rhetoric of, 102–12; scientific research and, 17–23, 55–59; speaking on behalf of others, 112–14; World War I and, 70–75
socialism, 24, 25
social-purity advocacy, 9–13, 20–23, 124, 152–53; "otherness" and, 33–34
soldiers. See post-war sex education; wartime sex education
Spingarn, Arthur, 71, 82

standards, double, 4–9
Stead, William T., 43
stereotypes, racial, 79–80, 81–83, 108–9
sterilization laws, 20
St. Petersburg Times, 54
suffrage movement, 44
Sumner, Walter T., 47
Survey, The, 142
sweethearts, women portrayed as, 75–80
syphilis, 18, 41, 75, 126, 127

Taboo: The Story of the Pioneers of Social Hygiene, 95
teacher unions, 64–65
temptresses, 75–80
Tilton, Elizabeth, 16
Traps for the Young, 5, 15
Trumbull, Charles, 5

Ulrich, Mabel, 88
unions, labor, 43, 64–65

Van Dis, J. A., 117
venereal diseases, xi, 18, 41, 96–97, 106, 109, 132–34, 151–52, 155, 159; "Keeping Fit" campaign, 117–23; tied to insanity, 74–75. See also post-war sex education; wartime sex education
Vigilance, 11, 57
visual rhetoric, xviii, 18–19

Ward, Mrs. Humphrey, 176n45
Warren, Earl, 145
wartime sex education, xiv, xxiii, 66, 94–95; for African American soldiers, 68–70, 81–86, 89, 150; patriotism and, 87–88; race and, 68–70; reasons for, 67–68, 150; social-hygiene movement and, 70–75; women portrayed as temptresses versus sweethearts in, 75–80. See also post-war sex education
Washington, Booker T., 137, 145
Wassermann syphilis blood test, 18

ROBIN E. JENSEN is an assistant
professor of communication
at Purdue University.

The University of Illinois Press
is a founding member of the
Association of American University Presses.

Composed in 10/13.5 Janson
with Electra display
by Celia Shapland
at the University of Illinois Press
Manufactured by Cushing-Malloy, Inc.

University of Illinois Press
1325 South Oak Street
Champaign, IL 61820-6903
www.press.uillinois.edu